BREAD OF LIFE
AND CUP OF JOY

W9-AYA-689

BREAD OF LIFE
AND
CUP OF JOY

Newer Ecumenical Perspectives
on the Eucharist

HORTON DAVIES

William B. Eerdmans Publishing Company
Grand Rapids, Michigan

Gracewing.

Leominster, England

Copyright © 1993 by Wm. B. Eerdmans Publishing Co.

First published 1993 in the United States by
Wm. B. Eerdmans Publishing Co.
255 Jefferson Ave. S.E., Grand Rapids, Michigan 49503
and in the U.K. by Gracewing
2 Southern Avenue, Leominster, HR6 0QF
All rights reserved

Printed in the United States of America

Library of Congress Cataloging-in-Publication Data

Davies, Horton.
    Bread of life and cup of joy: newer ecumenical perspectives
on the eucharist / Horton Davies.
        p.   cm.
    Includes index.
    ISBN 0-8028-0252-4 (pbk.)
    1. Lord's Supper. 2. Lord's Supper — History.
3. Lord's Supper and Christian union. I. Title.
BV825.2.D385   1992
234'.163 — dc20   92-37464
                                 CIP

Gracewing ISBN 0 85244 223 8

Cover illustration: "The Last Supper" by Sir Stanley Spencer
© Estate of Sir Stanley Spencer/VAGA, New York 1992

CONTENTS

PREFACE

INTRODUCTIONS can easily become no more than brief summaries of what is written in the chapters of a book. They can also take the form of anticipatory apologies for what the author has omitted. For these reasons I have concluded that a table of contents is indication enough of what is to follow and that any reader unfamiliar with liturgical jargon may find "A Short Glossary of Technical Terms" more useful.

My subtitle, *Newer Perspectives on the Eucharist,* is meant to imply that I concentrate on the most recent and unitive interpretations of the chief Christian sacrament, but that I also consider several older and cherished meanings given new life by modern scholarship. My longest chapters are those in which there has been the greatest controversy, namely, Chapters Three, Seven, and Eight.

I wish to thank three persons in particular for their help: Professor Daniel W. Hardy, for his sustained interest despite his many other responsibilities as Director of the Center of Theological Inquiry; Bill Eerdmans, who will have published books of three members of my immediate family, including my wife, Marie-Hélène, and my son, Hugh; and Donald Vorp, the very helpful Collection Development Librarian of the Princeton Theological Seminary Speer Library, that adjacent resource to which I and my congenial colleagues owe so much.

Horton Davies
The Center for Theological Inquiry
Princeton, New Jersey

A SHORT GLOSSARY
OF TECHNICAL TERMS

ANAMNESIS: This term, derived from I Corinthians 11:24, means the commemoration or recalling of past events so that they are made present through their effects. Its more specialized meaning is the prayer in the liturgy that recalls Christ's saving acts.*

CEREMONIAL: This refers to the actions that take place in worship as distinguished from the "ritual," which refers to the words used in worship.

CONSECRATION: The Prayer of Consecration, now often called instead "The Great Thanksgiving," is the central prayer in the Eucharist; it corresponds to the "canon" in the Roman Rite and the "anaphora" in the Eastern Orthodox rites.

EPICLESIS: This is an invocation either of God to send the Holy Spirit, or directly of the Holy Spirit to make the bread and wine of the Eucharist the body and blood of Christ. This was characteristic of all Eastern rites but has recently been included in most Roman, Anglican, and Protestant rites. It may have arisen from assuming that because the Holy Spirit was the agent in Christ's becoming human in the Incarnation, the Spirit could aptly be the agent of Christ's presence in the Eucharist.

ECUMENICAL MOVEMENT: This is the movement aiming at uniting the separate churches to fulfill Christ's high-priestly prayer

* N.B. Richard Buxton writes in Kenneth Stevenson, ed., *Liturgy Reshaped* (London: S.P.C.K., 1982), p. 98: "The word *anamnesis* is used because no one English word expresses the meaning of calling into present reality a fresh liberation of the salvific power of the event remembered."

that all his disciples might be one, as he and the Father are one, that the world might believe.

EUCHARIST: A title for the service of the Mass, Holy Communion, or the Lord's Supper, deriving from the Greek word meaning "thanksgiving." Jesus used the term at the Last Supper, and it expresses what is perhaps the supreme act of Christian thanksgiving.

FRACTION: This is the action of breaking the bread by the celebrant at the Eucharist. It was formerly thought of as symbolizing the breaking of Christ's body at the Crucifixion.

INSTITUTION NARRATIVE: This is the narrative of the actions of Jesus at the Last Supper that inaugurated the Eucharist. In the Roman and Anglican eucharists it forms part of the Prayer of Consecration because it contains the very word of the Word or Logos or Wisdom of God. This narrative, separated from a prayer, has been used in the Reformed churches as an assurance that the church is following Christ's intentions when he instituted it.

INTERCESSION: Prayer on behalf of others.

THE KISS OF PEACE (OR PAX): This is a sign of fellowship exchanged by Christians and can be a kiss or merely the shaking of hands. It was used in New Testament days, as Romans 16:16 and I Peter 5:14 testify.

THE LITURGICAL MOVEMENT: An interconfessional or interdenominational movement aimed at providing greater opportunities for the laity to share in and understand more fully the liturgy. Its founders in France were the Benedictine Dom Prosper Guéranger of the Abbey of Solesmes in 1832 and the Protestant Eugène Bersier at the Étoile in Paris in the 1880s. In England the Oxford Movement of the nineteenth century shared some of these aims, as did A. G. Hebert in the 1930s. In the U.S.A. Fr. Virgil Michel, O.S.B., was the founder of the movement.

LITURGY: This is an act of divine worship, usually culminating in the Eucharist. It derives from a Greek word found in the New Testament (e.g., in Phil. 2:30) and used in Hellenistic Greek to mean an act of public service. In Christian circles its meaning was restricted to service to God, and ultimately it was applied to the Eucharist as the supreme act of worship.

MASS: A title given to the Roman Catholic service of Holy Communion, which almost certainly derived from the concluding formula of dismissal: *Ite, missa est* ("Go, it is finished").

OFFERTORY: This refers to the bringing forward to the altar of the bread and wine, and sometimes also of the monetary offering of the people, which is the modern substitute for the bread and wine that the early Christians brought in some quantity so that what was left over after the celebration might be given to the sick, the poor, and prisoners for the faith.

PENTECOST: The fiftieth day after Easter is a Christian festival commemorating the descent of the Holy Spirit on the apostles (Acts 2:1-11).

RUBRIC: A direction for the conduct of divine worship, so called because it was originally written or printed in red.

SURSUM CORDA: A Latin phrase meaning "Lift up your hearts." From the earliest days it formed part of the dialogue introducing the eucharistic prayer, indicating the joy of the assembled body of Christ, the Christians.

TRANSUBSTANTIATION: This is the Roman Catholic teaching, expounded in the sixteenth century, that affirms the real presence of Christ in the Eucharist, explaining that while the appearance of the consecrated elements seems to be bread and wine, their substance or underlying essence has become the body and blood of Christ. It is an Aristotelian term that is negated by modern physicists.

TRANSIGNIFICATION: The term applied by modern interpreters of the Eucharist who are equally eager to maintain that bread and wine change their meaning — are transignified — by Christ to mean his body and blood, thus preferring a personalistic sign to a material substance or thing to refer to the gift of his own self donated in the Eucharist as body and blood for the nourishment of the Christian community. Coupled with this is another term, "Transfinalization," which indicates the *purpose* of the changed sign, or modified meaning.

ONE   The Eucharist as Memorial

A T FIRST GLANCE it would appear that a book designed to provide new or, at least, newer perspectives on the Eucharist by starting with its meaning as a memorial is merely stating the obvious. Moreover, Protestants have always considered this its primary significance, and both Roman Catholic and Orthodox theologians have generally recognized the element of reminiscence in the institution. Where then does the novelty arise? Recent understanding of the memorial aspect of the Eucharist maintains that this is no "mere memorialism" but the confession of the presence of the crucified and risen and ascended Lord in Holy Communion and is linked with an eschatological interpretation. Furthermore, we intend to show that the Greek term for memorial — *anamnesis* — emphasizes the present relevance of this special act of commemoration, and to demonstrate the importance of the context of the Jewish Passover for eucharistic interpretation, while also recognizing the differences between the Jewish and Christian celebration.

At the outset the commemorative aspect is clearly emphasized in the synoptic and Pauline accounts of the Last Supper. Luke 22:19 reports that when Jesus had broken the bread and given thanks, he said, "This is my body which is given for you. Do this in remembrance of me." Paul uses almost identical wording, after insisting that he has received this information from the Lord, "that the Lord Jesus on the night when he was betrayed took bread, and when he had given thanks, he broke

1

it, and said, 'This is my body which is for you. Do this in remembrance of me'" (I Cor. 11:23-24). It is generally acknowledged that the proper meaning of remembrance is recalling — that is, bringing to mind past events so that by their effects they become operative in the present. F. J. Leenhardt makes this meaning clear when he cites a saying of Gamaliel in explaining in the light of Exodus 13:8 the event of the Israelite Passover: "Every man in every generation must regard himself as having been personally delivered from Egypt. Every Israelite must know that he personally has been freed from slavery."[1]

Joachim Jeremias, in his thorough analysis of the words of Jesus at the Last Supper *(Die Abendmahlsworte Jesu)*,[2] finds it curious that Jesus had to remind the disciples who had been close companions during three years not to forget him. This is curious especially considering how dramatic the final events of Christ's earthly life were to prove immediately following the Last Supper. But what appears even more curious is Jeremias's own interpretation of the *anamnesis,* namely, that this a reminder to God, thus: "Do this that God may remember me." How could God ever forget the sacrifice of his eternal Son?[3]

The simplest interpretation of "Do this for my recalling" is to acknowledge the presence of Christ in the Eucharist and to apprehend his power, always remembering that the testimony of the gospels is both post-Resurrection and post-Pentecost. John Donne rightly insisted that "the art of salvation is the art of memory" because to remember is to receive the benefits of the Lord's passion and the fruits of his resurrection. This was

---

1. *Le Sacrament de la sainte Cène* (Neuchâtel and Paris: Delachaux & Niestlé, 1948), p. 18.

2. English translation, *The Eucharistic Words of Jesus* (London: SCM Press, 1966). A strong reaffirmation of the traditional interpretation of *anamnesis* is provided by Douglas Jones in his article "ἀνάμνησις *(anamnesis)* in the LXX; and interpretation of I Cor. XI.25," *Journal of Theological Studies,* vol. VII (1955), pp. 183-191. Leenhardt, *op. cit.,* p. 42, says that God does not need any reminder of Christ's sacrifice.

3. See Brian A. Greet, *Broken Bread in a Broken World* (Valley Forge, PA: Judson Press, 1971), p. 47.

not merely a retrospective reflection but a contemporary experience of his presence, as well as prospective anticipation, looking to the coming Kingdom of God in its fullness at the *parousia* and in the eschatological banquet in heaven.

Before moving on to the new understanding of memorial derived from the consideration of the Passover, it is worth mentioning the traditional values found in the memorial interpretation of the Eucharist. For these values our interpreters will be William Barclay, a Protestant New Testament scholar, and Alexander Schmemann, an Orthodox theologian.

Barclay finds four elements in the record of the institution of the chief sacrament:

> (i) A statement that the bread is the body of Jesus, and that it was for them. (ii) A statement that the cup represents the covenant blood of the new covenant, that is, the new relationship between man and God, made possible at the cost of the life and death of Jesus. (iii) An instruction to repeat this meal in the days to come, so that the memory of Jesus and what he had done and can do is always fresh. (iv) An eschatological saying in which Jesus affirms his confidence in the full coming of the Kingdom.[4]

When Barclay is asked what is the meaning of the recalling of Christ for today, he replies: "We remember to realize again what our blessed Lord has done and suffered for us" that we may reappropriate its many benefits, and we are remembering "someone who is gloriously alive. And therefore we remember Jesus Christ in the sacrament in order to encounter Jesus Christ."[5]

Alexander Schmemann in his *Eucharist: Sacrament of the Kingdom* insists that the whole liturgy is both a remembrance of Christ and a sacrament and experience of the presence "of the Son of God, who came down from heaven and was incarnate

---

4. William Barclay, *The Lord's Supper* (London: SCM Press, 1967), p. 55.
5. *Ibid.*, p. 111.

that he might in himself lead us up to heaven." He interprets
the Last Supper renewed in the Eucharist as the *telos,* that is,
"the completion, the crowning, the fulfillment of Christ's love,
which constitutes the essence of all his ministry, preaching,
miracles, and through which he now gives himself up, as love
itself." He sums it up as follows:

> From the opening words, "I have earnestly desired to eat this
> passover with you" (Luke 22:15), to the exit to the garden of
> Gethsemane, everything at the last supper — the washing of
> the feet, the distribution to the disciples of the bread and the
> cup, the last discourse — is not only concerned with love, but
> is *Love itself.* . . . And now at this table he manifests and grants
> this love as his kingdom, and his kingdom as "abiding" in love:
> "As the Father has loved me, so have I loved you; *abide in my
> love*" (John 15:9).[6]

The Passover Context of the Last Supper

Was the Last Supper a modified and transformed Passover?
Certainly many modern interpreters of the Eucharist think so.
But even if it was not, it took place as the chief Jewish feast at
the time of the Passion of Christ. It is surely important that Jesus
spoke of the New Covenant that he was inaugurating, that he
did so at the time when the inauguration of the Old Covenant
was being celebrated at Passover, and particularly that he made
the ideas of sacrifice and memorial central. Hence, at the very
least, the Passover is significant and telling background to the
institution of the Eucharist.

Before we can proceed to elaborate the probable influence
of the Passover on the Last Supper, we must consider the evidence. Matthew shows us the disciples asking Jesus, "Where do
you want us to prepare the passover?" (26:17 with parallels in

6. Published posthumously in 1988 by St. Vladimir's Seminary Press,
Crestwood, NY, pp. 199-200.

Mark 14:12 and Luke 22:8), and Paul wrote: "For Christ our passover [paschal] lamb has been sacrificed" (I Cor. 5:7).

There is, however, one important chronological difficulty to overcome if we are to assert it as highly probable that Jesus inaugurated the Eucharist during a celebration of the Passover. That is the fact that the synoptics and John's gospel disagree as to the date of the evening on which the Last Supper was held. John does not record the institution of the Eucharist, but his thought is impregnated with paschal ideas. He makes the death of Christ coincident with the slaughter of the paschal lambs, with the clear implication that the sacrifice of Christ replaced the sacrifice of the Law. Yet the fact remains that the lambs were slaughtered the day before the Passover was kept. The writers of the synoptic gospels clearly insist that the Last Supper and the Passover were held on the same evening.

Two fairly recent contributors to the discussion are of the opinion that the chronological difficulty can be overcome by holding that there were two different calendars for celebrating the Passover. Matthew Black, impressed by the Passover associations of John's Last Supper (narrative of 13:1ff. with intervening discourse material resumed at 18:2), asks whether this might have been an irregular passover. He finds some evidence for this supposition in the account of Mark, arguing that it was the illegality of the meal that gave Judas his chance to betray Christ. The dipping of the sop of bitter herbs was a distinctive and peculiar custom of the Passover, so that when Judas carried the sop, he brought evidence to the priests and Pharisees that an illegal feast had been celebrated. This would mean that Jesus was challenging the law of the Pharisees in their headquarters in Jerusalem.[7]

Now the question has to be settled as to whether there were calendars other than the official one. One exception is certainly the Qumran community's calendar. Mlle. A. Jaubert (*La Date de la Cène*, 1957) argued that there was an ancient calendar that

7. Black, "The Arrest and Trial of Jesus and the Date of the Last Supper," in *New Testament Essays* (Manchester: Manchester University Press, 1959), p. 32.

was not based on the twelve lunar months, but on a year of 364 days divided into four quarters of thirteen weeks, and that, according to this calendar, the Passover would always be celebrated on a Wednesday. It can be found in the apocryphal book of *Jubilees,* as well as in other books. So the chronological difference between the synoptic and the Johannine dating of the Passover is not an insuperable difficulty in relating the Last Supper to the origin of the Eucharist.

Leenhardt presents a reasonable conclusion: "When one knows the central importance for the piety of every Israelite of this solemn feast, which recalled the redemptive acts of God in making them actual, and His promises in renewing them, it is unthinkable that the soul of Jesus and his friends likewise, could for a single moment put it out of mind, even if the day did not coincide exactly with the directions of the liturgical calendar."[8]

The Purpose and Progress of the Passover

To trace the impact of the Passover on the Eucharist we must describe its progression and its purpose. The triple synoptic tradition (Matt. 26:17-19; Mark 14:12-16; Luke 22:7-13) prefaces the Last Supper with an account of the preparations for the paschal meal: "On the first day of Unleavened Bread, when the Passover lamb was sacrificed, his disciples said to Jesus, 'Where will you have us prepare for you to eat the Passover?'" In the mind of the evangelists, therefore, the Last Supper was celebrated in the context of the Jewish Passover.[9] It was a continuing annual celebration of the crossing of the Red Sea and the road to liberation from the galling servitude of Egypt. Lucien Deiss writes concerning its purpose:

8. Leenhardt, *op. cit.,* pp. 9-14ff.
9. Lucien Deiss, *It's the Lord's Supper: The Eucharist of Christians,* trans. Edmond Bonin (New York/Ramsey, NJ/Toronto: Paulist Press, 1976), p. 33.

To describe this liberation, Israel exhausted the vocabulary of human tenderness. In its mind, liberation from Egypt was like a mysterious birth, with God taking it in his arms as a father takes a newborn child (Hosea 11:1-3). God adopted this people in the wilds of the howling desert (Deuteronomy 32:10); there, the young maiden Israel was wed to her God (Jeremiah 2:2); and there she was loved "with an everlasting love" (Jeremiah 31:3).[10]

The Passover is designed to enable every Israelite to go through the drama of divinely directed freedom. The celebrants of the Lord's Supper merely mimed the Passover.

The meal was shared in a reclining position, appropriate to the status of free men who had experienced a great liberation. Four different times during the meal they drank from different cups of wine, each an emblem of joyful gratitude to God for having delivered their forefathers from Egyptian bondage, as had been ordered in Exodus 12.

After the preliminary benedictions the *harosheth* (i.e., a salad of bitter herbs) was brought to the table, followed by the unleavened bread and finally the lamb, each having a profound symbolical import. Then the father of the family gathered for the Passover would explain the meaning of the rite in response to the inquiry of the youngest son. The explanation essentially took the form of a commentary on Deuteronomy 26:5-11:

"And you shall make response before the LORD your God, 'A wandering Aramean was my father; and he went down into Egypt and sojourned there, few in number; and there he became a nation, great, mighty and populous. And the Egyptians treated us harshly, and afflicted us, and laid upon us hard bondage. Then we cried to the LORD the God of our fathers, and the LORD heard our voice, and saw our affliction, our toil, and our oppression: and the LORD brought us out of Egypt with a

10. *Ibid.*, p. 34.

mighty hand and an outstretched arm, with great terror, with
signs and wonders; and he brought us into this place and gave
us this land flowing with milk and honey. And behold, now I
bring the first of the fruit of the ground, which thou, O LORD,
hast given me.' And you shall set it down before the LORD
your God, and worship before the LORD your God; and you
shall rejoice in all the good which the LORD your God has
given to you and to your house, you, and the Levite, and the
sojourner who is among you."

The rest of the explanation derived from the account of the
liberation in Exodus 12. This passage tells how the preparation
for the deliverance took place. Each household was to take an
unblemished male lamb in the evening, kill it, and sprinkle some
of the blood on their doorposts and their lintels; the flesh was
to be roasted and eaten with bitter herbs, and in haste; "the
blood shall be a sign for you, upon the houses where you are,
and when I see the blood, I will pass over you"; and "This day
shall be for you a memorial day, and you shall keep it as a feast
to the LORD; throughout your generations you shall observe it
as an ordinance for ever."[11] In addition, the feast was to be
celebrated with unleavened bread, another sign of the haste in
which the Israelites were to depart. The bread, which could not
be baked, was "the bread of affliction" (Deut. 16:3); it was also
the bread of emergency. The bitter herbs also symbolized the
bitterness of Israel's lot before the divine redemption. The emergency was symbolized as well by the requirement that the
Israelites eat the lamb hastily, with a girdle round their waist,
sandals on their feet, and a staff in their hand, as if they were
escaping from some invisible pharaoh.[12]

The celebration of the Passover was not the memorial of an
historic event so much as it was a making it actual, like an event
in which each guest was taking part. Every guest knew that he
or she shared a redemption of which they were the beneficiaries.

11. Exodus 12:13-14.
12. Deuteronomy 16:1-8 and Exodus 12:11.

Thus, says Leenhardt, "Each one knew, not only what God had done once upon a time for his fathers, but also what God was doing for him."[13] The bitter herbs had to be chewed as an existential experience so that the contemporary person could be placed in the situation of the fathers and thus know that he had been freed from slavery. So the purpose of the paschal feast was to make real the covenant relationship established between God and Israel by divine grace.

However, the meaning of the Passover had changed in the time of Christ. Once more Israel was no longer free but existing under the suzerainty of the Romans, and the memory of the mighty deliverance of the past created the hope of a new liberation and a new deliverer. For this reason, the singing of the Psalms of the Hillel, an important component of the worship of the Passover, was given a messianic interpretation, and thus the fifth cup was given great significance. It was a large goblet kept for the prophet Elijah, a forerunner of the Messiah, in case he should come back. In this way, at the paschal meal, which Jesus shared with his disciples, their thoughts would be dominated by a past and a future redemption accomplished by God, by the recollection of the Covenant given at Sinai and the promise of a New Covenant, and by the thought of the paschal lamb and Christ as the Lamb of God.

The Transformation of the Passover in the Eucharist

If the background of the Passover was a very important context for the Last Supper, yet there was striking novelty in its explication, which constituted a transformation. Like the fifth cup in the Passover, this was a striking affirmation of the belief in a coming Messiah.

It has been pointed out that when their Master told the disciples of his forthcoming betrayal, they responded with

13. Leenhardt, *op. cit.,* p. 17.

anxious questions. When he spoke of his impending departure and return, Philip instantly asked to be shown the Father. Surprisingly, however, when Jesus made the striking pronouncement — "This piece of unleavened bread is my Body" — the disciples apparently accepted his words without further explanation. It is difficult, therefore, to assume that in the Passover liturgy in the time of Jesus there was not a reference to the messianic hope because that would have prepared the disciples for the equation of the unleavened bread with his body.[14]

In fact, it has recently been suggested that there survives even in the present-day Passover ritual a detail that requires a strongly messianic interpretation. Near the commencement of the celebration, after the president or host of the company has called upon God, Creator of the vine and the fruits of the earth, and the guests have drunk a cup of wine and eaten green vegetables, he breaks off a large part from the middle of three pieces of unleavened bread. He then covers it in a napkin and hides it.

The name of this portion that has been broken and concealed is *Afikoman*. The name is neither Hebrew nor Aramaic; it is of Greek derivation. Since this *Afikoman* is to be "discovered" and eaten at the end of the meal, some Jewish scholars have proposed that it means something akin to "dessert." However, Professor David Daube, an orthodox Jew who is very learned in Rabbinic Judaism, has affirmed in a London lecture, "*Aphiqoman* is the Greek *aphikomenos* or *ephikomenos*, 'The Coming One,' 'He that Cometh', Hebrew *habba*, Aramaic *'athe.'*"[15] A modern Jewish description of the Passover liturgy declares: "Since the meal cannot be ritually complete without eating the *Afikoman*, the

14. In this and in the following paragraphs concerned with the *Afikoman* and its significance in the Passover ritual I am greatly indebted to the second chapter of Thomas Corbishley, S.J., *One Body, One Spirit* (Leighton Buzzard, Eng.: Faith Press, 1973) in which he cites on two occasions an important lecture by Professor David Daube, "He That Cometh," given October 1966 at St. Paul's Cathedral, London.

15. David Daube's lecture cited by Corbishley, *op. cit.,* p. 22.

leader or host now calls for it. . . . The *Afikoman* is our substitute for the Paschal Lamb, which in days of old was the final food of the Seder feast. Each person is given a portion, which is eaten in a reclining position."

Thomas Corbishley views the drama of the Last Supper as follows:

Picture then the Leader, at the Last Supper, calling for the *Afikoman,* which, we remember, has been hidden since the beginning of the proceedings, and saying to his followers: 'The *Afikoman,* He who Comes, who was hitherto hidden, has now come. This piece of bread is my very self, no longer in type but in reality. When, therefore, you eat it, you are eating no longer a symbol, a foreshadowing of a future reality. You are eating my very self. Whenever, in days to come, you eat this same *Afikoman,* remember that I am truly present in it and therefore in you.'[16]

After the meal is completed, prayers are offered that include passages with a messianic application. We presume that they date back to the time of Christ, though this cannot be proved. One prayer includes the following statement:

We thank thee for thy covenant sealed in our flesh.

While this would originally refer to circumcision, yet it would have a fulfillment in the flesh of Christ's circumcised body soon to be broken on the cross to initiate the New Covenant. Soon afterward the assembly prays:

Hasten the Messianic era.

and also

May the merciful Father find us worthy of the Messianic era.

Almost immediately afterward the prayer follows:

16. Corbishley, *op. cit.,* p. 23.

> Blessed art thou, O Lord our God, king of the Universe who
> createst the fruit of the vine.[17]

Then the company drink the third of four cups that are drunk
during the Passover festival. As Corbishley rightly says, these
prayers, and particularly the ritual of the *Afikoman,* illuminate
Luke's account of the Last Supper:

> And when the hour came, he sat at table, and the apostles with
> him. And he said to them, "I have earnestly desired to eat this
> passover with you before I suffer; for I tell you I shall not eat
> it until it is fulfilled in the kingdom of God." And he took a
> cup, and when he had given thanks he said, "Take this and
> divide it among yourselves; for I tell you that from now on I
> shall not drink of the fruit of the vine until the kingdom of
> God comes." (22:14-18)

We need only add that the same gospel shows Jesus giving the
disciples the cup with the saying, "This cup which is poured out
for you is the new covenant in my blood" (22:20b).

David Daube, in his lecture delivered in St. Paul's Cathedral,
London, under the auspices of the Diocesan Council for Christian Jewish Understanding in October 1966, sums up the argument as follows:

> We are so used to Jesus's action on that occasion that we no
> longer wonder about its peculiar character, take it as, in the
> circumstances, the most natural thing in the world. A moment's
> reflection, however, will expose the untenability of this attitude.
> Let me put it this way: had no ritual of the kind preserved in
> the Jewish Passover eve service existed, and had Jesus suddenly
> distributed a cake of unleavened bread and said of it, "This is
> my body," His disciples, to put it mildly, would have been
> perplexed. With such a ritual referring to "The Coming One"
> in existence, the self-revelation made sense. Up to then, the
> fragment of unleavened bread was, so to speak, the Messiah in

17. The citations from the Passover liturgy are Corbishley's, *ibid.*

the abstract, the unknown Messiah; now He was known. The ritual of eating "The Coming One" . . . must precede the institution of the Eucharist, the decisive point of which was the identification: the ancient expectation was now fulfilled. If we did not find such a ritual in the Jewish background, we should have to invent it. As it does occur, the reasonable course seems to be to accept it for what it is.[18]

The Change from Passover to Eucharist

We have seen that there was one very important change in the movement from the Passover to the Eucharist, whether we consider the fifth cup prepared for Elijah the forerunner of the Messiah, or the *Afikoman* that was the piece of unleavened bread hidden and disclosed as a sign of the Messiah. Either would signify to the disciples in the upper room that Christ was the Messiah, and they would apprehend this not as a prophecy but a fulfillment. Such was not the case in the Passover liturgy as celebrated by the Jews.

Among the other notable differences between the Passover and the Eucharist was the matter of the frequency of the celebration. The Passover, the most solemn feast of the Jews, was an annual feast and the center of the Jewish year. But the Lord's Supper, or Eucharist, was not limited to those who were Jews; the Gentiles also participated, and it was from its origin almost a daily rite, as Acts 2:42, 46 attests.

Furthermore, none of the Psalms recited in the Passover, which made much of the so-called Hillel group of Psalms, was sung or recited during the Eucharist. Nor were the symbolic ceremonies of the Passover, such as the bitter herbs, the requirement of unleavened bread, and the inclining attitude at table, carried over into the Eucharist.[19] The climax of the paschal lamb was also

18. Daube cited by Corbishley, *op. cit.*, pp. 24-35.

19. The reason for the elimination of the details of the Passover from the reports of Paul and the synoptic writers of the Last Supper is suggested by H. Leclercq in his article, "La Messe," in the *Dictionnaire d'Archéologie*

omitted, except that in the course of time Christ himself was conceived as the ultimate substitute for it — and the end of sacrifices — since he was the Lamb of God. The five drinks had also disappeared in favor of a single drink from the chalice. In Roman Catholicism, as the tradition evolved, the people received the bread but not the wine, on the ground that the Body included the Blood.

But the striking differences were profoundly significant. Above all there was the recognition, as we have seen, that this meal proclaimed with the utmost clarity that Jesus was the Messiah and the inaugurator of the Kingdom of God and of the New Covenant that he had proclaimed in words and deeds, in preaching and parables, in miracles and in the actions of love. Moreover, the symbolism of this sacrament conveyed the awesome sublimity of the self-offering of the Son of God on the cross in the broken body and shed blood. But it differed from all other memorials, which were customarily souvenirs, or remembrances of deceased persons, in that the Eucharist symbolized and expressed Christ's promise: "Lo, I am with you always, to the close of the age" — a pledge from the risen, ascended Lord, who, according to the Epistle to the Hebrews, was seated beside God the Father in heaven and offered intercession for his faithful disciples of all times. These dramatic symbols conveyed what they represented: the uplifting and strengthening presence of the Eternal Savior, host and victim of the feast, the crucified leader of the new exodus from human slavery, "the pioneer and perfecter of our faith, who for the joy that was set before him endured the cross, despising the shame, and is seated at the right hand of the throne of God."[20] Thus, the Eucharist was an expression of three tenses: the past, the present, and the future.

Chrétienne et de Liturgie (Paris: Librairie Letouzey et Ane, 1933), Tome 11, I, p. 531B, as follows: "But — so as not to confuse the Jewish converts — the Eucharist had to give up the rites and formulas associated with the Passover." A further reason would be the extreme length of the Passover liturgy, which made it unsuitable for frequent celebration.

20. Hebrews 12:2.

Conclusion

In conclusion, the disciples would hear familiar echoes of the Passover in the Last Supper as well as meet two dramatically strange and novel elements. After the first dishes, the *hors d'oeuvres* of bitter herbs and the fruit *purée* the color of clay, grace was said before the main course of the Passover Lamb. At this point Jesus made the first unexpected innovation in the Passover ritual recorded in the New Testament. Here it was customary for the father of the household to take the unleavened bread in his hands and to say the prayer, "Blessed art Thou, who bringest forth bread from the earth." Then the father broke the bread into fragments. But at this point Jesus said instead, "Take, eat; this is my body." It would be slightly less of a surprise to the disciples if that fragment of unleavened bread was the *Afikoman*, but still a surprise, for he was affirming his messiahship.

As the meal proper continued with the eating of the Passover Lamb along with the side dishes, and with a concluding prayer of thanksgiving said over the third cup of wine, Jesus made his second change from the expected ritual. He then pronounced the words, "This is my blood which is poured out for many," or, "This cup is the new covenant in my blood."

The conclusion to be drawn from this selection of words and of these particular actions is that Jesus was inaugurating a New Covenant feast that would take the place of the Passover and the Old Covenant with Israel for his followers in the new, expanded Israel. Christ was, by these actions and interpretations, claiming for himself and his work a central and dominating place in the history of God's chosen people, and the hardest part for the disciples to understand was that he was shortly to become a crucified and agonized Messiah.

So in this new sacrament were linked the triple ideas of remembrance, sacrifice, and covenant, all of which had been included in the development of the historic Jewish Passover. The traditional Passover included recalling not only the dramatic exodus from slavery in Egypt to freedom in Canaan, but prior to that the readiness of Abraham to sacrifice Isaac, prefiguring Christ's own sacrifice to end sacrifices, the subsequent Covenant given to Moses on Sinai, and, still later, the future New Covenant promised by Jeremiah.

The details of the Passover and its significant symbolic acts and prayers did not need to be reported by Paul and the writers of the synoptic gospels because they were thoroughly familiar to the Jewish disciples. But the newer, revolutionary, and transformational elements added by Jesus had to be stressed, as, indeed, they were. And even today the degrees of meaning of the Eucharist are still far from being wholly understood.

TWO   The Eucharist as Thanksgiving

T HE TITLE of this chapter is redundant in that Eucharist is itself a Greek word best translated "thanksgiving." This was, in fact, one of the earliest terms used for the communion liturgy in the Hellenic world. It was also John and Charles Wesley's favorite name for the sacrament. It is the most frequently used term in the contemporary world as a consequence of the liturgical movement and the growing ecumenical sense that the disunity of the churches glaringly exhibited at the communion table is a denial of the central petition of Christ's high-priestly prayer that his disciples should be one, as he and the Father are one, "so that the world may know that thou hast sent me and hast loved them even as thou hast loved me" (John 17:23b). Furthermore, it is scandalous that this disunity should be revealed at the form of worship that is intended to produce the greatest degree of fellowship between Christ and his church. Thus, for both historic and ecumenical reasons there is growing acceptance of the term "Eucharist."

The alternative titles seem to stress divergence and difference rather than unity. The "Mass" derives from the formal conclusion of the service with its instruction, *Ite, missa est* ("Go, it is over"), which says nothing about the nature of this central communal act of the church. "The Lord's Supper" — a favorite Protestant designation — stresses the fact that it was instituted by Christ, which it was, but its emphasis is merely retrospective. "Communion" or "Holy Communion" — the favorite Anglican term for

17

the Eucharist — stresses the profound element of fellowship between God and humanity past and present, but leaves other
meanings of this service unexpressed. "Eucharist," on the other
hand, expresses the appropriate attitude of Christians contemplating their grateful and joyful encounter with the crucified and
risen Lord as the body of Christ. It also happens to be a term
historically used by the Orthodox churches.

An Etymological Excursus

In the first Christian centuries the Eucharist was designated by
different terms both in the New Testament and in classical Greek
and Latin usage. These included the following terms: *coena*
(supper), *coena dominica* (the Lord's supper) or *mensa Domini*
(kuriakon deipnon) (table of the Lord), *sacrificium (thusia)* (sacrifice), *oblatio* (oblation or offering), *fractio, fractio panis (klasis tou*
artou) (the breaking of bread), *to poterion tes eulogias* (I Cor.
10:16) (the cup of blessing), or simply *eulogia* (thanksgiving),
which was always an alternative Greek word for *eucharistia,*
leitourgia (the liturgy), and *anaphora* (the prayer of blessing).

Other alternative designations were *Agape* (love feast),
which ultimately became separate from the Eucharist; *synaxis*
(gathering); *invocatio* (or *epiklesis*), meaning invocation or the
word of invocation; *oratio* and *gratiarum actiones (euchai kai*
eucharistai), meaning words or acts of blessing, as in Justin
Martyr; *preces mystica* (mystical prayers); *solemnis oratio* (solemn
prayer); or again, *dominicum, dominicum collectam agere, offere*
(to make or offer the prayer of the Lord).[1]

However, among all these varied designations, the one term
that was more specially used to designate this mystery and that
is most frequently used nowadays is "the Eucharist." In classical

---

1. This catalogue of alternative designations for the Eucharist in early
Christian centuries is that supplied by Fernand Cabrol in Vol. Va, col. 686
of the *Dictionnaire d'Archéologie Chrétienne et da Liturgie.*

Greek the verb *eucharistein* has the meaning of being grateful or rendering thanks. The Septuagint uses the same Greek verb with exactly the same significance, as, for example, when Judith addresses her co-citizens of Bethulia thus: "Let us give thanks *(eucharistesomen)* to the Lord our God who, as He tested our ancestors, is now testing us" (Jud. 8:25), and the Jews who had been well treated in Scythopolis *thanked* the inhabitants for that kindness (II Macc. 12:29b), using the same verb, *eucharistein*.

The New Testament Use of the Term "Eucharist"

Before attempting to elucidate the New Testament use of the Greek verb *eucharistein,* it will be helpful to examine the use of the same verb in the Old Testament. Thanksgiving had a central place in Jewish piety, responding to the sense of triumphant and adoring gratitude experienced in the divine creation and in human history. The Psalmist spoke for all Jews in recording that "all the paths of the LORD are steadfast love and faithfulness, for those who keep his covenant and his testimonies" (25:10). Genesis 24:26-27 tells how Abraham sent his eldest servant to find Isaac a bride, and how God showed him the exquisitely beautiful Rebekah at the well of Nahor. His response is characteristic: "The man bowed his head and worshiped the LORD, and said, 'Blessed be the LORD, the God of my master Abraham, who has not forsaken his steadfast love and his faithfulness toward my master. As for me, the LORD has led me in the way to the house of my master's kinsmen.'" Here we have a profound sense of adoring obedience to God based upon admiration for God's marvelous guidance. This sense of wonder at God's creation and his control of the universe he made is central to the Psalms, and in the Eucharist as well evokes gratitude in the faithful.

The very earth is a vast temple where the creation shouts "Glory!" (Ps. 29:9), and the individual knows that every period of his life is in the hands of the Almighty (Ps. 31:16). His adoration is summed up in Psalm 31:21: "Blessed be the LORD, for he has wondrously shown his steadfast love to me. . . ," concluding in the imperative: "Love the LORD, all you his saints!" (Ps. 31:23).

The most typical lyrical prayer of Judaism is called the *Shemone Esre* or Eighteen Benedictions, and this is so representative that it is called *Tephillah* (the Prayer). Its initial stanza contains essential elements belonging to pre-Christian days:

> Blessed be you, O Yahweh,
> Our God and God of our fathers,
> God of Abraham, of Isaac and Jacob,
> Great God, redoubtable and mighty,
> Most high God, creator of heaven and earth,
> Our shield and the shield of our fathers,
> Our confidence in every generation.
> Blessed be you, O Yahweh, shield of Abraham!

As Lucien Deiss writes of this prayer, which is to be recited three times each day: "The soul of Israel reveals itself here unable to ask anything without giving thanks, unwilling to extend its hand to beg without first raising it to bless."[2] It is significant that Jesus, according to the report of Luke 10:21-22, echoes the *Shemone Esre,* for "Filled with the Holy Spirit," he said:

> "I bless you, Father,
> Lord of heaven and earth,
> for hiding these things from the learned and the clever
> and revealing them to mere children.
> Yes, Father, for that is what it has pleased you to do."

In the New Testament the word *eucharistein* is encountered frequently with its synonym *eulogein.* In the account of the miraculous feeding of the five thousand, Luke uses the latter

---

2. Deiss, *It's the Lord's Supper,* transl. Edmond Bonin (New York/Ramsey, NJ/Toronto: Paulist Press, 1976), p. 48.

verb: "And taking the five loaves and two fish he looked up to heaven, and blessed and broke them" *(eulogesen autous)* (9:16a), as do the parallel passages in Matthew 14:19 and Mark 6:41, while John 6:11 uses the synonymous verb *eucharistein* in the form *eucharistesas* translated "when he had given thanks. . . ." In the later miraculous feeding of the four thousand (Matt. 15:36; Mark 8:6) the verb used in blessing the seven fish is *eucharistein*. Yet when the risen Christ is with the Emmaus disciples and takes the bread, breaks it, and gives it to them, the verb used is *eulogein* (Luke 24:30). Furthermore, when in the midst of a tempest Paul encourages his companions by taking bread, giving thanks, breaking it, and eating it (Acts 27:35), the term used is *eucharistesen*. Thus, it is clear that the term for offering thanks or blessing can be used with or without any reference to the sacramental eucharist.

On the other hand, *eucharistein* is the preferred verbal form for referring to the institution of the sacrament. In each of the four eucharistic texts the word for blessing or giving thanks is *eucharistesas*. This is the case in the synoptic gospels and in I Corinthians 11, with the single exception of Mark 14, which used *eulogesas* for the bread and *eucharistesas* for the wine in verses 22 and 23.

It should be observed that the English translations of *eucharistesas* vary considerably. The RSV employs "when he had given thanks" consistently; the NEB uses "offered thanks," "gave thanks," and "after giving thanks"; and the JB has the renderings "when he had returned thanks," "when he had given thanks," "gave thanks," and "thanked God." *Eulogesas* is translated "blessed" in the RSV, "having said the blessing" in the NEB, and "when he had said the blessing" in the JB.

The Anaphora and Its Importance

Conservative critics have considered the category "eucharist" as too insubstantial an approach to understanding the meaning of the sacrament, but the research of J. P. Audet, "Literary Forms and Contents of a Normal Eucharistia in the First Century," has thrown a great deal of light on the dependence of the blessing in the primitive Eucharist on the Jewish *berakah* or "benediction."[3] Its importance can be gauged from Nicholas Lash's endorsement of Audet's conviction that too little attention has been paid to the concept of thanksgiving and blessing and its Jewish background, and too much attention given to the three short sentences: "This is my body," "This is my blood," and "Do this in remembrance of me."[4]

Audet's first conclusion is that the Eucharist is a solemn act of worship, addressed to God.

Second, the Eucharist is a communal action, a prayer made in the midst and in the name of an assembly of people, with the consequence that the individual deputed to "make the eucharist" in the assembly cannot be defined in abstraction from that community, and thus the priesthood of the community is protected from sacerdotal dominance.

In the third place, the "eucharist" has a threefold structure. The first element of the *berakah* is the "benediction" proper; it is invitatory in character and forms a brief but enthusiastic call to divine praise. The second component of the *berakah* is the assertion of the motive for the praise of the assembly. This motive is consistently declared to be a *mirabile Dei,* a wonderful work of God. Audet maintains that it is admiration and joy rather than gratitude that are dominant, for praise concentrates on the person praised and gratitude on the gift received, though in-

3. J. P. Audet's "Literary Forms and Contents of a Normal Eucharistia in the First Century" appeared in *The Gospels Reconsidered* (Oxford: Oxford University Press, 1960). It had first appeared in K. Aland *et al.,* eds., *Studia Evangelica: Papers Presented to the International Congress on 'The Four Gospels' in 1957* (Berlin, 1959), pp. 623-62. Although controversial, it has won the approval of Betz, Denis-Boulet, Jeremias, Kavanagh, Maertens, Thurian, and Vagaggini. For details see Nicholas Lash, *His Presence in the World: A Study in Eucharistic Worship and Theology* (London: Sheed and Ward, 1968), p. 78.

4. Lash, *op. cit.,* pp. 77-78.

creasingly the emphasis was bent toward thanksgiving. In the Christian Eucharist, however, the person and the gift coincide completely, as Nicholas Lash affirms.[5] One can readily see that the Christian anaphora also recalls the major *mirabilia Dei* in the orders of creation as well as redemption, in its anamnetic elements.[6] And this "recalling" of the mighty deeds of God in the past would not result in such permanent wonder and joy if it were only retrospective. But, as Professor Aidan Kavanagh insists, "the motive for blessing within a cultic action is a veritable kerygmatic annunciation to the assembly that this same *mirabile* is present here, active now, accomplishing its purpose still within the life of each and every member of the worshipping people."[7] The declaration of the link between the present rite and the saving acts of God is the central importance of the anaphora, and, Lash rightly claims, "it provides us with an essential insight towards an understanding of the relationship between that unique, unrepeatable, climactic, *mirabile Dei* which is the triumph of the cross, the sacrifice of Calvary, and the activity of the new people of God, assembled in the power of the Spirit of the risen Christ to celebrate that sacrifice."[8]

The third and concluding part of the *berakah* is a return to the initial "benediction" by way of a doxology, which is frequently "colored in different shades according to the particular theme which prevails in the anamnesis."[9]

In this brief summary of the structure of the *berakah* as a literary form, it can be seen that it has close parallels with the development of the eucharistic anaphora. Lash notes the parallels with the traditional Roman canon. He finds the initial "blessing" in the dialogue that precedes the Preface and in the opening phrases of the Prefaces themselves, the declaration of

5. *Ibid.*, p. 80, n. 33.
6. See my analysis of the concept *anamnesis* in the previous chapter.
7. Aidan Kavanagh, O.S.B., "Thoughts on the Roman Anaphora," in *Worship*, vol. XXXIX (1965), pp. 515-29, *ad loc.* 520.
8. Lash, *op. cit.*, p. 82.
9. Audet, *op. cit.*, p. 20.

the motive in the central part of most of the Prefaces and in the *Unde et memores,* and the concluding blessing in the final doxology.[10]

Although Professor Lash thinks that the Roman canon has a high content of joyful thanksgiving, another Roman Catholic, Fr. Lucien Deiss, would qualify the judgment, for he finds the reference to "eucharisticising" rather timid, even in the new Roman rites, with their praise "Father, you are holy indeed, and all creation rightly gives you praise," as Eucharistic Prayer III has it. In Eucharistic Prayer IV the day is anticipated when the glory of the Father will be celebrated when "freed from the corruption of sin and death, we shall with every creature" join in his praise. And Eucharistic Prayer II, modeled on Hippolytus's *Apostolic Tradition,* refers to Christ as follows: "He is the Word through whom you made the universe."[11]

The Term "Eucharist" in the Greek and Latin Fathers

It is worth taking a summary look at the use of the term "eucharist" in first the Greek and then the Latin Fathers. According to Fernand Cabrol, the word *eucharistia, eucharistein* was adopted by tradition to designate either the prayer that accompanied the consecration of the Eucharist, or the consecration itself.[12] St. Ignatius and St. Justin Martyr were the first to employ the term clearly in reference to the Eucharist.[13] The same usage is characteristic of the references of Irenaeus, Clement of Alexandria, and Origen, as also the *Didache.*[14]

10. Lash, *op. cit.,* p. 83.

11. Deiss, *op. cit.,* p. 53. It should be recalled, however, that the many Prefaces, varying with the Christian year, add considerably to the thanksgivings.

12. *Dictionnaire d'Archéologie Chrétienne et de Liturgie,* vol. Va, col. 689.

13. Justin, *Apol.* 1.66 (*Patrologia Graeca* VI, col. 428); Ignatius, *Ad Smyrn.* (P.G. V, col. 713).

14. Irenaeus 1.4.18, n. 5 (P.G. VII, col. 428); Clement, *Strom.* 1.4.25 (P.G. VIII, col. 1369); Origen, *Hom. in Num.* 5.1; the *Didache* 9.

St. John Chrysostom often speaks of the "eucharist," as does St. Cyril of Jerusalem. In the dialogue of the Preface the phrase *Eucharistesomen to Kurio* appears in the Liturgy of St. James, the Apostolic Constitutions, the Liturgy of St. Mark, and the Liturgy of St. Basil and St. John Chrysostom.[15]

The term used by the Latins is *eucharistia*, frequently found in the liturgies as in the Fathers. Tertullian refers to the *Eucharistiae Sacramentum* (*De Corona Militum* 3), and St. Cyprian often uses the term but prefers other alternatives such as *caro Christi, sanctum Domini, corpus Domini, sacrificium, solemnia,* and *oblatio*.[16] St. Augustine also uses the term *eucharistia* often, as in *Patrologia Latina* XLV, col. 1515. Fernand Cabrol notes that St. Thomas Aquinas provides a special etymology for *eucharistia: "dicitur eucharistia. id est BONA GRATIA: quia gratia Dei vita aeterna: vel quia realiter continet Christum qui est plenus gratia."* ("It is called eucharist because the grace of God is eternal life or because it contains in reality Christ who is full [of] grace.")

The Meaning of "Eucharist"

Our frequent references to the etymology of the Eucharist and its usage by the Scriptures, in Jewish piety, and by the Greek and Latin Fathers in the Latin and Oriental liturgies have established its widespread use in East and West from earliest Christian times. But we have barely touched the excitement and vitality that lies in the word. One modern theologian who has a romantic gift with words to enable the term "eucharist" to explode like a series of celestial fireworks before our eyes is Lucien Deiss. He takes as his example Clement of Alexandria, who rapturously

15. Chrysostom's references to "eucharist" are collected in F. E. Brightman, *Liturgies Eastern and Western* (London: Oxford University Press, 1896), pp. 474 and 479. For Cyril of Jerusalem's references see, for example, *Catecheses Mystagogica,* 1 (P.G. XXXIII, col. 1072).

16. Detailed source references are supplied by Fernand Cabrol, *op. cit.,* Va, col. 689.

describes Christ the Eternal Son's Eucharist chant with redeemed humanity: "Setting aside lyre and cithara as soulless instruments, the Word of God, through the Holy Spirit, has attuned to himself the world and especially man, who epitomizes it, together with his body and soul. With this thousand-voiced instrument, he sings of God and accompanies himself on this cithara which is man."[17]

As inspired as Clement of Alexandria, Deiss shows how the joint themes of creation and redemption are uplifted in the Eucharist. He writes:

> All these themes, naturally, have been "Christianized" in the passover of Christ, transfigured by the glory of the risen Lord. "To do this" in memory is to follow his example and praise the Creator for the seas and mountains he holds in the hollow of his hand, but especially for the new heavens and the new earth inaugurated by the resurrection; to bless the Father for fashioning the first man from the clay of the earth, but especially for forming the new Adam, whose resurrection flows back over the world in a ceaseless wave of life and joy (cf. Romans 5:12-21). Christians sing the "eternal light" of the spring equinox, but especially the Son of life and immortality who shines in their hearts (cf. 2 Timothy 1:10); they thank God for the springtime that mantles the hillsides in flowers and germinates the first fruits of the harvest for the passover, but especially for the unending springtime which the door of eternity now opens to them. Though they see that sin has flawed the harmony of creation and faded its beauty like a rose scattered on the autumn wind, they know the risen Lord restores everything — the universe of heaven and earth — in himself (cf. Ephesians 1:10, 22-23; I Corinthians 15:27; Revelation 21:6). Though they hear captive creation groaning under the yoke of sin and vanity (cf. Romans 8:19-22), they know these are no longer the throes of agony but the pangs of new life coming to birth. They know they are walking toward a new land, toward new heavens,

17. From the *Protrepticus* 1.5. Fr. Deiss's translation, *op. cit.*, pp. 53-54.

toward a new Jerusalem as beautiful as a bride (cf. Revelation
21:1-5). In a word, as the Jewish passover was the feast of
creation and springtime, so Christ's passover is the feast of the
new creation and eternal springtime, with the Eucharist commemorating and rendering thanks for both.[18]

Such poetical words are more suitable to describe the *mirabilia Dei* and the wonder they evoke than the usual diction of
liturgists who stumble amid the paradoxes and divine mysteries
and transcendences. So, again, I cite the words of Deiss as he
describes the transformation God makes in the Eucharist itself:

> But this process of divinization, this transformation of clay into
> a hymn of thanksgiving, is signified with particular intensity by
> the Eucharist. The grain of wheat, placed in the heart of the
> earth, germinated under the kiss of the springtime sun, crowned
> with golden heads ripe for harvesting, and baking into bread
> for man, is here changed into the body of the Son of God! And
> the blood of the grape, bronzed in autumn sunshine, is changed
> into the blood of the risen Christ. It is no longer just a sign of
> God (demonstrating his existence as does everything that comes
> from his hands), and no longer just a bearer of his grace (as in
> the other sacraments). Transubstantiated, it is eternal life, the
> body of the Son of God.
>   Thus the Eucharist reveals the ultimate meaning of God's
> creative act: the vocation of the entire universe. . . . This return
> of the creature Godward, this metamorphosis of slaves' groan-
> ing (cf. Romans 8:22) into a filial hymn of praise is signified
> by the Eucharist in a way which transcends all the other sacra-
> ments. The moment of consecration — when the bread and the
> wine, "fruit of the earth and work of human hands," become
> the body of Christ — consummates in the twinkling of an eye
> the march of the centuries toward God. Predestined by the
> Father, called to existence in the Son, "the first-born of all
> creation" (Colossians 1:15), and led by the Spirit, who moves

18. Deiss, *ibid.*

all the children of God (cf. Romans 8:4), man — and the creation he sums up in himself — returns "to the Father's heart" (John 1:18), that heart where the Son is found and the love of the Spirit reigns. . . . Born in the heart of God and transubstantiated in the Eucharist, creation returns into the heart of God, there eternally to "praise the glory of his grace" (Ephesians 1:6).[19]

Side by side with the eulogistic account of the meaning of thanksgiving in the sacrament are the grounds for thanksgiving as explained by a careful New Testament scholar of distinction. Professor William Barclay points out that the first eucharistic prayers, those of the *Didache,* are almost entirely prayers of thanksgiving, and cites the first prayer over the cup: "We give thanks to thee, our Father, for the Holy Vine of David, thy child, which thou didst make known to us through Jesus thy child; to thee be glory for ever." Over the bread the *Didache's* prayer goes: "We give thee thanks, our Father, for the life and knowledge which thou didst make known to us through Jesus thy child; to thee be glory for ever." He concludes by citing the post-Communion prayer:

> We give thanks to thee, O Holy Father, for thy Holy Name which thou didst make to tabernacle in our hearts, and for the knowledge and faith and immortality which thou didst make known to us through Jesus thy child; to thee be glory for ever. Thou, Lord Almighty, didst create all things for thy Name's sake, and didst give food and drink to men for their enjoyment, that they might give thanks to thee, but us hast thou blessed with spiritual food and drink and eternal light through thy child. Above all we give thee thanks that thou art mighty. To thee be glory for ever.

And Barclay's final comment on the first meaning of the Eucharist says it all without wasting a word: "The Eucharist is the

---

19. Deiss, *op. cit.,* pp. 54-55.

time for thanksgiving to God for his gifts in creation and redemption."[20]

Thanksgiving in Contemporary Eucharists

Already we have seen the divergence of opinion as to the adequacy or inadequacy of the element of thanksgiving in the Roman canons, along with the acknowledgment that the Prefaces in the anaphoras add several elements of thanksgiving according to the high and holy days of the Christian year. Is there much thanksgiving in the historic liturgy of the Eastern Orthodox churches still used relatively unchanged today? One is struck by the frequency of congregational affirmations of praise to the Holy Trinity that punctuate the liturgy. The depth of gratitude is most moving in a prayer of St. Simeon the new Divine in the Office of Preparation for Holy Communion, which after a profoundly penitential beginning concludes thus:

> . . . in merciful compassion thou dost cleanse and lighten them that earnestly repent, and makest them partakers of the light, freely imparting to them thy divinity: and, strange though it be to angels and to the mind of man, doest oftentimes hold converse with them, as with thy true friends. These things embolden me . . . O my Christ, and so, confiding in the riches of thy beneficence towards us, joyful at once and trembling, I who am grass partake of fire, and lo, a mighty wonder! I am bedewed and not consumed thereby, even as of old the bush burned and was not consumed. With thankful mind, with thankful heart, with thankfulness in every member of my soul and body now, I worship thee, my God, I glorify thee and I magnify thee, for blessed art thou, now and for evermore. Amen.[21]

20. Barclay, *The Lord's Supper* (London: SCM Press, 1967), p. 108.
21. *The Orthodox Liturgy being the Divine Liturgy of S. John Chrysostom and S. Basil the Great according to the Use of the Church of Russia* (London: S.P.C.K. for the Fellowship of SS Alban and Sergius, 1939), p. 13.

The Liturgy begins with the priest's affirmation: "Blessed is the kingdom of the Father, Son, and Holy Ghost, now and for ever and world without end,"[22] which sets the tone of the whole service. Psalm 146 (Praise the Lord, O my soul), later Psalm 93:1, 2, and 6 (The Lord is king and hath put on glorious apparel), follows, as does Psalm 95 (O come, let us sing unto the Lord), with intercalations of "O Son of God, who are wonderful in thy holy ones, who are risen from the dead, save us who sing unto thee: Alleluia."[23] There is thanksgiving also, as in the Roman and Anglican anaphoras, in the initiatory dialogue, "Let us give thanks unto the Lord"; and in the Liturgy of St. Basil, immediately before the words over the consecrated bread, the priest prays secretly in words that are charged with devotion and detailed thanksgiving to the "Master, lover of mankind" for his forgiveness to the sons of Adam, for sending the prophets and the saints, for sending the Law and angels for guardians, for the Incarnation of Christ, for his teaching, for his cross a ransom, his ascension to heaven, and his coming again.[24]

The entire point of the anaphora, according to Alexander Schmemann, is to be a thanksgiving. He wrote: "What, then, gives this chief, truly 'consummate' prayer of the liturgy its unity, transforms it into that *whole,* in and through which we affirm that this sacrament of sacraments is accomplished? The Church has answered this first and fundamental question literally from the first day of her existence by naming not only this prayer itself but also the entire liturgy with one word. This word is *eucharist, thanksgiving.*"[25] He concludes by asserting that the *praefatio* with the call of the celebrant "let us give thanks to the Lord" and the response of the assembly "it is meet and right"

22. *Op. cit.,* p. 32.
23. *Op. cit.,* found on pp. 37, 38, and 41.
24. *Op. cit.,* pp. 68-70.
25. *The Eucharist: Sacrament of the Kingdom* (Crestwood, NY: St. Vladimir's Seminary Press, 1988), p. 173.

are essentially "the beginning, the foundation, and the key to its entire contents, outside of which the most holy mystery of the eucharist remains hidden from us."[26]

Another indicator of the increased importance ecumenically of the term "eucharist" and its meaning can be seen in the fact that the majority of the recent liturgies of the Anglican communion of churches have changed the title of the Prayer of Consecration to the Prayer of Thanksgiving. Some of their newer thanksgivings put a lively stress on the importance of creation. A striking example is Eucharistic Prayer C in the second form of the Eucharist in *The Book of Common Prayer of the Episcopal Church in the U.S.A.* This goes as follows:

> At your command all things come to be: the vast expanse of interstellar space, galaxies, suns, the planets in their courses, and this fragile earth, our island home.
>
> All: *By your will they were created and have their being.*
>
> From the primal elements you brought forth the human race, and blessed us with memory, reason, and skill. You made us the rulers of creation. But we turned against you and betrayed your trust: and we turned against one another. . . .[27]

The same prayer continues with thanks for the sending of prophets and sages, and finally of Christ, as the assembly joins in praise with the communion of saints.

The Alternative Service Book 1980 of the Church of England has two *anamneses;* one is repeated in the first and second eucharistic prayers and the second is from the third eucharistic prayer. All three prayers allow an interesting variation in the initial dialogue:

---

26. *Ibid.,* p. 174.

27. Max Thurian and Geoffrey Wainwright, eds., *Baptism and Eucharist: Ecumenical Convergence in Celebration* (Geneva: World Council of Churches and Grand Rapids: Wm. B. Eerdmans, 1983), p. 165.

President: The Lord is here.
     All: *His Spirit is with us.*

Then the President continues:

It is indeed right,
it is our duty and our joy,
at all times and in all places
to give you thanks and praise,
holy Father, heavenly King,
almighty and eternal God,
through Jesus Christ your only Son our Lord.

Next follows the *anamnesis:*

For he is your living Word;
through him you have created all things from the beginning,
and formed us in your own image.

Through him you have freed us from the slavery of sin,
giving him to be born as man and to die upon the cross;
you raised him from the dead
and exalted him to your right hand on high.

Through him you have sent upon us
your holy and life-giving Spirit,
and made us a people for your own possession.[28]

Eucharistic Prayer III has the following *anamnesis:*

Father, we give you thanks and praise,
through your beloved Son Jesus Christ,
your living Word through whom you have created all things;

Who was sent by you, in your great goodness, to be our
    Saviour;
by the power of the Holy Spirit he took flesh and, as your

28. *The Alternative Service Book 1980,* pp. 130-31, 133.

Son,
born of the blessed Virgin, was seen on earth
and went about among us;

He opened wide his arms for us upon the cross;
he put an end to death by dying for us
and revealed the resurrection by rising to new life;
so he fulfilled your will and won for you a holy people.[29]

The Lutheran churches also emphasize creation in their eucharistic prayers. For example, the German Lutheran Church includes the following grateful recollection:

> Lord, our God, Ruler over all: We praise you for the wonder of your creation. You bless human labour and endow us with life and joy. You have given us bread and wine that we may celebrate the supper of your Son. We thank you for the mystery of your love. Receive us anew as your own that our conduct may honour you, through Jesus Christ, our Lord.[30]

A fuller *anamnesis* commemorating the creation and God's mighty acts in history is found in *The Lutheran Book of Worship* (1978), prepared by the Inter-Lutheran Commission on Worship, including the Lutheran Church in America, the American Lutheran Church, the Evangelical Lutheran Church of Canada, and the Lutheran Church–Missouri Synod. This liturgy is also remarkable for its ecumenical commemoration of the contribution of Christian leaders of all denominations in many centuries. Its *anamnesis* proceeds as follows:

> Holy God, mighty Lord, gracious Father:
> Endless is your mercy and eternal your reign.
> You have filled all creation with light and life;

---

29. *Ibid.*, p. 136.
30. Taken from *Agende für evangelisch-lutherische Kirchen und Gemeinden*, I (1955), with trial use revisions of 1976 and 1977. The English translated source is in Thurian and Wainwright, eds., *Baptism and Eucharist*, p. 139.

heaven and earth are full of your glory.
Through Abraham you promised to bless all nations.
You rescued Israel, your chosen people.
Through the prophets you renewed your promise;
and at this end of all the ages, you sent your Son,
who in words and deeds proclaimed your kingdom
and was obedient to your will, even to giving his life.[31]

The eucharistic prayers of the French Reformed Church are remarkable for their combination of joy, lively invocations of the Holy Spirit, and sense of the communion of saints. After the introductory dialogue one prayer goes as follows:

> Yes, it is our joy,
> O God of love and holiness, our Creator and our Father,
> to give you thanks always and everywhere.
> In your image you made us all,
> your universe you put in our care;
> your creation you entrust to our hands,
> with all its wonders and its travail.
> You make us partners in your labours
> and invite us to share in your rest,
> through Christ our Lord,
> whom the earth and the heavens
> with all the angels and archangels
> acclaim for ever and ever, singing:
>
> > *Holy, Holy, holy Lord,*
> > *God of the universe!*
> > *Heaven and earth are filled with your glory.*
> > *Hosanna in the highest.*
> > *Blessed is he who comes in the name of the Lord.*
> > *Hosanna in the highest.*

Lord, send upon us and upon this thanksgiving meal the
          Spirit of Life,
who spoke through Moses and the prophets,

31. *Lutheran Book of Worship*, p. 69.

who descended upon Jesus at the river Jordan,
and upon the apostles at the first day of Pentecost.
Send this same Spirit of fire,
that its coming may transfigure our humanity
by the power of Christ's body and blood.[32]

The Reformed churches of the world have followed the example of the Reformed Church of France in returning to the standard anaphora. For example, the Church of Scotland's eucharistic prayer, after the introductory dialogue, continues:

> Truly at all times and in all places we should give thanks to thee, O Holy Lord, Father Almighty, everlasting God; who didst create the heavens and the earth and all that is therein; who didst make man in thine own image and whose tender mercies are over all thy works.

> We praise thee for Jesus Christ whom thou hast sent to be the Saviour of the world.

> Blessed be the hour in which he was born and the hour in which he died.

> Blessed be the dawn of his rising again and the high day of his ascending.

> We praise thee that he, having ascended up on high, and sitting at thy right hand, sent forth the Holy Spirit upon the Church to be the light and guide of all those who put their trust in thee.

32. Eucharistic Prayer II, authorized in 1982 by the National Council of the Reformed Church of France. The English translation is from Thurian and Wainwright, eds., *op. cit.,* p. 152. The Fourth Eucharistic Prayer of this rite includes the following commemorative summary:

> For he is your living Word,
> through whom you created all things,
> whom you sent to us our Saviour,
> to do your will to the very end,
> and to gather together from our human race
> a holy people for your own possession. (*Op. cit.,* p. 153)

Blessed be the Spirit, the Giver of Life, enabling thy people to
proclaim the gospel among all nations and to fulfill with Christ
their royal priesthood until he comes again.[33]

The United Church of Christ in the United States dates
from the union of the Congregational and the Evangelical and
Reformed Church in 1957. Our citation will be from its book,
The Service of Word and Sacrament I (1957). Prior to the traditional dialogue, the leader in worship begins:

Luke the Evangelist records that on the evening of the first day
of the week, the same day on which our Lord rose from the
dead, when he was at table with two of the disciples, he took
bread and blessed and broke it, and gave it to them, and their
eyes were opened, and they knew him. Beloved, this is the joyful
feast of the people of God. Come from the East and the West,
and from the North and the South, and gather about the table
of the Lord. Behold how good and pleasant it is when brothers
and sisters dwell together in unity. The peace of the Lord Jesus
Christ be with you all.

The dialogue ensues, and the commemoration follows:

We give thanks to you, O holy Lord, Father Almighty, everlasting
God, for the universe which you have created, for the heavens
and the earth, and for every living thing. We thank you that you
have formed us in your own image and made us for yourself.
We bless you that when we rebelled against you, you did not
forsake us, but delivered us from bondage, and revealed your
righteous will and steadfast love by the law and the prophets.
    Above all we thank you for the gift of your Son, the Re-
deemer of all men, who was born of Mary, lived on earth in
obedience to you, died on the cross for our sins, and rose from
the dead in victory; who rules over us, Lord above all, prays
for us continually, and will come again in triumph.

33. *The Book of Common Order* (1979), the Second Order for Holy
Communion, included in Thurian and Wainwright, eds., *op. cit.*, p. 157.

We thank you for your Holy Spirit and for your holy church, for the means of grace and for the promise of eternal life. With patriarchs and prophets, with your church on earth and with all the company of heaven, we magnify and praise you, we worship and adore you, O Lord Most Holy.[34]

In this prayer God is praised in three tenses, past, present, and future (the latter in the *parousia*), within a trinitarian structure of devotion, and in a spirit of joyful sanctity.

A Book of Services (1980) of the United Reformed Church of the United Kingdom includes an impressive commemoration in relevant contemporary language, as follows, in what it calls "Thanksgiving III":

We thank you,
Lord God almighty,
that you are a God of people,
that you are not ashamed
to be called our God,
that you know us all by name,
that you hold the world in your hands.
You have created us
and called us in this life
that we should be made one with you
to be your people here on earth.
Blessed are you,
creator of all that is.
Blessed are you
for giving us space and time for living.
Blessed are you for the light of our eyes
and for the air we breathe.
We thank you for the whole of creation,
for all the works of your hands,
for all that you have done among us
through Jesus Christ, our Lord.

34. Included in Thurian and Wainwright, eds., *op. cit.,* 154-55.

Therefore with all the living
and all who have gone before us in faith,
we praise your name,
O Lord our God,
bowing before you, saying. . . .

After the *Sanctus,* the *Benedictus,* and the *Hosanna,* the prayer
continues:

We thank you, holy father,
Lord our God,
for Jesus Christ,
your beloved son,
whom you called and sent
to serve us and give us light,
to bring your kingdom to the poor,
to bring redemption to captives
and to be for ever
and for us all
the likeness and embodiment
of your constant love and goodness.
We thank you
for this unforgettable man
who has fulfilled everything that is human —
our life, our death.
We thank you
because he gave himself,
heart and soul, to this world. . . .[35]

The extraordinary simplicity (reflected in the multitude of mono-
syllabic words), relevance, and modernity of this prayer and of
the seasonal Prefaces is particularly striking.

The Methodist Churches in the U.S.A. and in Britain have

35. From *A Book of Services* (Edinburgh: The Saint Andrew Press, 1980,
2nd impression, 1984), pp. 34-35. The United Reformed Church is the
result of the union of the Congregational Church and the Presbyterian
Church of England in the United Kingdom.

also been busy liturgically. "The Great Thanksgiving" eucharistic prayer of The United Methodist Church, U.S.A. of 1980 is divided by the traditional *Sanctus, Hosanna,* and *Benedictus* into two sections, each of which deserves citation. The first part goes:

> Father, it is right that we should always
> and everywhere give you thanks and praise.
>
> Only you are God. You created all things and called them
>   good.
> You made us in your own image.
> Even though we rebelled against your love you did not
>   desert us.
> You delivered us from captivity,
> made covenant to be our sovereign God,
> and spoke to us through your prophets.

The second part continues:

> We thank you, holy Lord God,
> that you loved the world so much
> you sent your only Son to be our Saviour.
> The Lord of all life came to live among us.
>
> He healed and taught, ate with sinners,
> and won for you a new people by water and the Spirit.
> We saw his glory.
> Yet he humbled himself in obedience to your will,
> freely accepting death on a cross.
> By dying he freed us from unending death;
> by rising from the dead, he gave us everlasting life.[36]

The final couplet has a memorable concision and much illumination, and the emphasis on creation and redemption is balanced.

36. This is the "alternative rite" of the United Methodist Church of the United States as revised in *We Gather Together* (1980) and is also found in Thurian and Wainwright, eds., *op. cit.,* p. 171.

The Methodist Service Book is authorized by the British
Methodist Conference and was first published in 1975, to which
additions were made in 1984. It includes five impressive long
forms of thanksgivings arranged as litanies for use on Sundays
when the Eucharist is not celebrated. The eucharistic Thanksgiving proceeds as follows:

> Father, all-powerful and ever-living God,
> it is indeed right, it is our joy and our salvation,
> always and everywhere to give you thanks and praise
> through Jesus Christ your Son and Lord.
> You created all things and made us in your own image.
> When we had fallen into sin, you gave your only Son to
>   be our Saviour.
> He shared our human nature, and died on the cross.
> You raised him from the dead, and exalted him to your right
>   hand
> in glory, where he lives for ever to pray for us.
> Through him you have sent your holy and life-giving Spirit
> and made us your people, a royal priesthood, to stand
>   before you
> to proclaim your glory and celebrate your mighty acts.
> And so with all the company of heaven we join in the
>   unending
> hymn of praise. . . .[37]

Thanksgiving in Ecumenical Liturgies

Three ecumenical liturgies in particular deserve consideration for
their prayers of thanksgiving and the extent of the commemoration in them. The most important is the liturgy prepared for the

---

37. *The Methodist Service Book* (London: Methodist Publishing House,
reprint of 1984), pp. 56-57. The Alternative Thanksgivings are on pp.
76-81. Prayer B in this series would fit perfectly into the anamnetic section
of the anaphora in Holy Communion.

plenary session of the Faith and Order Commission of the World Council of Churches in Lima and used for the first time on January 15, 1982. It was later used at the Sixth Assembly of the World Council of Churches, with the Archbishop of Canterbury as the celebrant. It was devised by Max Thurian, distinguished liturgist of the Taizé Community, whose aim was "to illustrate the solid theological achievements of the Faith and Order document, *Baptism, Eucharist and Ministry.*"[38]

In the Eucharistic Liturgy of Lima there is a brief preparation before the dialogue using two benedictions from the Jewish liturgy (also found in the revised Roman Catholic liturgy) and a prayer for unity inspired by the *Didache*. It is completed with the ancient eucharistic acclamation, *"Maranatha"* ("Come, Lord!"), as in I Corinthians 16:22. After the dialogue the prayer continues:

> Truly it is right and good to glorify you, at all times and in all places, to offer you our thanksgiving, O Lord, Holy Father, Almighty and Everlasting God. Through your living Word you created all things, and pronounced them good. You made human beings in your own image, to share your life and reflect your glory. When the time had fully come, you gave Christ to us as the Way, the Truth and the Life. He accepted baptism and consecration as your Servant to announce the good news to the poor. At the last supper Christ bequeathed to us the eucharist, that we should celebrate the memorial of the cross and resurrection, and receive his presence as food. To all the redeemed Christ gave the royal priesthood and, in loving his brothers and sisters, chooses those who share in the ministry, that they may feed the Church with your Word and enable it to live by your Sacraments. Wherefore, Lord, with the angels and all the saints, we proclaim and sing your glory: . . .

Then follow the *First Epiclesis,* the Institution Narrative, and thereafter the *Anamnesis:*

38. These words are part of Max Thurian's introduction to the Lima Liturgy in Thurian and Wainwright, eds., *op. cit.*, p. 244.

> Wherefore, Lord, we celebrate today the memorial of our re-
> demption: we recall the birth and life of your Son among us, his
> baptism by John, his last meal with the apostles, his death and
> descent to the abode of the dead; we proclaim Christ's resurrec-
> tion and ascension in glory, where as our Great High Priest he
> ever intercedes for all people; and we look for his coming at the
> last. United in Christ's priesthood, we present to you this
> memorial: Remember the sacrifice of your Son and grant to
> people everywhere the benefits of Christ's redemptive work.[39]

This full *anamnesis* stresses the role of Christ, the eternally pre-
existent Son, as Creator, and emphasizes his mighty acts as the
incarnate Son on earth and as the eternal High Priest in heaven
who makes intercession for his people. Other commemorations,
already cited, have laid more stress on the wonders of creation
from a human standpoint, or the marring of creation by human
rebellion. Still others have emphasized the splendor of human
faculties of reason and memory and love and the fruits of the
earth. This one, however, concentrates on the mightiest act of
God in our redemption through Christ.

The Consultation on Church Union of the U.S.A., which
includes ten churches, has authorized its liturgy in *Word, Bread, Cup*.
Its commemoration begins with the dialogue, and continues thus:

> It is truly right to glorify you, Father, and to give you thanks;
> for you alone are God, living and true, dwelling in light inac-
> cessible from before time and for ever. Fountain of life and
> source of all goodness. You made all things and fill them with
> your blessing: you created them to rejoice in the splendour of
> your radiance.

Then follow the *Sanctus, Benedictus,* and *Hosanna,* and the prayer
continues:

> We remember with joy the grace by which you created all things
> and made them in your own image.

39. *Ibid.,* pp. 252-53.

We rejoice that you called a people in covenant to be a light to the nations. Yet we rebelled against your will. In spite of prophets and pastors sent forth to us, we continued to break your covenant. In the fullness of time, you sent your only Son to save us. Incarnate by the Holy Spirit, born of your favoured one, Mary, sharing our life, he reconciled us to your love.

At the Jordan your Spirit descended upon him, anointing him to preach the good news of your reign. He healed the sick and fed the hungry, manifesting the power of your compassion. He sought out the lost and broke bread with sinners, witnessing the fullness of your grace. We beheld his glory.

The Institution Narrative then follows, and the prayer continues:

After the meal our Lord was arrested, abandoned by his followers and beaten. He stood trial and was put to death on a cross. Having emptied himself in the form of a servant, and being obedient even to death, he was raised from the dead and exalted as Lord of heaven and earth.

Through him you now bestow the gift of your Spirit, uniting your Church, empowering its mission, and leading us into the new celebration you have promised. Gracious God, we celebrate with joy the redemption won for us in Jesus Christ. Grant that in praise and thanksgiving we may be a living sacrifice, holy and acceptable in your sight, that our lives may proclaim the mystery of faith.[40]

This commemoration in the eucharistic prayer is remarkable in its summation of the major events and activities in the life of

40. *Ibid.,* pp. 184-85. C.O.C.U. includes in its membership the following churches: African Methodist Episcopal Church, African Methodist Episcopal Zion Church, Christian Church (Disciples of Christ), Christian Methodist Episcopal Church, Episcopal Church, National Council of Community Churches, Presbyterian Church in the United States, United Church of Christ, United Methodist Church, and United Presbyterian Church in the U.S.A. *Word, Bread, Cup* was published by Forward Movement Publications, Cincinnati (1978); the eucharistic prayer is the second included in that book.

Christ, but unique in describing in vivid detail the earthly events that followed after the Last Supper.

Finally, among the ecumenical liturgical thanksgivings we select one prepared by the British Joint Liturgical Group, which has exercised great influence on liturgical reforms in Great Britain. Its members come from the Church of England, the Church of Scotland, the Baptist Union, the Episcopal Church in Scotland, the Methodist Church, the Churches of Christ, the Roman Catholic Church, and the United Reformed Church. The group published in 1978 a "eucharistic canon." It begins as follows:

> Almighty God, Eternal Father, it is our duty and delight at all times and in all places to give you thanks and praise. You are the creator of all things and the source of all life, in whom we live and move and have our being. You have given us your only Son, Jesus Christ, to free us from the slavery of sin and to make us heirs of eternal life. He was born as one of us, was obedient to your will, and accepted death upon the cross: you raised him from the dead and have made him Lord of all. You send us your Spirit to guide us into the truth, and to bring us reconciliation and peace, and to renew us as the Body of your Son.
>
> (And now we give you thanks . . .)
>
> We praise you, for you are God.
>
> *All:* We acclaim you, for you are the Lord. We worship you, eternal Father: and with the whole company of heaven we sing in endless praise: Holy, holy, holy Lord, God of Power and might. Heaven and earth are full of your glory. Hosanna in the highest.
>
> (Blessed is he who comes in the name of the Lord. Hosanna in the highest.)
>
> Heavenly Father, we offer you this praise through Jesus Christ, your only Son our Lord, who hallowed your name, accom-

plished your will, established your kingdom, and gave himself
to be our spiritual food. And now we pray that by the power
of your Holy Spirit these gifts of bread and wine may be to us
his body and his blood.

The Institution Narrative follows, succeeded by the following:

Therefore, heavenly Father, obeying the command of your dear
Son, and looking for his coming again in glory, we celebrate
the perfect sacrifice of his death upon the cross, his mighty
resurrection and his glorious ascension.

All: Christ is Victor. Christ is King. Christ is Lord of all.

Father, accept through Christ our sacrifice of thanks and praise:
and as we eat and drink these holy gifts, kindle in us the fire
of your Spirit that with the whole Church on earth and in
heaven we may be made one with him. Count us worthy to
stand before you as your people and to offer without ceasing
our adoration and service, through Jesus Christ our Lord.
Through him, with him, and in him, in the unity of the Holy
Spirit, all honour and glory are yours, Father Almighty, now
and for ever.

All: Amen.[41]

It should be observed that this canon is generally to be used in
ecumenical celebrations of the Eucharist, although not exclusively so, and that an attempt has been made to express God's
mighty acts in terms of present rather than past activity. In
addition, the ideas are borrowed from Scripture; for example,

41. Thurian and Wainwright, eds., *op. cit.,* pp. 182-83. The accompanying notes of the Joint Liturgical Group, which we have summarized,
also include the comment that the *Sanctus,* with the Introduction, has been
taken from the *Te Deum,* and is supported by the theory of P. Cagin, *Te
Deum ou Illatio* (Solesmes, 1906), and E. Kähler, *Studien zum Te Deum*
(Göttingen, 1956), that this hymn was originally the Preface, *Sanctus,* and
Post-Sanctus of a Mass for the Easter Vigil.

the reference to creation derives from Acts 17:28. It should also be noted that the *Post-Sanctus* has deliberate echoes of the Lord's Supper.

Conclusion

In the many forms of eucharistic thanksgiving we have considered, it is clear that the synagogue and the church have much in common, as we also saw in our chapter entitled "The Eucharist as Memorial," where the present and future benefits of God's mighty acts of the past are or will be appropriated. Another common element in the worship of both is the *Sanctus,* which persists in nearly all liturgies. Moreover, it should be noted that it is a thanksgiving for the whole of creation, whether in heaven or on earth. George Every suggests that the *Sanctus* was probably originally the conclusion of a thanksgiving for creation, but in later times it was abbreviated in the Eastern liturgies, and in the West largely displaced by the proper Prefaces.[42] Thus the modern recovery of a fuller thanksgiving for the being of God and for the creation of the world that is so strong a characteristic of recent and especially ecumenical liturgies fills an important gap in worship; it has great importance for the Christian doctrine of creation and for humanity made in the image of God. The same author also suggests that prayers are needed that express a more contemporary cosmology. He even provides an example:

> It is meet, right, and our bounden duty, that we should at all times and in all places give thanks to you, O Lord, holy Father, Almighty God, the origin and end of all the worlds, of outer space and the infinitely small, you who penetrate the universal whole as a ray of light a crystal, who called us, despite our sin,

42. Brother George Every, S.S.M., *Basic Liturgy: A Study of the Structure of the Eucharistic Prayer* (London: The Faith Press, 1961), p. 7.

to a rational understanding, that we might glorify you in the ordering of this world, and with angels and archangels evermore praise you, saying. . . .[43]

The most successful example of a modern cosmology was cited in Eucharistic Liturgy II, the third thanksgiving in the *Book of Common Prayer of the Episcopal Church in the U.S.A.,* and few have dared to follow this example.

It is cheering that the modern liturgical movement is increasingly recognizing that for historical and ecumenical reasons the term "Eucharist" is appropriate and meaningful for the chief sacrament, for it prescribes the true corporate response of obedient adoration that should characterize Christian worship. It is also increasingly felt that the deepest meaning of Holy Communion should be looked for in the anamnetic part of the Prayer of Thanksgiving, for this becomes a confessional, and even a kerygmatic, statement of the meaning of the Trinity and the summary of the revelation of Christ's acts, past, present, and future. We also noted in the Joint British Liturgical Group's prayer of thanksgiving a characteristic shared with the Jewish commemoration of the Passover, namely, a determination wherever possible to use verbs in the present or future tense to show the relevance of the mighty acts of God in the past. This has been admirably expressed by Gregory Dix, the Anglican Benedictine, in recalling that the intention of the Eucharist as the early church understood it was "the 'recalling' before God of the one sacrifice of Christ in all its accomplished fullness so that it is here and now operative by its effects in the souls of the redeemed."[44]

Our historical etymological hunts have shown conclusively

---

43. *Ibid.,* p. 116.
44. Dix, *The Shape of the Liturgy* (Westminster, MD: Dacre Press, 1946), p. 243. W. Jardine Grisbrooke in J. Gordon Davies, ed., *The New Westminster Dictionary of Liturgy and Worship* (Philadelphia: Westminster Press, 1983), p. 18, makes the following correction of Dix: ". . . so far as the doctrine of the Early Church is concerned, he ought to have written 'bodies and souls.'"

that in the New Testament the verb *eucharistein* ("to give thanks") and its derivatives were almost exclusively used in the four accounts of the Last Supper, as well as in the Septuagint and in the Greek and Latin Fathers.

Further, we have considered the dominant use of the triple structure of the Jewish *berakoth* or benedictions and their probable impact on the eucharistic thanksgiving with a stress on the appropriate sheer adoring and grateful wonder at the marvelous acts of God in both creation and redemption. Further consideration of the development of the *anamnesis* in the eucharistic thanksgivings might well have encouraged us to accept George Every's suggestion that the anaphora developed its increasingly trinitarian structure (retained most fully in the Eastern liturgies with the high role of the Holy Spirit stressed in their use of the Invocation of the Holy Spirit [the *epiclesis*] because this was derived from the simple baptismal confessions of faith).[45] Here again we see the preaching role of the thanksgiving prayer as a summary of the Christian faith.

Thus, the title, the form, and the content of the eucharistic Prayer of Thanksgiving are seen to have even greater significance and relevance today than in the past, because it determines both the meaning of the Eucharist and the Christian response that is most appropriate.

45. Every, *op. cit.*, p. 6.

THREE   The Eucharist as Sacrifice

WHEN THE Eucharist was chiefly regarded as a memorial, traditionally the Protestant stress, then Roman Catholics derided it as "mere memorialism" or antiquarianism. When the dominant stress, as in Roman Catholicism, was to regard the Eucharist as a sacrifice, the Protestants of Reformation times scorned it as a combination of magic and priestcraft. Many Protestants consider the concept itself very controversial unless it is reinterpreted, and for some it remains controversial even after reinterpretation. But it is also true that among Lutherans and Anglicans there is a striking convergence in the new reconsideration of sacrifice, which will be detailed later.

It is worth recalling the words of the former Anglican Archbishop of Canterbury, A. M. Ramsey: "Of these elements in the Christian Eucharist it is probable that those of *thanksgiving* and *commemoration* have aroused the least controversy and misunderstanding, while the meaning of *mystery* and *fellowship* and *sacrifice* has been the subject of many disputes in the history of the Church."[1] Despite the convergence mentioned, there is a continuing debate in the Church of England between the Evangelicals and the high Anglicans as to the appropriateness of using the term "sacrifice" for the Eucharist. A single citation will testify to the objection of a distinguished Evangelical: "The Holy Com-

1. *The Gospel and the Catholic Church* (London: Longmans, Green and Co., 1936), p. 111.

49

munion, as we find it in the New Testament, *contains no statement or act indicating that any sacrifice is being offered in the service, except the giving of thanks.*"[2] Clearly, the question of sacrifice in the Eucharist leads to controversy between churches and within a single church. It is important, therefore, to consider the arguments for and against the use of the concept of sacrifice in Holy Communion.

Arguments in Favor of Sacrifice as an Interpretive Category

It seems important, as evidence of the reconsideration of the relevance of sacrifice in eucharistic interpretation, to expound the revisionary views of three distinguished French-speaking Protestants, as well as those of a Scandinavian Lutheran, of an American Episcopalian, and of a British Baptist. The first is the Taizé community's liturgist, Brother Max Thurian, a Reformed Church member as well as a leading "ecumaniac." Thurian claims that there are three grounds for the necessary use of the term "sacrifice" to interpret the meaning of the Eucharist. First, the Eucharist is "the sacramental *presence* of the sacrifice of the cross . . . and it is the liturgical *presentation* of the Son's sacrifice by the church to the Father, in thanksgiving for all his blessings and in that he may grant them afresh." In the second place, it is "the *participation* of the church in the intercession of the Son before the Father in the Holy Spirit, that salvation may be accorded to all . . . and that the kingdom may come in glory." Third, it is "the *offering* which the church makes of itself to the Father, united

2. R. T. Beckwith and J. E. Tiller, eds., *The Service of Holy Communion and its Revision* (Latimer Monographs III; Appleford: The Marcham Manor Press and Nashville: Abingdon, 1972), p. 35. The words are italicized in the original for emphasis. See also Alan M. Stibbs, *Sacrament, Sacrifice and Eucharist* (London: The Tyndale Press, 1961), pp. 29ff. See also Donald Bridge and David Phypers, *Communion: The Meal that Unites?* (Wheaton, IL: Harold Shaw Publishers, 1982), *passim*.

in the Son's intercession, as its supreme act of adoration and its perfect consecration in the Holy Spirit."[3] Among Protestants generally the *sacrificium laudis* (sacrifice of praise) would be acknowledged — the third point made by Thurian — but the other two statements would be disputed. All three points would be welcomed by Roman Catholics, the Orthodox, and high Anglicans.

The most extensive reinterpretations of the Eucharist as a sacrifice have been undertaken by F. J. Leenhardt and J. J. von Allmen, both Reformed professors of theology. Leenhardt's major work is *Ceci est Mon Corps: Explication de Ces Paroles de Jesus-Christ* ("This is My Body: An Explanation of These Words of Jesus Christ"). Acutely aware of the serious misuse of the concept of sacrifice in the eucharistic theology and praxis of the past, he insists on the recovery for Protestants of a guarded concept of sacrifice. The holy supper, he affirms, like the entire life of Christ, is a sacrifice for sinners. But it is unacceptable to imply that the eucharistic sacrifice is added to that of Christ's sacrifice on the cross.[4] Further, it is God who in the sacrament actualizes his gift anew so that the sacrifice of Christ becomes available for all believers.[5]

The gift of bread by Christ prolongs the Passion with the same love for sinners, so that both on the cross and in the Eucharist Christ gives his body.[6] In addition, Leenhardt insists

---

3. Thurian's essay, "The Eucharistic Sacrifice and the Real Presence," is found on pp. 74-101 of Michael J. Taylor, ed., *Liturgical Renewal in the Christian Churches* (Baltimore and Dublin: Helicon, 1967). The citations come from p. 74.

4. Leenhardt's *Ceci est Mon Corps* was published by Delachaux & Niestlé, Neuchâtel, in 1955 as the third in the series of *Cahiers Théologiques*. The reference is to p. 47.

5. *Ibid.*, p. 52.

6. *Ibid.*, p. 53. The original reads: "la donation du pain prolonge cette passion parce qu'elle est une manifestation renouvelée de l'amour qui a inspiré le Christ dans tout son ministère et l'a conduit à la Croix. Sous des formes apparentes diverses, il se passe la même chose, Dieu poursuit le même but. L'unité des actions apparait meme clairement dans la parole explicative prononcée par le Christ: dans les deux cas, *il donne son corps*."

that the efficacy of the rite is dependent neither on the authority
of the church, nor on the faith of the recipient, nor on the act
of the presiding priest or minister, but solely on the action of
Christ that makes the Eucharist an *opus operatum* and safeguards
its efficacy.[7]

J. J. von Allmen has a deep sense of reverence and understanding of the Holy Supper. Examining I Corinthians 10:17 ("Because
there is one loaf, we who are many are one body, for we all partake
of the same loaf"), he observes that this Pauline claim, "which only
makes sense if this unique bread is the Body of Christ, means that
the Supper constitutes the church and reveals her."[8] He further
insists that at the moment the church meets in eucharistic worship,
the total Christ, head and body *(Christus totus, caput et corpus)* —
to use the Augustinian formula — is present, "the Christ who
came, who reigns and is coming, and in Him and with Him, the
whole communion of saints, in whom the history of salvation is
accomplished."[9] In answering why Jesus instituted the Eucharist,
Von Allmen says that it was because "He interpreted His death as
a sacrifice offered to God for the world's salvation." It was also
"because Jesus knew that He was the Messiah and gave to His
death a Messianic significance: the significance of a sacrifice which
was decisive for the history of the world." His aim was "that what
He did might remain fresh, so that those who enact the *anamnesis*
might benefit from the reconciliation accomplished by Christ
through the very *anamnesis* which they re-enact. In this way the
Crucified might remain present among His followers to give
Himself to them in the gift of what He had done for them."[10] But
Jesus also had a second reason, namely, to give his followers an
example and a command. He invited them through their own
sacrifice to share his sacrifice. Hence, "The Eucharist is the moment when the Church makes an offering of herself, when, if I may

7. *Ibid.,* pp. 55-57. But he also insists that unbelief is an obstacle to
receiving the gift of Christ *(ibid.).*

8. *The Lord's Supper* (London: Lutterworth Press, 1969), p. 37.

9. *Ibid.,* p. 49.

10. *Ibid.,* p. 90.

dare say so, she rushes towards God through the breach made by the death of Jesus in a heaven otherwise walled up, when she moves forward in procession to give herself in and through what she is bringing with her."[11] The third reason, according to Von Allmen, for the institution of the Eucharist by Christ, was that Jesus was giving his disciples a foretaste of the eschatological banquet in the expectation of which he himself fasted on the night in which he was betrayed.[12] He concludes with these ringing words: ". . . since the Eucharist is a sacrament of the sacrifice of Christ and a channel of the Church's sacrifice, it must also be interpreted in sacrificial categories."[13]

The fourth witness to a radical reappraisal of sacrifice in the Eucharist is a Lutheran, the eminent Professor Regin Prenter. One has only to recall what Luther thought of the sacrificial interpretations of the sacrament in his *Babylonian Captivity* to realize what a change this represents in Lutheranism. Luther wrote: "The third shackle imposed upon this sacrament is by far the most wicked abuse of all. The result of it is that there is no belief more widely accepted in the church today, or one of greater force, than that the mass is a good work and a sacrifice. And this abuse has brought in its train innumerable other abuses; and these, when faith in the sacrament has completely died away, turn the sacrament into mere merchandise, a market, and a business run for profit."[14]

11. *Ibid.*, p. 92.
12. *Ibid.*, p. 93.
13. *Ibid.*, p. 96. It is also worth mentioning that in this explication of the Lord's Supper Von Allmen is warning against a misinterpretation of the sacrifice as if it were a matter of magic, that is, operating without taking into account Christ's action and the believer's acceptance of it in faith, or as if it were considered as merely a symbolical rather than an efficacious act.

14. *Reformation Writings of Martin Luther, Translation with Introduction and Notes from the Definitive Weimar Edition* by Bertram Lee Woolf (London: Lutterworth Press, 1952), vol. I, p. 231. In the same *Pagan Servitude of the Church* Luther added that the Canon of the Roman Mass seemed to express the belief that the Mass is a sacrifice in the words "these gifts, these offerings, these holy sacrifices" and later "this oblation." Luther added: "Moreover, the request is very definite that the sacrifice will be accepted as was Abel's

Prenter's work in systematic theology is entitled *Skabelse og Genloesning* (Creation and Redemption). It has not been translated into English, but is considered carefully by A. M. Allchin, who provides many citations in English.[15] Prenter sees the Eucharist as "the sacrificial meal of fulfilment," the fullest expression of divine love and an anticipation of the life to come. "Love is, like faith and hope, a death to all righteousness of our own, a turning to the other righteousness (*justitia aliena*) of Christ. At no stage does the character of faith as a denial of self and taking refuge in Christ appear so sharply as in its fulfillment in love. For in love, the fight with the old Adam comes to an end with its complete submission in death as a sacrifice." Thus love can be differentiated from every sort of Pelagian self-offering made in our own strength. This emphasis is made vivid by distinguishing between the death of a hero and the death of a martyr. Further, our death can only be an offering (sacrifice) to God if we surrender any thought that our death as a gift means anything. This giving up of our own life is reflected in the Holy Supper, where Jesus' offered (sacrificed) body and blood are given to us as food for our journey into our own death. So our death becomes an offering of love when envisaged not as our ruin or surrender, but as included in Jesus' death on the cross, his death which is our real death, offered to God for our sake, as the highest offering of love.[16]

What is so remarkable about this sacrificial understanding of the Lord's Supper is that it preserves the central Pauline doctrine of justification by faith, attributing all to the crucified

---

sacrifice. Then, too, Christ is said to be the victim on the altar" (*ibid.*, vol. I, p. 249). (The Latin term used for "victim" is *hostia*.)

15. The article of Allchin is entitled "The Eucharistic Offering." It is found in *Studia Liturgica* (Amsterdam), vol. I, pp. 101-14. The citations of Allchin are translations of Prenter's *Skabelse og Genloesning*, 2nd edn. 1955, pp. 531-33. Later citations are Prenter's, pp. 533, 550, and 551; Allchin's are from pp. 109 and 110.

16. Allchin, *op. cit.*, p. 109.

Lord. Prenter, like Leenhardt and Von Allmen, insists on the necessity of leaving behind the traditional Protestant fears of words like sacrifice and offering. "In this sense," says Prenter, "we must insist, not only that the Eucharist is a true sacrifice, but even that it is the eternal presence of the sacrifice of Calvary in the Church. Yet it must be said that in the Eucharist we present only the eucharistic elements and prayer as offerings, but Jesus' offered body and blood, which is the one gift of love we can bring."[17] Prenter concludes his consideration of the Eucharist with the confident affirmations that follow, expressing the real presence in the sacrament:

> *The body and blood really present are nothing else than the body and blood which were offered on Calvary.* The ascended Christ is identical with the crucified. And the miracle of the Eucharist is not that a heavenly substance is called down to earth, but that the risen and ascended Lord is continually present, as the suffering and offered son of man. *The miracle is that the sacrifice of Calvary has not been past, but remains eternally present.* . . . The real presence means that the sacrifice on Calvary is eternally in Christ's Church, till He comes, in the form of the bread and wine of the new covenant feast, and makes it possible for His disciples to have a part in His sacrificial passage through death to life.[18]

Our American Anglican witness is Professor Cyril Richardson, who begins by insisting that the sixteenth-century antitheses between Catholic and Protestant must be overcome and argues that the notion of sacrifice cannot be restricted to death. He sees four aspects or moments of the sacrificial act: first there is offering or the abandonment of the self to God; next there is dying: "the actual experience whereby the ego-centered nature is crucified"; this in turn leads to resurrection, which means that we rise with Christ and share in the anticipation of the heavenly banquet uniting both realized and future eschatology. Thus at

17. *Ibid.*, p. 110.
18. *Ibid.*, p. 110.

the Eucharist we experience the larger conception of sacrifice
and see "worship as the total act in which there is presented the
whole work of Christ in such a way that we are able to live
through it ourselves and participate in that which he has accomplished in terms of human nature." Richardson concludes: "It
is necessary at this point to go beyond the once-for-allness of
the cross, to appreciate its significance as the historic expression
of the eternal reality of the divine nature. It is because the divine
nature is love that the sacrifice of Christ is an eternal act and is
thus able to be made present in worship here and now."[19]

Another liturgiologist, and, perhaps surprisingly, a British
Baptist, the Reverend Neville Clark, offers great illumination on
the connection between sacrifice and the Eucharist in a lecture
given to the Ecumenical Liturgical Conference in Swanwick in
January 1961.[20] After expounding the sacrifice of Christ on Calvary as expiatory and substitutionary, he asserts that the sacrament
is a recalling of the once-for-all sacrifice, making it operative and
effectual here and now, and that this is made possible by the Holy
Spirit overwhelming time. He continues: "We do not offer Christ's
sacrifice. We make memorial of it, we proclaim it." Then he asks:

> What then do we offer — and how? There is indeed a eucharis-
> tic offering, but its keynote is not substitution but participation
> and incorporation. We share in Christ's offering, are taken up
> into his offering, become united with him in his offering; not
> that we may offer Him, nor that He may offer us, but that our
> self-offering may be made one with His, that *pro nobis* may
> become *in nobis,* that the Whole Christ, Head and members,
> may offer the Totus Christus.

His conclusion is that by this clarification barren controversies
may be avoided, with some crying "sacrifice" and others "com-

---

19. Richardson's essay, "Word and Sacrament in Protestant Worship,"
appears in Michael J. Taylor, ed., *Liturgical Renewal in the Christian Churches*
(Baltimore and Dublin: Helicon, 1967). The references are to pp. 48-50.
20. See *Studia Liturgica,* vol. II, p. 193.

munion" when in fact both are necessary, for the Eucharist is communion *in* sacrifice, and "altar and table are inevitably and necessarily one." Clark asserts that it is pointless to argue whether the "offertory" should be made before communion at the Offertory or at the post-communion prayer of oblation. He argues that the "offering" occurs in the eucharistic prayer, for it is by thanksgiving that offering is made, and the "offering" occurs in communion since we offer by communicating. He concludes, "The 'offering' is made in word at the eucharistic prayer, and in deed at communion; and in the mystery and wholeness of the eucharistic drama, these two are one."[21]

Criticism of the Sacrificial Interpretation

The question is inevitable: if the sacrificial interpretation can be maintained in such a way as to stress justification by faith, what objections can there be to the dominant Catholic interpretation?

The first answer must be that the sacrificial interpretation is open to abuse, as is the prior dominant Protestant interpretation of memorialism linked with the notion that the bread and wine are merely reminders of a past action of importance. What, then, are the abuses?

Leenhardt claims that the interpretation of the Eucharist has been faulty in three ways. The first error is that of sheer magic — the belief that the Eucharist is effectual of itself apart from the presence of Christ merely through the pronouncement of the consecratory formula. This is always the danger of insisting upon the *opus operatum*. One vivid example of such an error may be given. It was reported by Dr. F. W. Dillistone that he heard a concerned Vermont monsignor at a conference describe many of the great town churches of his own communion " as perilously like efficiently run sacramental filling stations."[22] For them, the

21. *Ibid.*
22. *Christianity and Symbolism* (London: Collins, 1955), p. 285.

act had become automatically efficacious and the change in the matter of the oblation was regarded as having been automatically produced.

The second error, according to Leenhardt, is the conviction that it is the priest's invocation of the formula of consecration that makes the sacrament effectual. This has led to the story (whether apocryphal or not) that glorifies the celebrant at the Mass ludicrously by asserting that the priest is more powerful than the Blessed Virgin because she bore Christ only once, whereas the priest brings him to life again at every Mass.[23] This story exposes a double defect of the *ex opere operato* explanation: it is presumed to be magical, and it denies the royal priesthood of all believers.

The third error, also according to Leenhardt, is a Protestant one, namely, that it is the faith of the individual that makes the Eucharist effectual. Its Pelagianism is crudely obvious, and its individualism breaks all sense of the essentially corporate nature of the church as the body of Christ. Even so, the partial truth in its falsity is the recognition that the unbeliever will not receive the sacrament of Holy Communion, but only believers. But it is the crucified and risen and ascended Lord alone who actualizes his presence in the sacrament.[24]

Another serious error occasionally made is to interpret the Eucharist as a reminder to God the Father of Jesus' sacrifice. This is, in fact, a grossly anthropomorphic notion of God. Is he to be regarded as an absent-minded emeritus professor? And what sort of doctrine of the Trinity makes such a consideration that God needs reminding? Professor C. F. D. Moule has concluded that "For myself I remain wholly unconvinced by the attempts to make the *anamnesis* ('this do in remembrance of me') mean that God is here reminded of what Christ has wrought:

23. Reported by Allchin, *op. cit.,* p. iii; see n. 15 above.
24. See *Ceci est Mon Corps,* chap. V, entitled "Le probleme de l'efficacité du rite" (pp. 50-57). The same three errors are evaluated in Oscar Cullmann and F. J. Leenhardt, *Essays on the Lord's Supper* (London: Lutterworth Press, 1958), pp. 68f.

i.e. as though Christ's words meant 'Do this to remind God of me!'"[25] On this matter Douglas Jones believes that "Do this in remembrance of me" is still the most natural conclusion for the translation of *anamnesis* and urges that the alternative "seems to come near to transforming the community of disciples, and therefore the Church, into some sort of mediator between God and his Christ, presenting to the divine memory at every Eucharist the story of his obedience and sacrifice that God may remember him and so effect his vindication on the last day."[26]

Several Protestant theologians are disturbed by the sacrificial view of the Eucharist because it seems to them to imply the repetition of Christ's sacrifice at each celebration of the Holy Communion, and this denies the unique once-for-allness of the Crucifixion on Calvary, so strongly emphasized in Hebrews 9:28. The Greek term for *once* is *hapax*. Alan Stibbs, an Anglican Evangelical, in *Sacrament, Sacrifice and Eucharist* (1961) devotes much of his argument to denying the New Testament validity of the view that the sacrament is a re-presentation of Christ's sacrifice to God. He quotes the following assertion from a sermon preached by Archbishop Ramsey in 1958 at the Eucharistic Congress: "In the Eucharist the sacrifice is that of Christ Himself. Having nothing of our own to offer, trusting only in Christ's one offering of Himself, it is that which we represent to the Father as ourselves members of Christ's body, accepted only in Him."[27] The view of Stibbs himself is that "the one fatal objection to the offering before God of the consecrated bread

25. Moule, *The Sacrifice of Christ* (Philadelphia: The Muhlenberg Press, 1964), p. 47. Dean Norman Hook, in *The Eucharist in the New Testament* (London: Epworth Press, 1964), p. 149, concurs with Professor Moule, stating that when the concept of *anamnesis* "implies that God needs to be reminded, or induced, to remember, then we should recognize that this is an Old Testament idea which has no place in the Christian doctrine of God."

26. The article of Douglas Jones, a most careful analysis, is found in *Theological Studies*, vol. VII (1955), pp. 183-91. The citation is from p. 191.

27. A. M. Stibbs, *Sacrament, Sacrifice and Eucharist* (London: The Tyndale Press, 1961), p. 23.

and wine in order to express this worship is that the Lord's Supper has not been ordained to be used in this way." He explains that this is to turn the sacrament into a means of making our sacrifice to God, and to "divert it from its intended exclusive reference to the one unique, atoning sacrifice, once offered by Christ alone, to secure remission of sins for us."[28] To the question, Can the church offer Christ to God? Stibbs insists that the proper Scriptural answer is "No." And in rejecting A. G. Hebert's claim that it is right to speak of "presenting before God," "pleading" or "offering" before him the one sacrifice of Christ, he approves Gustaf Aulén's criticism of this claim:

> In reality no man has ever "offered" the sacrifice of Christ. Christ's sacrifice is and remains His own act. We look in vain for any New Testament statement to the effect that we offer Christ. The sacrifice of Christ is and remains His own sacrifice, eternally valid, present in the Eucharist, but entirely His own, not the Church's sacrifice.[29]

The problem seems to be the concentration on the Offertory in the eucharistic liturgy — that is, setting apart, prior to the canon or major prayer of thanksgiving, the bread and wine as symbols of the offering of the congregation. In a strictly narrow sense, even if the president insists that we offer God of his own, echoing the words of David, "For all things come from You, and of Your own have we given You" (2 Chron. 29:14b), or even adds that these offerings are the products of divine gift and human labor (as bread and wine clearly are), it must appear that our *offering* or offertory is important. As we have seen, Prenter insisted that it is Christ's offering alone that is prolonged in the Eucharist, that ultimately and without heroism or self-satisfaction it is only our own death we can offer, and that that is made possible by Christ's death, which ends death in the Resurrection.

28. *Ibid*.
29. The three consecutive Aulén citations come from his *Eucharist and Sacrifice* (Philadelphia: Muhlenberg Press, 1958), pp. 37, 166, and 182.

Norman Hook, formerly Dean of Norwich, contends that the only offering we make is the *sacrificium laudis,* in expressing our gratitude for the benefits of the mighty acts of Christ and our renewed promise of obedience, which is certainly not our oblation of Christ's sacrifice. The completeness and uniqueness of Christ's perfect sacrifice ended the need for other oblations, which surprised the pagans contemporary with the early church to such a degree that they called Christians "atheists." Of the first Christians Hook says: "True they had abandoned the offering of any sacrificial victim, for Christ's sacrifice was a once-for-all affair, but the sacrificial meal remained, and that meal was the Eucharist. The early Christians, therefore, did not hesitate to speak of their Eucharist in terms of sacrifice, but they were careful to speak of it as 'the sacrifice of praise and thanksgiving.'"[30]

The difficulties faced by maintaining a doctrine of eucharistic sacrifice have been graphically as well as carefully exposed in an important article written by an Anglican clergyman and liturgical expert, the Reverend Dr. Kenneth Stevenson. It is entitled "Eucharistic Sacrifice — An Insoluble Liturgical Problem?"[31] The first difficulty he envisages concerns the offertory and the various ways it is dealt with. When bread and wine are placed upon the communion table, ". . . the president may say nothing at all; may quote I Chronicles 29 — 'Of thine own do we give Thee,' or may yet say words that formally present the gifts to God, in sometimes quite elaborate language; another option is to point to Christ as the only offering other than that of ourselves (Romans 12:1)."[32] The difficulty is caused partly by the different and apparently uncertain ways of affirming the offertory, or by the conviction that an offertory is utterly inappropriate. Stevenson indicates the latter embarrassment by citing another liturgiologist, the Reverend Bryan D. Spinks, who insists: "The Church cannot

30. *The Eucharist in the New Testament* (London: Epworth Press, 1964), p. 127. The New Testament reference is to Hebrews 13:15.
31. *The Scottish Journal of Theology,* vol. XLII (1989), pp. 469-92.
32. *Ibid.,* p. 469.

offer Christ, because the Head and Body, though one, are united only by the action of the Head. We therefore cannot identify the self-offering and the eucharistic memorial with the sacrifice of the Cross."[33]

One rarely sees, as in Stevenson's constructive historical analysis of the possibilities of linking the past sacrifice with the present recalling of that sacrifice, such fairness to the alternatives proposed. He suggests, in a summary of his own book *Eucharist and Offering,* that the liturgies of East and West have looked at three different ways of regarding offering. One criterion is the offering of "story" in which the narrative of salvation is found in the sermon and in the eucharistic prayer. The second way is that of "response." By this is meant listening to the story in Word and Eucharist, but also acting upon it. Here the church is not a passive recipient but dares to act boldly in imitation of the Savior, and daring to "do" the Eucharist as well as intercessory prayers is part of that response. The third way is that of "gift." "Here we come to the most sensitive part of all," says Dr. Stevenson, ". . . because of the paradox that in bread and wine God speaks to us, in ordinary food that is itself the result of dying and rising, wheat crushed and baked, grapes crushed and fermented. In acted parable, as of old, Jesus plays it slant. The bread and wine are neither formally 'offered' nor ritually 'held back'. They are just there on the table, eloquent testimony of the parable to end all parables, that it is in dying that we live to him."[34]

He continues by claiming that there are four ways through the *anamnesis* in the historic and contemporary liturgies. The first is by linking "remembering . . . we offer" (used by the West Syrian and Roman liturgies), which has the advantage that it claims what the church is doing, but without any direct relation to Christ's death it is open to the criticisms of the Reformation.

The second anamnetic route is that used by the English

33. *Ibid.,* p. 484.
34. *Ibid.,* p. 486.

Anglican rites of 1980: "With this bread and cup . . . we re-member." It emphasizes very strongly the sacrifice of Calvary, but it does not explain what the bread and wine are there for.

The third route is "in union with Christ we offer," and this is employed by both the American United Methodist rite and the ecumenical Lima Liturgy. It relies heavily on what Christ is doing now in his intercession, rather than what the church is doing now in remembering and offering. Its weakness may be that it places too little emphasis on the paradox that this is both Christ's and the church's action.

The fourth route is a variation of the third and is used by the Church of Scotland. Its key phrase is "pleading the eternal sacrifice." This approach ties the eternal sacrifice with the spir-itual sacrifice of the church, and with the invocation of the Holy Spirit on the Eucharist.

Stevenson's conclusion is that the story needs to have both vertical and horizontal emphases "so that what God is supposed to have done engages with how human beings are involved."[35] And, in the second place, it needs to be spread throughout the anaphora, "but it is finely focused in the anamnesis-epiclesis, because that is where, in traditional-style texts, the Church says what it thinks that it is doing."[36] His final admonition runs: "Above all, however, the twentieth-century *rapprochement* and *retour aux sources* may have left a few marks from the past that show the scars of old battles which are not quite so necessary to fight any more. They also show us, at root, how sacrifice keeps returning to give us new perspectives on that feast on which we shall endeavor to feed until the end of time."[37]

We have encountered both the conviction of even some Protestants that sacrifice is an essential component of the Eu-charist (and not merely a memory of it) and the difficulties and even potential dangers that evangelical Anglicans and many

35. *Ibid.,* pp. 486-88.
36. *Ibid.,* p. 489.
37. *Ibid.*

Protestants still find in such an approach. It is important, how-ever, to look ecumenically at the remarkable convergences and agreements that have been reached in the conviction that the Eucharist is the actualization of the historic sacrifice on Calvary made available by the eternal Christ.

Convergences on the Concept of Sacrifice in the Eucharist[38]

First, we shall consider important denominational agreements on the interpretation of sacrifice in the Eucharist in official conversations and agreements between representatives of these denominations. Such are those between Roman Catholics and Lutherans, between Roman Catholics and Anglicans, between Roman Catholics and the French Reformed Church, and *The Eucharist in Ecumenical Thought,* the Louvain Statement of the Faith and Order Commission of the World Council of Churches in 1971 — a multidenominational document.

The four statements we are to consider are important in their agreement "on the uniqueness of Jesus' *sacrifice* in his death upon the cross, but then also on its continuing availability to people today as a means of forgiveness and life — something with which believers themselves are united in sacrifice (though

---

38. Several volumes and articles have highlighted these convergences, including Michael J. Taylor, ed., *Liturgical Renewal in the Christian Churches* (Baltimore and Dublin: Helicon, 1967); Alexander Schmemann, *The Eu-charist: Sacrament of the Kingdom* (Crestwood, NY: St. Vladimir's Seminary Press, 1988); and especially Thurian and Wainwright, eds., *Baptism and Eucharist: Ecumenical Convergence in Celebration* (Geneva: World Council of Churches; Grand Rapids, MI: Wm. B. Eerdmans, 1983), and *Modern Eu-charistic Agreement* (London: S.P.C.K., 1973). Two important essays on the same theme are Ottfried Jordahn's "The Ecumenical Significance of the New Eucharistic Prayers of the Roman Liturgy" (*Studia Liturgica,* vol. XI [1976], pp. 101-17), and E. Glenn Hinson's "The Lima Text as a Pointer to the Future: A Baptist Perspective" (*Studia Liturgica,* vol. XVI [1986], pp. 92-99). The first article was written by a German Lutheran, and the second by an American Baptist.

expression of this point remains under debate)." This is Reumann's major conclusion on ecumenical dialogues in his critical study *The Supper of the Lord: The New Testament, Ecumenical Dialogues, and Faith and Order on Eucharist.*[39] Our citations will bear this out.

A Lutheran–Roman Catholic Statement comes from theologians of both churches looking for unity in their respective traditions. It is an American document. It rejects an understanding of the sacrament as "only commemorative or figurative." What was immediately agreed was:

> I(a) Lutherans and Roman Catholics alike acknowledge that in the Lord's Supper 'Christ is present as the Crucified who died for our sins and who rose again for our justification, as the once-for-all sacrifice for the sins of the world, who gives himself to the faithful'. On this Lutherans insist as much as Catholics, although, for various reasons, Lutherans have been reticent about speaking of the eucharist as a sacrifice.

> I(b) The confessional documents of both traditions agree that the celebration of the eucharist is the Church's sacrifice of praise and self-offering or oblation. Each tradition can make the following statement its own: 'By him, with him, and in him who is our great High Priest and Intercessor we offer to the Father, in the power of the Holy Spirit, our praise, thanksgiving and intercession. With contrite hearts we offer ourselves as a living and holy sacrifice which must be expressed in the whole of our daily lives.'[40]

Then comes the acknowledgment that the difficulty is whether the worshiping assembly "offers Christ" in the sacrifice of the Eucharist. The Lutherans denied this, believing that only in this way could they preserve the unrepeatable character of

---

39. Published by Fortress Press, Philadelphia (1984), p. 187.

40. All citations from the four ecumenical dialogues are found in *Modern Eucharistic Agreement* (London: S.P.C.K., 1973). The first reference is from p. 37.

the sacrifice of the cross. Now they recognize their agreement
in the assertion that "What God did in the incarnation, life,
death, resurrection, and ascension of Christ, he does not do
again. The events are unique; they cannot be repeated, or
extended or continued. Yet in this memorial we do not only
recall past events: God makes them present through the Holy
Spirit, thus making us participants in Christ (I. Cor. 1.9)."[41]
The Lutherans add that they accept the Roman Catholic view
which asserts that through "this Union between Christ and
Christians, the eucharistic assembly 'offers Christ' by consenting
in the power of the Holy Spirit to be offered by him to the
Father. Apart from Christ we have no gifts, no worship, no
sacrifice of our own to offer to God. All we can plead is Christ,
the sacrificial lamb and victim whom the Father himself has
given us." The further issue of the nature of the presence of
Christ in the Lord's Supper was also considered at length, but
it does not concern us here. The frankness with which the
Lutheran difficulties were stated and faced and the strong ecumenical desire for unity are the two strongest impressions made
by this statement.

In the same year, 1971, the Anglican–Roman Catholic
International Commission meeting at Windsor produced *An
Agreed Statement on Eucharistic Doctrine*. Beginning with a
section on "The Mystery of the Eucharist," it continued with
a second section entitled "The Eucharist and the Sacrifice of
Christ." Like the Lutheran–Roman Catholic Statement it affirms the once-for-all, unique, and perfect sacrifice on the
cross:

> Christ's redeeming death and resurrection took place once for
> all in history. Christ's death on the cross, the culmination of his
> whole life of obedience, was the one, perfect and sufficient
> sacrifice for the sins of the world. There can be no repetition
> of or addition to what was then accomplished once for all by

41. *Ibid.*, p. 38.

Christ. Any attempt to establish a nexus between the sacrifice of Christ and the eucharist must not obscure this fundamental fact of the Christian faith. Yet God has given the eucharist to his Church as a means through which the atoning work of Christ on the cross is proclaimed and made effective in the life of the Church. The notion of *memorial* as understood in the passover celebration at the time of Christ — i.e., the making effective in the present of an event in the past — has opened the way to a clearer understanding of the relationship between Christ's sacrifice and the eucharist. The eucharistic memorial is no mere calling to mind of a past event or its significance, but the proclamation of God's mighty acts. Christ instituted the eucharist as a memorial *(anamnesis)* of the totality of God's reconciling action in him. In the eucharistic prayer the church continues to make a perpetual memorial of Christ's death, and his members, united with God and one another, give thanks for all his mercies, entreat the benefits of his passion on behalf of the whole Church, participate in these benefits and enter into the movement of his self offering.[42]

While the once-for-allness of Christ's sacrifice is strongly emphasized, it is not clear how to interpret the "nexus" between Christ and the church. In the third section, "The Presence of Christ," we have a sense of the presence of the great High Priest in eternity who intercedes for his people: "It is the Lord present at the right hand of the Father, and therefore transcending the sacramental order, who thus offers to the Church, in the eucharistic signs, the special gift of himself."[43] Unfortunately, the issue of the offertory is not mentioned in the *Agreed Statement*, whereas the *Lutheran–Roman Catholic Statement* met the issue head-on.

The Dombes Agreement, entitled *Towards a Common Eucharistic Faith?* (also issued in 1971) is an agreement between Roman Catholics and Protestants made by the Group of Les Dombes. This was a group of Christian ecumenists founded as

42. *Ibid.*, pp. 27-28.
43. *Ibid.*, p. 28.

far back as 1937 by the Abbé Paul Couturier and comprising a French Reformed and Roman Catholic membership. *Towards a Common Eucharistic Faith?* consists of two parts: a doctrinal agreement and a pastoral agreement.

It begins by defining the Eucharist:

> 4. The eucharist is the sacramental meal, the new paschal meal of God's people, which Christ, having loved his disciples unto the end, gave them before his death that they might celebrate it in the light of his resurrection until his coming.
>
> 5. This meal is the effective sign of the gift Christ made of himself as the bread of life, through the sacrifice of his life and his death and by his resurrection.
>
> 6. In the eucharist, Christ fulfils in a surpassing manner his promise to be amongst those who gather together in his name.[44]

The Agreement continues by defining the Eucharist as an Act of Thanksgiving to the Father, which is the *berakah* or blessing for all that God has achieved in the creation and redemption of the world and all he seeks to accomplish by the coming of his Kingdom. Also:

> 8. The eucharist is the great sacrifice of praise in which the Church speaks in the name of all creation. For the world which God reconciled with himself in Christ is present at each eucharist: in the bread and wine, in the persons of the faithful and in the prayers they offer for all mankind. Thus the eucharist opens up to the world the way to its transfiguration.[45]

The third section, "Memorial of Christ," emphasizes that the whole life of Christ was sacrificial and that this sacrifice is re-presented in the Eucharist:

> 9. Christ instituted the eucharist as a memorial *(anamnesis)* of his whole life and above all of his cross and resurrection. Christ,

44. *Ibid.*, p. 57.
45. *Ibid.*, p. 58.

with everything he has accomplished for us and for all creation, is present himself in this memorial, which is also a foretaste of his kingdom. <u>The memorial, in which Christ acts through the joyful celebration of his Church, implies this re-presentation and this anticipation.</u> Therefore, it is not only a matter of recalling to mind a past event or even its significance. The memorial is the effective proclamation by the church of the great work of God. By its communion with Christ, the Church participates in this reality from which it draws its life.[46]

The reference to the high priesthood of Christ in eternity is powerfully expressed in the next paragraph:

10. The memorial, being at once re-presentation and anticipation, is lived out in thanksgiving and intercession. Making the memorial of the passion, resurrection, and ascension of Christ, our High Priest and Mediator, the Church presents to the Father the one perfect sacrifice of the Son and asks him to accord every man the benefit of the great work of redemption it proclaims.

11. Thus united to our Lord, who offers himself to his Father, and in communion with the universal Church in heaven and on earth, we are renewed in the covenant sealed with the blood of Christ and we offer ourselves as a living and holy sacrifice which must be expressed in the whole of our daily life.[47]

Other sections deal with the Eucharist as "Gift of the Spirit," "The Sacramental Presence of Christ," "Communion in the Body of Christ," "A Mission in the World," and "Banquet of the Kingdom." This comprehensive analysis ends with a striking request: "we think that access to communion should not be refused for reasons of eucharistic belief to Christians of other denominations whose own faith is that professed above."[48]

The parallels between the Les Dombes statement and *The*

46. *Ibid.*
47. *Ibid.*
48. *Ibid.*, p. 64.

Eucharist in Ecumenical Thought, the Louvain Statement of 1971 prepared by the Faith and Order Commission of the World Council of Churches, are close. The various sections of the statement are "The Lord's Supper," "Thanksgiving to the Father," "Memorial (Anamnesis) of Christ," "Gift of the Spirit," "Communion of the Body of Christ," "Mission to the World," and "End of Divisions." The only difference from the Dombes Group statement is that there is no heading for "Banquet of the Kingdom," though the eschatological anticipation is included in other sections, and Dombes deals with "The Presidency of the Eucharist," which Faith and Order omits, while Faith and Order emphasizes the importance of unity, which is shattered by the unwillingness of some Communions to admit believers of other churches to their Eucharists. Yet the stirring practical conclusion of the Les Dombes statement is missing.

The element of sacrifice is stressed in the first section:

> The eucharist is the sacramental meal, the new paschal meal of the people of God, which Christ, having loved his disciples until the end, gave to them before his death, shared with them after his resurrection and commanded them to hold until his return.
>
> This meal of bread and wine is the sacrament, the effective sign and assurance of the presence of Christ himself, who sacrificed his life for all men and who gives himself to them as the bread of life; because of this, the eucharistic meal is the sacrament of the body and blood of Christ, the sacrament of his real presence.
>
> In the eucharist the promise of the presence of the crucified and risen Christ is fulfilled in a unique way for the faithful, who are sanctified and unified in him, reconciled in love to be his servants of reconciliation in the world.[49]

The *sacrificium laudis* is expressed in the second part of the second section:

49. *Ibid.,* p. 83.

The eucharist is the great sacrifice of praise by which the Church speaks on behalf of the whole creation. For the world which God has reconciled to himself is present at every eucharist: in the bread and wine, in the persons of the faithful, and in the prayers they offer for themselves and for all men. As the faithful and their prayers are united in the Person of our Lord and to his intercession they are transfigured and accepted. Thus the eucharist reveals to the world what it must become.[50]

It will be observed that the term "offer" is included in this description, but without reference to a specific "offertory," which is disappointing. But the implication is that an offertory would be appropriate.

Sacrifice in Contemporary Eucharists

The new Roman Catholic eucharistic prayers move in an ecumenical direction, since Form IV with its Eastern emphasis on the *epiclesis,* and Forms II and III show the institution narrative incorporated in the thanksgiving recital instead of being a simple historical recital or an independent consecration formula. However, the emphasis on the offertory is still strong, too strong in Form I, where it is written: "Vouchsafe, we beseech you, O God, to make this offering wholly blessed, approved, ratified, reasonable and acceptable. . . ."[51] The Roman Missal of 1970 includes the following offertory prayers that emphasize the divine gift rather than the human offering:

C: Blessed are you, Lord, God of all creation. Through your goodness we have this bread to offer, which earth has given and human hands have made. It will become for us the bread of life.

---

50. *Ibid.,* p. 84.
51. Thurian and Wainwright, eds., *Baptism and Eucharist: Ecumenical Convergence in Celebration,* p. 130. See also Ottfried Jordahn's article "The Ecumenical Significance of the New Eucharistic Prayers of the Roman Liturgy," in *Studia Liturgica,* vol. XI (1976), pp. 101-17.

P: By the mystery of this water and wine may we come to share in the divinity of Christ, who humbled himself to share in our humanity.

C: Blessed are you Lord, God of all creation. Through your goodness we have this wine to offer, fruit of the vine and work of human hands. It will become our spiritual drink.

P. Blessed be God forever.

C: Lord God, we ask you to receive us and be pleased with the sacrifice we offer you with humble and contrite hearts. . . .[52]

Even so there is too much stress on our offering.

Among several alternative modern German Lutheran texts, we select one example mentioning the sacrifice and the offering:

P: We thank you for the salvation, you have prepared for us through the holy and all-sufficient sacrifice of his body and blood on the tree of the cross. Gathered in his name and for his remembrance, we pray: Lord, send down upon us the Holy Spirit, sanctify and renew us in body and soul, and grant that under this bread and wine we receive in true faith the very body and blood of your Son to our salvation, since even now we make use of Christ's own testament according to his command. . . .

Then follows the Institution Narrative, and the prayer continues:

Therefore we remember, Lord, heavenly Father, the saving passion and death of your dear Son Jesus Christ. We praise his victorious resurrection from the dead, and are comforted by his ascension into your heavenly sanctuary where he, our High Priest, continually intercedes for us. . . .[53]

52. Thurian and Wainwright, eds., *op. cit.*, p. 132. From the *Agende für evangelisch-lutherische Kirchen und Gemeinden,* I (1955), incorporating revisions of 1976 and 1977 offered for trial use.
53. *Ibid.*, p. 137.

A second prayer has a commendable brevity:

> We praise you for the wonder of your creation. You bless human labour and endow us with life and joy. You have given us bread and wine that we may celebrate the supper of your Son. We thank you for the mystery of your love. Receive us anew as your own that our conduct may honour you, through Jesus Christ our Lord.[54]

The Church of Sweden's Lutheran Liturgy of 1975 has an admirably succinct reference to both sacrifice and offering, as follows:

> Look upon the perfect and everlasting sacrifice (or offering) through which you reconciled us to yourself in Christ. Through the Holy Spirit let us all be joined in one body and perfected to a living sacrifice in Christ.[55]

Here the vertical stress is recognized even in the horizontal response of the sacrifice of praise.

The relevant part of the eucharistic prayer provided by the American *Lutheran Book of Worship* of 1978 proceeds:

> P: Therefore, gracious Father, with this bread and cup we remember the life our Lord offered for us.
>
> And, believing the witness of his resurrection, we await his coming in power to share with us the great and promised feast.
>
> C: Amen. Come, Lord Jesus.
>
> P: Send now, we pray, your Holy Spirit, the spirit of our Lord and of his resurrection, that we who receive the Lord's body and blood may live to the praise of your glory and receive our inheritance with all the saints in light.[56]

54. *Ibid.,* p. 139.
55. *Ibid.,* p. 141.
56. *Ibid.,* p. 143.

As one might expect from the liturgists of France, the eucharistic prayers of the Reformed Church of France are comprehensive and vivid. We cite from Eucharistic Prayer IV, immediately after the triple acclamation of the people:

> Lord Jesus, we proclaim your death,
> we celebrate your resurrection,
> we await your coming in glory.

The prayer continues:

> Therefore, Lord, we make before you the memorial
> of the incarnation and passion of your Son,
> of his resurrection from the dead,
> of his ascension in glory,
> of his perpetual intercession;
> we await and earnestly pray for his return,
> rejoicing in the Holy Spirit
> whom you have given to your Church.
> O God our Father, we remember that the Crucified
> ever lives to intercede for us;
> we therefore pray you to transform our lives,
> that they may be consecrated to you; . . .[57]

The Church of Scotland 1979 Communion Order follows the Institution Narrative thus:

> Therefore, having in remembrance his work and passion, we now plead his eternal sacrifice and set forth this memorial which he has commanded us to make.

After the *epiclesis* and a prayer of intercession, the prayer continues:

> Accept this our duty and service, O Father, and graciously accept us also as, in fellowship with all the faithful in heaven and on

57. *Ibid.*, p. 154.

earth, we pray thee to fulfil in us and in all men the purpose of thy redeeming love. . . .[58]

The Church of England's *Alternative Service Book* (1980) in Rite A links Christ's sacrifice with the responsive sacrifice of praise:

> *President:* Therefore, heavenly Father, we remember his offering of himself made once for all upon the cross, and proclaim his mighty resurrection and glorious ascension. As we look for his coming in glory, we celebrate with this bread and this cup his one perfect sacrifice.
>
> Accept through him, our great high priest, this our sacrifice of thanks and praise; and as we eat and drink these holy gifts in the presence of your divine majesty, renew us by your spirit, inspire us with your love, and unite us in the body of your Son, Jesus Christ our Lord.[59]

There is a parallel prayer, the third in Rite A, which links Christ's "perfect sacrifice made once for the sins of all men" with "our duty and service, a spiritual sacrifice of praise and thanksgiving."

The Episcopal Church in the U.S.A. in its *Book of Common Prayer* of 1979 also makes the same links, Christ's and the church's sacrifice of praise. In Holy Eucharist II, Eucharistic Prayer C, the Celebrant prays:

> Remembering now his work of redemption, and offering to you this sacrifice of thanksgiving,

and the faithful respond:

> We celebrate his death and resurrection, as we await the day of his coming.[60]

---

58. *Ibid.*, p. 157.
59. *Ibid.*, p. 163.
60. *Ibid.*, p. 166. Also *ibid.*, p. 168. Form 1 prayer reads: "Father, we now celebrate the memorial of your Son. By means of this holy bread and cup, we show forth the sacrifice of his death, and proclaim the resurrection,

One is impressed by the naturalness of the transition and the creation of the link in several of the anaphoras in the American *Book of Common Prayer.*

As far as the eucharistic prayers of Methodism are concerned, the astute Anglican analyst, the Reverend Kenneth Stevenson, has praised the prayer in the president's book, *At the Lord's Table: A Communion Service for Use by the Minister* (1981) for the United Methodist Church of the U.S.A., as perhaps "the most nuanced formulation we have seen so far for the eucharist as a memorial sacrifice, but it is at the same time the action of Christ Himself, through his heavenly intercession."[61] The prayer reads in part:

> Therefore,
> in remembrance of all your mighty acts
> in Jesus Christ,
> We ask you to accept this our sacrifice
> of praise and thanksgiving
> which we offer
> in union with Christ's sacrifice for us,
> as a living and holy
> surrender of ourselves.[62]

Finally, we look at The Eucharistic Liturgy of Lima (1982), an important ecumenical liturgy in which Max Thurian tried to include the major insights of the Faith and Order Movement of the World Council of Churches. After the first *epiclesis* and the Institution Narrative, the *anamnesis* follows:

> P: Wherefore, Lord, we celebrate today the memorial of our redemption: we recall the birth and life of your Son among us,

---

until he comes again. Gather us by this Holy Communion into one body in your Son Jesus Christ. Make us a living sacrifice." See also the parallel form 2 on p. 169.

61. *The Scottish Journal of Theology,* vol. XLII (1989), pp. 469-92, article entitled "Eucharistic Sacrifice — An Insoluble Liturgical Problem?" The citation is from p. 476.

62. *At the Lord's Table* (Nashville: Abingdon Press, 1985), p. 24.

his baptism by John, his last meal with the apostles, his death and descent to the abode of the dead; we proclaim Christ's resurrection and ascension in glory, where as our Great High Priest he ever intercedes for all people; and we look for his coming at the last. United in Christ's priesthood, we present to you this memorial: Remember the sacrifice of your Son and grant to people everywhere the benefits of Christ's redeeming work.

C: *Maranatha, the Lord comes!*

Epiclesis II

P: Behold, Lord, this eucharist which you yourself gave to the Church and graciously receive it, as you accept the offering of your Son whereby we are reinstated in your Covenant. As we partake of Christ's body and blood, fill us with the Holy Spirit that we may be one single body and one single spirit in Christ, a living sacrifice to the praise of your glory.[63]

Conclusion

The following major conclusions can be arrived at in consideration of the complicated matter of the concept of sacrifice and the appropriateness or inappropriateness of any offering on the part of the church except the sacrifice of praise.

In the first place, the definition of sacrifice must include not only the passion and death of Jesus Christ, the incarnate Lord, but the recognition that his entire life of obedience to the Father and his continuing intercession in heaven for all is an everlasting sacrifice, making sinners holy through his unstinted compassion. Increasingly, the anamnetic elements of the anaphora make this clear. It was strikingly manifested in the Lima Liturgy, which seemed insensitive only at the point where God was repeatedly asked to "remember" as if his memory needed jogging.

63. Thurian and Wainwright, eds., *Baptism and Eucharist*, p. 252.

Second, the more contemporary liturgists stress that the link between the historic sacrifice on Calvary that was unrepeatable and perfect, and all eucharists in history, is explained increasingly, like the Jewish understanding of the Passover that was the background of the Eucharist, as a recalling or representing or prolongation by the eternal Christ, victorious over time, and is therefore an actualization of sacrifice by Christ the eternal High Priest and Intercessor. Here there is a recollection that is more than antiquarianism or notionalism, but the actual making present of the past in the sacrament, together with the stress of the Epistle to the Hebrews on the eternal High Priest who ever lives to intercede for humanity with the Father.

Third, it is, as the *epiclesis* implies, the Holy Spirit, the Inspirer, Illuminator, and Sanctifier, who unites the church in the Eucharist with the Father and the Son, for the Spirit is the *vinculum unitatis et caritatis,* the very bond of unity and love, and therefore of the deepest communion, of union with the Holy Trinity in the church on earth and in heaven.

What matters most in the final analysis is the recognition that in the cross as in the Eucharist, God conveys his own sacrificial self-giving. Rowan Williams expresses it excellently:

> God acts, offers, gives, in order to bring creation into fellowship with him; and, because that fellowship is so strange to fearful, self-enclosed, human beings, it requires a uniquely creative gift — a gift which involves God's manifesting himself without power or threat. He 'distances' himself from the stability of his divine life in order to share the vulnerability and darkness of mortal men and women. By the 'gift' of his presence — the presence in our world of an unreserved compassion and unrestricted hope — he establishes communion; but this can be clearly shown only in conditions of final rejection and dereliction. The gift is consummated on the cross.

Moreover, the same author insists that for humans, sacrifice and justice are interrelated, and that the ultimate response to God's sacrificial action is our own sacrifices:

'To make remembrance' of Christ is more than the performance of an act of worship; it is to accept living under the sign of the cross and in the hope of the resurrection. It is to accept the meaning of a life that was given over to death — at the hands of the powerful — for the love of others.[64]

64. *Eucharistic Sacrifice — The Roots of a Metaphor* (*Grove Liturgical Studies,* no. 31; Bramcote, Nottinghamshire: Grove Books, 1982).

FOUR

The Eucharist as
Eschatological Banquet

FOR EVEN an initial understanding of the Eucharist, it is essential to realize that it comprises three tenses: past, present, and future. As we saw in Chapter One, the sense of memorial is not merely retrospective, but has implications for the present. The present tense of the Eucharist emphasizes the real presence of Christ. The eschatological element of the Eucharist not only refers to the future banquet in eternity, but actually anticipates its fulfillment and joy. The words of Donald Baillie are worth pondering in this connection: "For the Real Presence in the sacrament," he writes, "is in a paradoxical sense a presence-in-absence. There is a sense in which, as St. Paul puts it, 'we are absent from the Lord.'[1] His presence with us is not of the same mode as it was with His disciples in the days of His flesh, nor of the same mode as it will be when we come to see 'face to face.'"[2] Thus the anticipated presence in eternity is a fuller presence with Christ than that of his presence with the disciples while on earth, a presence in which the triumphant Spirit overcomes the limitations of corporeal existence.

1. II Corinthians 5:6.
2. I Corinthians 13:12. The citation from Donald Baillie comes from *The Theology of the Sacraments and Other Papers* (New York: Charles Scribner's Sons, 1957), pp. 100-101.

The Newly Found Relevance of the Eschatological

The Eucharist as celebrated in the New Testament was a strongly eschatological experience for the first Christians. The apostles and their converts were so convinced of God's power through the resurrection of Christ and the sending of the Holy Spirit at Pentecost that they expected the *parousia* or second coming of Christ in their own lifetime and with it the triumphant establishment of the Kingdom of God over all its enemies. In the course of history, when the *parousia* was delayed, the growing prominence of the memorial aspect of the Eucharist made the eschatological element fade into the background.

The renewed interest in the eschatological implications of the Eucharist began with the research of Johannes Weiss and the widely read book of Albert Schweitzer, *The Quest of the Historical Jesus,* published in 1911. Until their emphasis on its importance, eschatology had been reduced to little more than an appendix to systematic theology dealing with "the last things" — the general resurrection and the final judgment, which, since they followed the conclusion of the history of the world, seemed indefinitely remote. As Alasdair Heron expresses it, "The sense, so present to St. Paul, that in Jesus Christ the final, saving act of God had been realised, that, in him, the 'end' has already broken in, that our own existence is directed and drawn towards the conclusion and consummation realised in his death and resurrection, had largely faded from Christian consciousness."[3] The same author points out that the Eucharist was then interpreted either as a memorial of the past or as a celebration of the present, which had two further consequences. It resulted, in the Reformers, in treating the Eucharist as a completed past, and in the Roman Catholics, in treating the once-for-all-sacrifice as being *continued,* not repeated in the present. The eschatological perspective of the New Testament means that what Christ "was,

3. A. I. C. Heron, *Table and Tradition* (Philadelphia: The Westminster Press, 1983), p. 152.

suffered and did for us he makes ever and again contemporary in its completeness for us who are still *in via*. We have to do not only with past and present, but with past, present, *and future* meeting in Him, and making Him the ground, accompaniment *and goal* of our journey."[4]

There are three inspirational sources for the newer eschatological emphasis. One is seen in the theology of hope that has received special attention among contemporary German theologians and is exemplified by Jürgen Moltmann, Gerhard Sauter, and Johannes Metz.[5] Another factor is the unusual attention given in our time to the future, in planning, projecting, and extrapolating, or even in the anticipation of political and social revolutions. But whatever the causes, it has had the effect of changing the perception of some liberal theological estimates of Jesus as a gentle teacher or a model social reformer into viewing him as a spiritual revolutionary of a Kingdom of God whose members trusted in the transforming love of God, forgave their enemies, and followed the suffering Christ through martrydom in the hope of resurrection. But the chief difference in the new theologians is that they are no longer oriented toward the past, but expectant and future-oriented. The third source of inspiration for a theology of hope is the refusal to be overwhelmed by the dreadful alternative of paralyzing despair so characteristic of our century, caused by the world wars, the Nazi holocaust, the millions who die of hunger, and the other millions who live a penurious, marginalized existence with only crumbs to eat and without shelter. Life is not worth living without hope, and Christianity can galvanize hope.

4. *Ibid.*, p. 153.

5. Moltmann's work is *Theologie der Hoffnung*, the fifth edition of which appeared in 1965 and was translated as *The Theology of Hope* (New York: Harper & Row, 1967). Gerhard Sauter's book is *Zukunft und Verheissung* (Zurich: Zwingli Verlag, 1965). Johannes Metz has two important essays, "The Church in the World," in T. P. Burke, ed., *The Church in History* (New York: Sheed and Ward, 1966), and "Die Verantwortung der Christlichen Gemeinde," in Adolf Exeter, ed., *Die Neue Gemeinde* (Mainz: Matthias Grunewald Verlag, 1966).

Faith and love are still part of the important triad of virtues, but the theologians of hope insist that in our situation the chief virtue is hope. The medieval credo of St. Anselm of Canterbury was *credo ut intelligam* ("I believe in order to understand"). The new motto is *spero ut intelligam* ("I hope in order to understand").[6] Moltmann has written:

> From first to last, and not merely in the epilogue, Christianity is eschatology, is hope, forward looking and forward moving, and therefore also revolutionizing and transforming the present. The eschatological is not one element of Christianity, but is the medium of Christian faith as such, the key in which everything in it is set, the glow that suffuses everything here in the dawn of an expected new day.[7]

For Moltmann the church must become "the Exodus of people." Metz insists that the tension between the church and the world is not spatial but temporal, for the church should be ahead of the world leading the world to the establishment of the Kingdom of God. It will be clear that the theologians of hope are eager to prevent the church from becoming a static antiquarian institution, but, as Harvey Cox argues, "the theology of hope comes perilously close to identifying God with the *future*" and forgets that the doxological formula acclaims the God who was and is as well as is to come.[8]

It is, then, not surprising that within the theological emphasis on the necessity of hope, liturgists should seek for its expression in the Eucharist. Moreover, as we shall see, the eschatological element in the Eucharist was there from the beginning, even if, after the postponement of the *parousia*, it was overlaid by the retrospective emphasis on the memorial of the cross. It is important, therefore, to turn to the New Testament records of the

6. Moltmann, *op. cit.,* p. 16.

7. *Ibid..,* p. 33.

8. Harvey Cox, *The Feast of Fools: A Theological Essay on Festivity and Fantasy* (Cambridge, MA: Harvard University Press, 1969), p. 130.

institution of the Last Supper for any eschatological clues, and afterward to the reflections on the eschatological elements of faith in the Epistle to the Hebrews and the Book of Revelation.

Eschatological Elements in the Record of the Last Supper

It is important to recognize at the outset that three gospel narratives of the Last Supper end their reports with a significant renunciation, that is, by a vow of renunciation made by Jesus. Mark as well as Matthew records the saying of Jesus that he will not drink again of the fruit of the vine until the coming of the Kingdom. This suggests, though without the outright statement, that while Jesus had shared the bread and the cup, he was now forswearing the use of wine. Luke, however, begins his account in a way that suggests that Jesus neither ate the Passover himself nor tasted the wine at all: "And he said to them, 'I have earnestly desired to eat this passover with you before I suffer; for I tell you I shall not eat it until it is fulfilled in the kingdom of God.' And he took a cup, and when he had given thanks he said, 'Take this, and divide it among yourselves; for I tell you that from now on I shall not drink of the fruit of the vine until the kingdom of God comes.' "[9]

In any case, whether Jesus shared the meal and the cups or not, he certainly renounced their future use until the Kingdom, for which he was offering his life, should come. As Alasdair Heron comments: "His mind was travelling forward to the kingdom, and to the feast that he would share with his disciples then. Here lies in the background the thought of the Messianic banquet which indeed is specifically mentioned a little later in Luke's account of the Last Supper — at 22:30 — that you may eat and drink at my table in my kingdom."[10]

From this two conclusions may be drawn. The first is that

9. Luke 22:15-18.
10. Heron, *op. cit.,* p. 153.

the Kingdom of God will be a great feast, but only through Christ's own renunciation of feasting as the vow of renunciation foreshadows his death. But, in the second place, the wine he offers the disciples is a foretaste of the wine of the Kingdom, when the hunger and thirst of the disciples will finally be satisfied in the eschatological banquet in the house of the Father. It is clear, then, that the Last Supper was itself an eschatological meal, which manifestly already anticipates the end. Moreover, this meaning was carefully retained in the earliest days of the history of the Christian church when the eucharistic prayers regularly included the cry *Maranatha,* "Come, Lord!" Furthermore, St. Paul insisted that each Eucharist anticipates the second coming: "For as often as you eat this bread and drink the cup, you proclaim the Lord's death until he comes."[11]

Thus, each celebration of the Eucharist points beyond itself to the final coming of Christ at the end of time. Each Eucharist is, as Jeremy Taylor expressed it, "an antepast of heaven." While the followers of Christ already share in his Kingdom, yet this Kingdom must expand until its fellowship is complete in the heavenly Jerusalem. St. Paul in the Epistle to the Ephesians sees the body of Christ as an eschatological fellowship: "Blessed be the God and Father of our Lord Jesus Christ, who has blessed us in Christ with every spiritual blessing in the heavenly places. . . . For he has made known to us in all wisdom and insight the mystery of his will, according to his purpose which he set forth in Christ as a plan for the fulness of time, to unite all things in him, things in heaven and things on earth."[12] History's most decisive event has taken place in the person and work of Jesus Christ through whom the old age has been brought

11. I Corinthians 11:26. Baillie (*op. cit.,* p. 105) reminds us that Oscar Cullmann maintained that the early Christian ejaculatory prayer, so early that it was handed down in the Aramaic form of *Marana tha,* "Come Lord," had two tenses, an eschatological and a present tense. Thus simultaneously it meant "Come and grant us now Thy presence in worship" as well as "Come in power and glory."
12. Ephesians 1:3, 9, and 10.

to an end and the new ushered in. In the Eucharist we anticipate
the end of this present age. As a result the prevailing tone of
each celebration is expectancy and exultation, for in each eucharistic celebration, as one shares in the cost of redemption,
namely, the agony of Christ's death on the cross, one also shares
in the last great sacrament when, in the words of our great Host,
"I drink it new with you in my Father's kingdom."[13]

C. H. Dodd explains part of the mystery of the Eucharist
in the following passage: "In the Eucharist, therefore, the Church
perpetually reconstitutes the crisis in which the Kingdom of God
came into history. It never gets beyond this. At each Eucharist
we are *there* — we are in the night in which He was betrayed,
at Golgotha, before the empty tomb on Easter Day, and in the
upper room where He appeared; *and* we are at the moment of
His coming, with angels and archangels and all the company of
heaven, in the twinkling of an eye at the last trump. Sacramental
communion is not a purely mystical experience, to which history,
as embodied in the form and matter of the sacrament, would
be in the last resort irrelevant; it is bound up with a corporate
memory of real events."[14] Edmund Schlink summarizes: "In the
Lord's Supper we already share here on earth in that future glory.
In the Lord's Supper we are present at the death of Christ and
at His return, at His first and second advent."[15]

Eschatological Eucharistic Elements
in Hebrews and Revelation

Having examined the eschatological words of Jesus at the Last
Supper, we must now consider the eschatological eucharistic
elements in both the Epistle to the Hebrews, which speaks at

13. Matthew 26:29.
14. C. H. Dodd, *The Apostolic Preaching and Its Developments* (London:
Hodder and Stoughton, 1936), pp. 234f.
15. In Donald Baillie and John Marsh, eds., *Intercommunion* (London:
SCM Press, 1952), p. 296.

length about the eternal, heavenly priesthood of Christ, and the
Book of Revelation, which describes the marriage feast of the
Lamb.

The author of the Epistle to the Hebrews makes the highest
claims for Christ as the supreme high priest, who renders other
priests unnecessary because his sacrifice on the cross was the
ultimate and efficacious sacrifice, making all other sacrifices unnecessary. Christ was the "pioneer of salvation" who was made
"perfect through suffering."[16] Christ is also "a merciful and
faithful high priest in the service of God to make expiation for
the sins of the people."[17] This high priest has experienced temp-
tation without surrendering to it, and so can sympathize with
human weakness and thus enable sinners to "find grace to help
in time of need."[18] Previous priests were numerous because death
prevented them from remaining in office, but since Christ is the
risen and ascended Lord, "he holds his priesthood permanently,
because he continues for ever. Consequently he is able for all
time to save those who draw near to God through him, since
he always lives to make intercession for them."[19] As the permanent Divine Intercessor, Christ pleads for his own members
of the body in the Eucharist. And it is in an adoring response
to his intercession at God's right hand that the author of the
Epistle urges his readers, "Through him then let us continually
offer up a sacrifice of praise to God, that is, the fruit of lips that
acknowledge his name."[20] These convictions of the writer of
Hebrews have found lodging in the historical liturgies and have
been important in the exposition of eucharistic theology because
they combine emphases on the suffering of Christ as making his
obedience perfect, on the new covenant that his sacrifice to end
all other sacrifices made possible, on the body of Christ's *sacrificium laudis* as its proper response, and on the important es-

16. Hebrews 2:10.
17. Hebrews 2:17.
18. Hebrews 4:16.
19. Hebrews 7:24-25.
20. Hebrews 13:15.

chatological assertion that the enthroned Christ in heaven loves to make intercession for his people.

In the Old Testament there is anticipation of the eschatological feast of joy for the righteous, but also of a threatening feast for the unrighteous. The former is prophesied by Isaiah: "On this mountain the LORD of hosts will make for all peoples a feast of fat things, a feast of wine on the lees, of fat things full of marrow, of wine on the lees well refined."[21] The feasts of judgment are found in Isaiah 34:1-6ff., in Jeremiah 46:10, and in Zephaniah. Thus, while there is a sense of the great assize at the end of history, with the exception of Isaiah, there is little sense of God's joyful celebration with the godly at the end of history.

The eschatological banquet, as envisioned by the author of the Book of Revelation, is a complicated fusion of three rich metaphors relating to the exalted Christ in heaven. In concentrated form it is contained in a single verse: "And the angel said to me: 'Write this: Blessed are those who are invited to the marriage supper of the Lamb.'"[22] This cryptic saying requires careful unraveling.

First we must expound the concept of Christ as the Lamb of God, a term that is employed no less than twenty-eight times in Revelation. It evokes the description the Gospel of John gives of John the Baptist seeing Jesus approaching him, and declaring, "Behold, the Lamb of God, who takes away the sin of the world!"[23] This means that Jesus blots out the sin of the world by the expiatory blood of his sacrifice on the cross. Furthermore, the Christian community in describing Christ as the Lamb expresses the patience of his suffering (Acts 8:32), his sinlessness (I Pet. 1:19), and the efficacy of his sacrificial death (John 1:29, 36; I Pet. 1:18-19).[24] The image of the paschal lamb is also recalled, for the Lamb bears on his neck the marks of his slaugh-

---

21. Isaiah 25:6.
22. Revelation 19:9.
23. John 1:29.
24. J. Jeremias in G. Kittel and G. Friedrich, eds., *The Theological Dictionary of the New Testament* (Grand Rapids: Wm. B. Eerdmans, 1964-76), vol. I, p. 340.

tering (Rev. 5:6, 9, 12; 13:8); but the Lamb overcame death (5:5-6) and rules the world, taking over the book of destiny in the heavenly council (4:2ff.; 5:7ff.). He also establishes the rule of peace and celebrates his marriage festival with the community (19:9).

The image of Christ as a bridegroom has rich allegorical implications. This image is found in St. Paul, where the community is compared with a bride and Paul is the best man who guards the bride's virginity and will lead her to Christ, the bridegroom, as his pure community.[25] The image is repeated in Ephesians 5:22ff., a passage that emphasizes the love of Christ for his community, which is selfless to the point of self-sacrifice, and obliges the community to obedience and bridal purity.[26] The same image is found in the gospels, where the synoptic writers applied the saying of Jesus in Mark 2:19a ("Can the wedding guests fast while the bridegroom is with them? As long as they have the bridegroom with them, they cannot fast") to the historical Jesus.[27] In the Book of Revelation the image of the messianic bridal community is found in the final chapters depicting the ultimate consummation of history (19:7, 9; 21:2, 9; 22:17) and the image of the bride has been transferred from the earthly community to the heavenly Jerusalem, which descends to the transfigured earth when the millennial kingdom of God terminates. This heavenly city of God is "prepared as a bride adorned for her husband."[28] Jeremias finely describes the fulfillment as follows: "Final fulfilment, certainly of salvation, joy, hope, and longing are all expressed here in what is said about the Lamb's wife."[29]

The third element in the mélange of metaphors is, of course, the feast or festival. It is a marriage festival, and therefore one of the utmost joy, for it proclaims the indissoluble union of

25. *Theological Dictionary of the New Testament*, vol. IV, p. 1105.
26. *Ibid.*, vol. IV, p. 1104.
27. The changes are made in context in Matthew 9:15 and Luke 5:34.
28. Revelation 21:2, in a direct echo of Isaiah 61:10.
29. *Theological Dictionary of the New Testament*, vol. IV, p. 1104.

Christ and his faithful disciples of all the centuries, the communion of saints. Nothing can be more appropriate than to anticipate in the celebration of the Eucharist, which recalls the sacrifice of the Lamb of God on the cross, affirms his invisible
presence and union with the church as his body, and looks
forward to sharing eternity in his visible presence with un-
bounded joy.

This recovered emphasis seems an important rectification of
eucharists in the past that have stressed the agony and death of
Christ with an excessively retrospective look, and that transformed the marriage feast of the Lamb into a funeral repast. The
Last Supper takes into account both the death and the joyful
second coming of the Lord, for, as St. Paul put it, we "proclaim
the Lord's death till he comes."[30] Its significance is expressed by
G. D. Yarnold: "The Eucharist is the fellowship meal of the
Kingdom here and now: the marriage supper, the perfect fellowship meal when the Kingdom is delivered up to the Father."[31]
Thus the church on earth participates in the worship of heaven,
and its true citizenship is renewed and deepened because the
church in its eucharistic worship looks forward to the second
coming of Christ in which the Lord will return in joy.

Our concentration will now be on the fact that the eschatological banquet is, above all, a festivity, a meal that expresses
abounding and exhilarating joy.

The Banquet of Joy

Joy was an original emphasis of the Eucharist, but it is one that
has not been characteristic of its celebration for many, many
centuries. It has returned as a feature of the present-day Eucharist, but it is far from dominant. For it to be a true celebration

30. I Corinthians 11:26.
31. *The Bread Which We Break* (London: Oxford University Press,
1960), p. 76.

of salvation in Christ, the emphasis of joyful celebration must be fully recovered.

Protestants tend to think of the Eucharist as a sacred meal because of the central table and its frequent designation as the Lord's Supper — even though it is held almost always in the morning rather than at night, and despite the fact that the quantity of food and drink is minimal. Catholics, however, almost evitably think of the central and dominating altar and of a sacrifice, rather than a meal. It is customary for them to partake only of a wafer, which is hardly a meal in itself. If these limitations make it difficult to imagine a meal either at the Lord's Supper or at Mass or Holy Communion, even more difficult is perceiving this service as a celebration. For us its character is solemn, sacred, and staid; not joyful, jubilant, and celebratory. What, then, should be the characteristics of a Christian celebration, and can we find appropriate elements or parallels in social life?

The nearest parallels of what might be appropriate forms of celebration are birthday parties, or important wedding anniversaries, or public recognitions of achievements of distinction. In each case there are the gatherings of colleagues and friends. In each case individuals are honored for their characters or achievements. In each case there are informal or formal speeches recognizing the values of the person honored. In each case the party or communal function is a delightful break from the humdrum routine of daily business life.

Frederic Debuyst, a Benedictine, has analyzed "Feast Day and Festive Occasions."[32] He finds that they are powerfully *communitarian* experiences, and that the more successful they are, the more they induce "a phenomenon of participation, an experience of communion, and . . . one who truly enters into its spirit must give up every inclination to egotism, arbitrary exclusivism and individualistic expropriation or possessiveness."[33] Furthermore, it gives

32. In Christopher Duquoc, O.P., ed., *The Gift of Joy,* in *Concilium,* vol. 39 (New York: Paulist Press, 1968), pp. 7-16.
33. *Ibid.,* pp. 12, 13.

members of the party a sense of the joy of existence and the primordial unity of the human race.

Debuyst claims that a genuinely festive occasion requires three essential traits: universality, unanimity, and a participation in eternity beyond the boundaries of time.[34] The universality means that there are no strangers at the festive board. If, in fact, a stranger appears at the door, he must become a guest, for if he is turned away or prevented from entering, this becomes a sin against openness and can ruin the spirit of the celebration. The second characteristic is unanimity; it clearly requires everyone to share the same intentions and values. At this point Debuyst cites a text of St. John Chrysostom to make the point that a festive occasion makes its own communion. That profound text is "Where charity radiates its joy, there we have a feast." It is *agape* — the divine love — that finally makes the feast.

The third trait necessary concerns the temporal duration of the festivity. Even if every human festive occasion has a beginning and an end, it is still possible to think of a perduring festival that is interior to the guests at the temporal feast — grounded in the sheer goodness of creation and the deeply rooted brotherhood and sisterhood of humanity.

The Christian feast, which is what the Eucharist is, both recapitulates and deepens the three traits that are part of every human festivity. It begins by thanking God for the whole of creation. The joy of Sunday recapitulates the joy of sabbath as it celebrates God's approval of his work of six days. But, further than this, the Christian feast celebrates the *second* creation, for, as Debuyst expresses it, "By the incarnation of God's Son and the power of the redemption, this second creation has rescued everything from the bottomless abyss of sin. The Christian feast is essentially a joyous remembrance *(anamnesis)* of the Lord's death and resurrection, a participation in the superabundance of life and love that has been ever present and available to us since Easter morning."[35] The

34. *Ibid.*
35. *Ibid.,* p. 14.

Christian communion is a complete circle, not even broken by death, for the King of Kings and Lord of Lords is the risen, ascended, interceding, and victorious Christ.

The Hebraic Understanding of Joy

The contrast between the biblical and our modern conception of joy is striking. It may well be, as Fr. Pietro Dacquino suggests, the result of the duality of Western civilization in which we split soul and body. Consequently joy is either a spiritual and abstract experience or synonymous with base and forbidden pleasures.[36] This dichotomy was not experienced by ancient peoples. For them true joy was the simultaneous expression of physical, psychological, and spiritual well-being. Consequently, joy was unembarrassingly associated with the body in the pleasure of a good meal (Tob. 2:1) and a drink of good wine (Judg. 9:13; Ps. 104:15: "and wine to gladden the heart of man"). Music and dancing were the expressions of this joy (Job 21:12; Lam. 5:15). Many reasons were given for the expression of joy, among them the birth of children, especially sons (Jer. 20:15b), long life (Ecclus. 30:23), love of a spouse (Prov. 5:18b), and, of course, prosperity and abundance at the harvest of grain and vintage (I Chron. 12:41b; Isa.16:10). Deliverance from enemies or victories also were occasions of joyful feasting (I Sam. 18:6; II Chron. 20:27). Joy was seen as a gift of God and was often associated with religious feasts and liturgical worship.[37]

Joy was also a characteristic of the sacrificial banquets of the Hebrews when they made pilgrimages to the temple and gave the tithe offering (Deut. 12:7, 18; 14:23). This was felt to be a joy of the heart, deeply internal, the joy of the benevolent who fulfilled God's Law. This joy, says Canon Dacquino, was opposed to the

36. "Human Joy and the Hereafter in the Biblical Books," in *Concilium*, vol. 39, pp. 17-31.
37. For the joy of Passover see Isaiah 30:29; Ezra 6:22; for Pentecost see Deuteronomy 16:10; and for Tabernacles see Psalm 81:2-4.

materialistic joys of some of their contemporaries (see Isa. 22:13) and to the orgiastic pleasures of neighboring peoples (see Hos. 9:1). It was a gift of God for his faithful people.

To that joy of the Hebrews there was one dire threat — the fear of death and the sheer desolation of Sheol, the place of the dead (see Eccl. 6:4; 9:5-6). Here in complete inertia and oblivion all happiness came to an end. But, concomitant with this darkest pessimism, there appeared in the writings of the prophets a sense of joy in the future eschatological era. It begins with Isaiah 9:2a in the eighth century B.C., and a century later Zephaniah and Habakkuk speak of it. It is mainly the exilic writings Deutero-Jeremiah (31:7; 33:9b, 11) and Deutero-Isaiah (44:23; 49:13; 52:9) that make reference to it, and it becomes most clear in the third part of Isaiah (60:15; 65:18-19; 66:10-14). In the so-called Apocalypse of Isaiah (25:6), the work of the prophet's disciples in the third century B.C., we have the splendid and dominant image of the feast: "On this mountain the Lord of hosts will provide for all peoples a feast of rich food and choice wines, juicy rich food and pure, choice wines."[38] This may rightly be called a dominant image because it appears and reappears in Jewish apocalyptic.[39]

This eschatological joy is the gift of salvation, and it is prepared by God not only for Israel but for mankind (Isa. 66:18ff.; 25:6). This joy is essentially a return to the joy at the very outset of creation when it came forth "good" at the hands of God, Eden anew.

Christ and Messianic Joy

A striking characteristic of Luke's gospel is the association of Jesus with great joy. Luke writes of the joy announced by the angel to Mary (1:28), who herself proclaims joy in the *Magnificat,* while the angels proclaim their joy to the shepherds in

---

38. For the references in the two preceding paragraphs I am indebted to the compilation of Canon Dacquino, *ibid.,* pp. 18-22.

39. See Ethiopic Enoch 62:14 and Slavic Enoch 42:5.

Bethlehem (2:10). Another of the gospels, Matthew, recalls the joy of the three magi in meeting the child Jesus (2:10).

Inevitably the Messiah himself, Jesus, described the salva,ion to be inaugurated as a great feast, a wedding banquet given by a monarch to celebrate the wedding of his son (Matt. 22:4), or as a great supper prepared by a wealthy landowner (Luke 14:16ff.). John's gospel, too, emphasizes joy. In John 8:35 Jesus speaks of Abraham's joy at the thought of the eschatological era, and during the discourse of the Last Supper the Savior often mentions joy, a joy that is his own and must be in "his own" (15:11; 17:13), which will increase at his resurrection (16:20b) and no one will be able to take away from his disciples (16:22). It stresses that this is a complete, an eschatological, joy (15:11b; 17:13; see also I John 1:4; 2 John 12). Such is the climax of happiness in the life to come in the presence of Christ and his friends. It is this abounding and unceasing joy that is the dominant characteristic of the eschatological banquet, and the Bible stresses its importance.

The Present Meaning of the Eschatological Banquet in the Eucharist

The fullest explication of the correlation of the Eucharist with the eschatology of the New Testament has been made in the pioneering study of Geoffrey Wainwright, *Eucharist and Eschatology*, published in 1971. He envisages the Eucharist as projecting the *parousia* in four major ways: (a) the Eucharist is a memorial of Christ himself as well as a promise of greater things to come; (b) the church claims that promise in its cry of *Maranatha* in the Eucharist; (c) the Eucharist promises to the penitent forgiveness of sins and eternal life, but judgment to the impenitent; and (d) the Eucharist is a projection in the temporal sense — throwing forward Christ's final advent into the present.[40]

40. Wainwright, *Eucharist and Eschatology* (London: Epworth Press, 1971), pp. 91-93.

Some explanation and filling out of the summary is necessary. In the first place, the church at the Eucharist prays that
the Father will complete the bringing in of his Kingdom by
sending the same Messiah again to accomplish his final work.
In the second place, the church at the Eucharist claims the
promise the Lord made at his first coming: "Where two or
three are gathered in my name, there am I in the midst of
them."[41] The church longs impatiently for the day when God's
loving rule will be universally acknowledged, but the Father
keeps that a secret. So the church claims Christ's promise here
and now in the equivalent of the *Maranatha*, "Our Lord,
come!" As Wainwright affirms: "The Church prays for the final
advent of the Lord; but if the moment for that is not yet come,
the Church may still acclaim the presence of Christ even now
to confirm His people's hope."[42] In Christ's present coming in
the Eucharist he offers pardon to the penitent, assuring them
of their acquittal and granting them a foretaste of the delights
to come in the eternal kingdom.[43] At the same time there is
for the impenitent and the unbelieving the threat of condemnation in the great assize. This negative element of the *parousia*
must not be neglected by sentimentalism. It is significant that
Revelation mentions the dreadful opposite of the final banquet
of the blessed in the threatening words: "Then I saw an angel
standing in the sun, and with a loud voice he called to all the
birds that fly in mid-heaven, 'Come, gather for the great supper
of God, to eat the flesh of kings, the flesh of captains, the flesh
of mighty men, the flesh of horses and their riders, and the
flesh of all men, both free and slave, both small and great.'"[44]
This threat recalls a parallel in Ezekiel, where the prophet is to
foretell the doom of God, in which the birds of prey and

41. Matthew 18:20.
42. *Eucharist and Eschatology*, p. 93.
43. This is seen in Matthew 26:27, which, when the cup is offered,
reads: "Drink of it, all of you; for this is my blood of the covenant, which
is poured out for many for the remission of sins."
44. Revelation 19:17-18.

predatory animals will gorge themselves on a sacrificial feast, eating flesh and drinking blood.[45]

It is also possible that Paul's vehement condemnation of the Corinthians for "not discerning the body" at the Eucharist through their disregard of their brethren who are left hungry by their greed may not only be intended to refer to their future condemnation at the great assize, but also to be applicable to every Eucharist. In this way the meal designed to give the benefits of salvation from Christ may be the very meal at which he executes judgment.

It is worth stressing that Luke testifies to the gladness that the primitive Christians experienced in their celebrations of the Eucharist: "And day by day, attending the temple together and breaking bread in their homes, they partook of food with glad and generous hearts, praising God and having favor with all the people."[46] There was a profound sense of exhilaration, if not of hilarity, in the triple assurance that the Resurrection was the validation of Christ's words and actions, that their own sins were forgiven, and that their eternal future was guaranteed. The eucharists of the primitive church had no alternative except to be exuberant but holy celebrations of joy.

Furthermore, the dominating sense of overwhelming joy so characteristic of those early eucharists was, according to J. Gordon Davies, due in part to the recollection of the post-Resurrection meals that the disciples had shared with Christ, for here the messianic banquet promised by Jesus at the Last Supper was partly anticipated.[47] Furthermore, joy is a quality of the eschatological existence founded by the Holy Spirit, since "the kingdom of God is . . . righteousness and peace and joy in the Holy Spirit" (Rom. 14:17). Even in the fourth century the sense

45. Ezekiel 39:17 reads: "As for you, son of man, thus says the Lord GOD. Speak to the birds of every sort and to all beasts of the field, 'Assemble and come, gather from all sides to the sacrificial feast which I am preparing for you, a great sacrificial feast upon the mountains of Israel, and you shall eat flesh and drink blood.'"

46. Acts 2:46. See also Acts 16:34.

47. Introductory essay to *An Experimental Liturgy* (London: Lutterworth Press, 1958), p. 24.

of gladness had not disappeared from the Eucharist, for as St. Ambrose declared, "in joy the Church calls Christ, having ready a feast which can seem worthy of heavenly banqueting."[48]

The eucharistic meal has several other implications as well. It is a meal of the Kingdom because it emphasizes the continuity and the difference that mark the present and future forms of the Kingdom of God. The Eucharist is a taste of the Kingdom, but the eschatological banquet is the fullness of the Kingdom. While the church eats at the table of the Lord only at intervals in time, the feeding at the eternal table is uninterrupted. Further, the eucharistic meal reveals not only God's provision of daily food for mankind, but also that the bread and wine are signs that God feeds his chosen in Christ on his own being. "Christ is food, table-fellow and host."[49] The Eucharist indicates the positive value of the material creation for humanity, and thus there is no ultimate opposition between the earthly and the heavenly, for the bread and wine, which are material, mediate communion between God and human beings. At the same time it points to the eschatological meal in which that communion will be the closest possible. Finally, the Eucharist reveals the communal nature of the Kingdom of God both here in part and later in fullness. The community of the Kingdom shares in the one loaf at the one table of the Lord, as indicated by I Corinthians 10:16b-17: "The bread which we break, is it not a participation in the body of Christ? Because there is one bread, we who are many are one body, for we all partake of the one bread."

The great historic liturgies all remind us that at the Eucharist the church joins in the worship of heaven in both the acclamation of the *Sanctus,* "Holy, holy, holy, LORD God of hosts; heaven and earth are full of your glory,"[50] and in the recitation of the Lord's Prayer, which anticipates that all the saints will be called children of God.

48. *De Sacramentis* 5.14.
49. *Eucharist and Eschatology,* p. 58.
50. Isaiah's acclamation "the whole earth is full of your glory" (6:3) has the addition of "heaven and" to make it "Heaven and earth are full of your glory."

Some theologians who are universalists see another eschatological meaning in the Eucharist. Disregarding St. Paul's warning about receiving the sacrament to one's own condemnation, and convinced of the ultimate victory of God's love over all human disobedience, they would approve a passage in a letter of the Scottish theologian D. S. Cairns, who wrote, after citing the words of Jesus at the Last Supper, "Verily I say unto you, I will drink no more of the fruit of the vine until the day that I drink it new with you in the Kingdom of God," these words: "At the very nadir of defeat and solitude, He founds a rite and sends it down through all history, which will be a continual prophecy of victory. In the sacrament we are really rehearsing, or rather anticipating, the day when the whole human race will be home, gathered round the Father's table, after Iliads and Odysseys yet to be! Retrospect and prophecy is one; that is what the sacrament is to me, with the renewal of the covenant face to face."[51] In this expression of conviction we can hear the heavenly choirs singing in full-throated exultation, and the trumpets and the drums of the celestial orchestra sounding the ecstatic triumph of Christ and his saints, echoing in the earthly Eucharist.

A final eschatological meaning in the Eucharist is that its emphasis on the completion and perfection of the Kingdom of God in history should be a further incentive in prosecuting the evangelizing mission of the church, thus proving its fidelity to the post-Resurrection command of Christ. The command, "Go, therefore, and make disciples of all nations. . . ," was, it should be recalled, linked to the glowing promise, "Lo, I am with you always, to the close of the age" (Matt. 28:19, 20).

Eschatological Elements in Modern Eucharistic Liturgies

Because of its powerful eschatological emphases in the anaphora of the leading historic liturgy of the Eastern Orthodox churches,

---

51. David Cairns, *An Autobiography* (London: SCM Press, 1950), p. 201.

namely that of Saint John Chrysostom, still used widely in this
day, we shall cite the major part of that anaphora:

The Priest says: The grace of our Lord Jesus Christ, and the love
of the God and Father, and the fellowship of the Holy Spirit
be with you all.

People: And with your spirit.

Priest: Let us lift up our hearts.

People: We have lifted them with the Lord.

Priest: Let us give thanks to the Lord.

People: It is fitting and right (to worship the Father, the Son,
and the Holy Spirit, the consubstantial and undivided Trinity).

The priest begins the holy anaphora: It is fitting and right to hymn
you, (to bless you, to praise you), to give you thanks, to worship
you in all places of your dominion. For you are God, ineffable,
inconceivable, invisible, incomprehensible, existing always and
in the same way, you and your only-begotten Son and your
Holy Spirit. You brought us out of not-being to being; and
when we had fallen, you raised us up again; and did not cease
to do everything until you had brought us up to heaven, and
granted us the kingdom that is to come. For all these things
we give thanks to you and to your only-begotten Son and to
your Holy Spirit, for all that we know and do not know, your
seen and unseen benefits that have come upon us. We give you
thanks also for this ministry; vouchsafe to receive it from our
hands, even though thousands of archangels and ten thousands
of angels stand before you, cherubim and seraphim, with six
wings and many eyes, flying on high *(aloud)* singing the trium-
phal hymn (proclaiming, crying, and saying:)

People: Holy, (holy, holy, Lord of Sabaoth; heaven and earth are
full of your glory. Hosanna in the highest. Blessed is he who
comes in the name of the Lord. Hosanna in the highest.)

The priest, privately: With these powers, O Master, lover of man, we cry and say, holy are you and all-holy, and your only-begotten Son, and your Holy Spirit; holy are you, all-holy and magnificent is your glory; for you so loved the world that you gave your only-begotten Son that all who believe in him should not perish, but have eternal life.

*   *   *

The priest, privately: We therefore, remembering the saving commandment and all of the things that were done for us: the cross, the tomb, the resurrection on the third day, and the ascension into heaven, the session at the right hand, the second and glorious coming again; *(aloud)* offering you your own from your own, in all and through all.

*   *   *

The invocation of the Holy Spirit on the gifts follows:

Priest privately, so that they may become to those who partake for vigilance of soul, for forgiveness of sins, for fellowship with the Holy Spirit, for the fullness of the kingdom (of heaven), for boldness towards you: not for judgment or condemnation. . . . [Then a prayer follows for those who rest in faith, including the Virgin, St. John the Baptist, and the apostles] and all your saints: at their entreaties, look upon us, O God. And remember all those who have fallen asleep in hope of resurrection to eternal life, and grant them rest where the light of your countenance looks upon them.[52]

The anaphora ends with a triune doxology. In a remarkable way it has never allowed us to forget heaven, where God, Father, Son, and Holy Spirit, and all the saints share the life and love of God. By comparison both the ancient and modern Western liturgies are much more earthbound.

52. Thurian and Wainwright, eds., *Baptism and Eucharist: Ecumenical Convergence in Celebration,* pp. 117-18.

It is significant, however, that in the Roman Missal of 1970 the fourth eucharistic prayer is modeled on the Orthodox liturgy. After the initial dialogue the canon proceeds thus:

Father in heaven, it is right that we should give you thanks and glory: you are the one God, living and true. Through all eternity you live in unapproachable light. Source of life and goodness, you have created all things, to fill your creatures with every blessing and lead them to the joyful vision of your light. Countless angels stand before you to do your will; they look upon your splendour and praise you, night and day. United with them, and in the name of every creature under heaven, we too praise your glory as we say: *Holy, holy, holy Lord, God of power and might, heaven and earth are full of your glory. Hosanna in the highest. Blessed is he who comes in the name of the Lord. Hosanna in the highest.*

[Then follow the commemoration of creation and of redemption, the *epiclesis,* and the institution of the Eucharist, concluding with: Let us proclaim the mystery of faith:

(1) *Christ has died, Christ is risen, Christ will come again.*

OR

(2) *Dying you destroyed our death, rising you restored our life. Lord Jesus, come in glory.*

OR

(3) *When we eat this bread and drink this cup, we proclaim your death, Lord Jesus, until you come.*

OR

(4) *Lord, by your cross and resurrection you have set us free. You are the Saviour of the world.*

*   *   *

Remember those who have died in the peace of Christ and all the dead whose faith is known to you alone.

Father, in your mercy grant also to us, your children, to enter into our heavenly inheritance in the company of the Virgin Mary, the Mother of God, and your apostles and saints. Then, in your kingdom, freed from the corruption of sin and death, we shall sing your glory with every creature through Christ our Lord, through whom you give us everything that is good.

Through him, with him, in the unity of the Holy Spirit, all glory and honour is yours, almighty Father, for ever and ever.

P: *Amen.*[53]

The Third Roman Eucharistic Prayer, which also includes the four splendid alternative responses and an *epiclesis*, has this *anamnesis:*

Father, calling to mind the death your Son endured for our salvation, his glorious resurrection and ascension into heaven, and ready to greet him when he comes again, we offer you in thanksgiving this holy and living sacrifice. . . .

May he make us an everlasting gift to you
and enable us to share in the inheritance of your saints . . .
on whose constant intercession we rely for help. . . .

Welcome into your kingdom our departed brothers and
sisters and all who have left this world in your friendship.
We hope to enjoy for ever the vision of your glory,
through Christ our Lord, from whom all good things
come.[54]

53. *The Sunday Missal. A New Edition: Sunday Masses for the Entire Three Year Cycle* (London: Collins Liturgical Publications, 1984), pp. 52-55.
54. *The Sunday Missal,* pp. 48-50.

The eschatological references of the new Roman Masses mark a considerable advance in this respect over the Tridentine canon.

The Church of England has, in addition to the traditional rite of 1662, four new eucharistic prayers in *The Alternative Service Book, 1980*. Each contains the response:

> *Christ has died:*
> *Christ is risen:*
> *Christ will come again.*

Following the dialogue, the *Sanctus*, and the *Benedictus* there is a commemoration of creation and redemption, an *epiclesis*, the record of the institution, followed by the response cited. The First Eucharistic Prayer then proceeds:

> Therefore, heavenly Father,
> we remember his offering of himself
> made once for all upon the cross,
> and proclaim his mighty resurrection and glorious ascension.
> As we look for his coming in glory,
> we celebrate with this bread and this cup
> his one perfect sacrifice. . . .

and the prayer concludes:

> Through him, and with him, and in him,
> by the power of the Holy Spirit,
> with all who stand before you in earth and in heaven,
> we worship you, Father almighty,
> in songs of everlasting praise:

> *All: Blessing and honour and glory and power be yours for ever and ever.*[55]

The Third Eucharistic Prayer, after commemorating the cross, the Resurrection, and the Ascension and anticipating the *parousia*, concludes:

55. *The Alternative Service Book, 1980*, pp. 130-32.

Send the Holy Spirit on your people
and gather into one in your kingdom
all who share this one bread and one cup,
so that we, in the company of all the saints,
may praise and glorify you for ever,
through him from whom all good things come,
Jesus Christ our Lord,

By whom, and with whom, and in whom,
in the unity of the Holy Spirit,
all honour and glory be yours,
Almighty Father, for ever and ever. *Amen.*[56]

The American *Book of Common Prayer* (1979) has many alternative Great Thanksgivings, but, apart from the seasonal Prefaces for Advent (which refer to the Final Judgment), for Easter (referring to everlasting life), for Ascension Day (referring to heaven "to prepare a place for us"), and, of course, for All Saints, and the traditional use of the *Sanctus,* the eschatological references are few and very condensed. For example, Holy Eucharist II, Prayer A, asks: "and at the last day bring us with all your saints into the joy of your eternal kingdom,"[57] while an alternative final prayer of gratitude for the sacrament praises God for the assurance "that we are living members of the Body of your Son, and heirs of your eternal kingdom."[58] Eucharistic Prayer B of Rite II is more expansive:

In the fullness of time, put all things in subjection under your Christ, and bring us to that heavenly country where, with [_____] all your saints, we may enter the everlasting heritage of your sons and daughters.[59]

Eucharistic Prayer C includes the congregational response:

56. *Ibid.,* pp. 130-32.
57. *Book of Common Prayer . . . according to the Use of the Episcoopal Church* (New York: Church Hymnal Corporation, 1979), p. 363.
58. *Ibid.,* p. 366.
59. *Ibid.,* p. 369.

We celebrate his death and resurrection,
as we await the day of his coming.

In addition, there is in Eucharistic Prayer D a much fuller preparation for the *Sanctus* and *Benedictus:*

> It is truly right to glorify you, Father, and to give you thanks;
> for you alone are God, living and true, dwelling in light inac-
> cessible, from before time and for ever.

> Fountain of life and source of all goodness, you made all things
> and fill them with your blessing; you created them to rejoice
> in the splendor of your radiance.

> Countless throngs of angels stand before you to serve you night
> and day; and, beholding the glory of your presence, they offer
> you unceasing praise. Joining with them, and giving voice to
> every creature under heaven, we acclaim you, and glorify your
> Name, as we sing (say). . . .[60]

It is very disappointing that this *American Book of Common Prayer,*
which has an innovative prayer of gratitude for the creation and
a marvelously compassionate form of thanksgiving for the birth
or adoption of a child, offers such slight treatment of eschatology
in the liturgy.

The German Lutheran Rite (1955 with revisions of 1976
and 1977) has an extensive act of glorification between the
dialogue and the *Sanctus:*

> It is truly estimable and right, just and salutary, that at all times
> and in all places we give you thanks, holy Lord, almighty Father,
> eternal God, through Jesus Christ our Lord. You sent him for
> the salvation of the world that by his death we might have
> forgiveness of sins and by his resurrection we might have life.
> Through him the angels praise your majesty, the heavenly hosts
> adore you, and the powers tremble; together with the blessed
> Seraphim all the citizens of heaven praise you in brilliant jubi-

60. *Ibid.,* p. 373.

lation. Unite our voices with theirs and let us sing praise in endless adoration.

After the Institution and the Consecration Alternative Prayer B continues:

> Therefore we remember, Lord, heavenly Father, the saving passion and death of your dear Son, Jesus Christ. We praise his glorious resurrection from the dead and are comforted by his ascension into your heavenly sanctuary where he, our high priest, continually intercedes for us. And as all of us are one body in Christ through the fellowship of his body and blood, so gather your faithful people from the ends of the earth, that together with all the faithful we may celebrate in his kingdom the marriage feast of the Lamb. Through him be praise and honour, glory and adoration, almighty God, in the Holy Spirit, now and forever, and to the ages of ages.[61]

This is splendidly comprehensive and is one of the rare prayers that actually uses the term "the marriage feast of the Lamb." Several prayers of thanksgiving (alternatives to B) also stress the eschatological aspect. For example, one, after the response: "We proclaim your death, O Lord, and we praise your resurrection, until you come again in glory," continues:

---

61. Thurian and Wainwright, eds., *Baptism and Eucharist: Ecumenical Convergence in Celebration,* pp. 136-37. The English translation of the official *Agende für evangelisch-lutherische Kirchen und Gemeinden,* I, is borrowed from the Lutheran/Roman Catholic Joint Commission, *The Eucharist* (Geneva: The Lutheran World Federation, 1980).

I am also indebted to Professor Gerhard Sauter of Bonn University for drawing my attention to the *Arnoldshainer Thesin* (1958), a document prepared by theologians of the Lutheran, Reformed, and United churches in West Germany to overcome doctrinal differences in the Eucharist deriving from the Reformation, which stressed the importance of the eschatological motif. The respective churches accepted this document and also the right of ministers of each church to celebrate in the other two churches. Professor Sauter himself believes that a true interpretation of the doctrine of justification by faith of sinners requires open admission to the Eucharist for the penitent, which is an eschatological reference, as Romans 8:24 indicates.

So we remember, heavenly Father, the suffering and death of your Son. We praise his resurrection and ascension, and we rely on his lordship over all the world. We pray: Just as all who receive his body and *one* body in Christ, so gather together your people from the ends of the earth, and let us with all faithful people celebrate the eternal feast of joy in his kingdom. . . .[62]

The President: Therefore, gracious Father, with this bread and cup we remember the life our Lord offered for us. And, believing the witness of his resurrection, we await his coming in power to share with us the great promised feast.

Congregation: Amen. Come, Lord Jesus.

P: Send now, we pray, your Holy Spirit, the spirit of our Lord and of his resurrection, that we who receive the Lord's body and blood may live to your praise and glory and receive our inheritance with all your saints in light.

C: Amen. Come, Holy Spirit.

P: Join our prayers with those of your servants of every time and every place, and unite them with the ceaseless petitions of our great high priest until he comes as victorious Lord of all.[63]

Here we have in a natural succession the eschatological banquet, the primitive *Maranatha*, a parallel simple *epiclesis*, and the communion of saints in a notable liturgical achievement.

The British *Methodist Service Book* (1975) in "The Thanksgiving" carefully combines the recognition of Christ's eternal priesthood in heaven with the priesthood of all believers, as it commemorates God's mighty acts:

You raised him from the dead, and exalted him to your right hand in glory, where he lives for ever to pray for us.
Through him you have sent your holy and life-giving Spirit

62. *Ibid.*, p. 138.
63. *Ibid.*, p. 143.

and made us your people, a royal priesthood,
To stand before you to proclaim your glory and celebrate
your mighty acts.
And so with all the company of heaven we join in the
unending hymn of praise. . . .

After the mention of the Institution and the *epiclesis,* the prayer
continues:

Make us one body with him.
Accept us as we offer ourselves to be a living sacrifice,
and bring us with the whole creation to your heavenly
kingdom.[64]

"The Great Thanksgiving" of the "alternate rite" of the
United Methodist Church of the U.S.A. published in 1980 has
an excellent *anamnesis* in which the following finely balanced
references appear:

By dying, he freed us from unending death;
By rising from the dead, he gave us everlasting life.

It also has few eschatological references, with the exception of:

When we eat this bread and drink this cup,
we experience anew the presence of the Lord Jesus Christ
and look forward to his coming in final victory.[65]

The Reformed Church of France in its official Liturgy of
1982 includes the following petitions in its Fourth Eucharistic
Prayer, following the congregational response:

Lord Jesus, we proclaim your death,
we celebrate your resurrection,
*   we await your coming in glory.*

64. *Ibid.,* p. 170.
65. *Ibid.,* pp. 171-72.

Therefore, Lord, we make before you the memorial
of the incarnation and passion of your Son,
of his resurrection from the dead,
of his ascension in glory,
of his perpetual intercession;
we await and earnestly pray for his return,
rejoicing in the Holy Spirit
whom you have given to your Church.
O God our Father, we remember that the Crucified
ever lives to intercede for us;
we therefore pray to you to transform our lives,
that they may be consecrated to you;
grant us the joy of your presence,
and fill our hearts with your Spirit,
through Christ our Saviour.[66]

It is comprehensive and yet pellucidly clear.

A Book of Services of the United Reformed Church in the United Kingdom (1980) in its Third Thanksgiving prays as follows:

So whenever we eat of this bread
and drink from this cup,
we proclaim the death of the Lord
until he comes.

Therefore, Lord our God,
we present this sign of our faith
and therefore we call to mind now
the suffering and death of your son,
his resurrection from the dead,
his entry into your glory,
rejoicing that he
who is exalted at your right hand
will speak up for us
and will come

66. *Ibid.,* p. 154.

> to do justice to the living and the dead
> on the day that you have appointed.[67]

This prayer is an admirable lesson in edification and is unique in reminding the communicants not only of eternal life but also of the day of judgment that precedes it.

The "Great Thanksgiving" of the United Church of Christ in the U.S.A. includes in its commemoration "the gift of your Son . . . who rules over us, Lord above all, prays for us continually, and will come again in triumph" and prefaces the prayer by inviting Christ's modern disciples in the cheerful words: "Beloved, this is the joyful feast of the people of God. . . . Behold how good and pleasant it is when brothers dwell in unity." The failure to include sisters in the invitation is a sure indication that the prayer was composed before the days of inclusive language. It did not fail to include, however, the sense of joy in the feast and, as the following citation will clarify, the *parousia* and the communion of saints:

> Above all we thank you for the gift of your Son, the redeemer of all men, who was born of Mary, lived on earth in obedience to you, died on the cross for our sins, and rose from the dead in victory; who rules over us, Lord above all, prays for us continually, and will come again in triumph.

> We thank you for your Holy Spirit and for your holy Church, for the means of grace and for the promise of eternal life. With patriarchs and prophets, apostles and martyrs, with your Church on earth and all the company of heaven, we worship and adore you, O Lord Most Holy:[68]

The Free Churches have always felt a sense of imprisonment in relatively fixed liturgies, but nonetheless their ministers can often frame prayers of deep spiritual insight. One celebrated

---

67. *A Book of Services: The United Reformed Church in the United Kingdom* (Edinburgh: The Saint Andrew Press, 1980), p. 36.

68. Thurian and Wainwright, eds., *Baptism and Eucharist*, p. 153.

example is Edward Reynolds, a distinguished Presbyterian Puritan in seventeenth-century England, who, becoming Anglican, produced the classic General Thanksgiving. So, as a reminder of the possibilities of free prayer, let me include a Baptist prayer for Easter Day:

> God our Father, accept the Easter thanksgiving of your
>   people.
>
> We thank you for Christ who is with us now
> standing among us in the fellowship of the church
> present at our table in the companionship of family and
>   friends
> beside us in our daily work
> beneath us as a rock in the stress, upheaval and change
> of our daily lives.
>
> We thank you for the Christ who will be with us in our
>   death
> may his presence free us from anguish
> may the light of his resurrection scatter the shadows
> that death may cast back across our lives.
>
> For the knowledge of Christ's presence in this life and the
> assurance of his presence in the life to come, we praise you, O
> God. In his name. Amen.[69]

Conclusion

We have reached the end of this chapter with a sense of disappointment that, for reasons of time and space, some material had to be left out. If too much has been made of the apocalyptic visions of the Book of Revelation in constructing the marriage

---

69. *Praise God: A Collection of Resource Material for Christian Worship*, compiled by Alex Gilmore, Edward Smalley, and Michael Walker, and published by The Baptist Union, London, England, 1980, p. 31.

banquet of the Lamb, then one could have examined the promising hypothesis of Massey H. Shepherd, Jr., that the very structure of Revelation is based upon the liturgy for Easter of the primitive church. His thesis is: "We propose to show that the outline and plan according to which the visions unfold is possibly — we would say probably — laid out in a scheme that follows the church's paschal liturgy."[70] We might also have made use of the suggestion that while the fourth gospel omits any institution of the Lord's Supper, yet the discourse on Jesus as the Bread of Life, which ends with the words "the bread which I shall give for the life of the world," is not only a parallel to the manna that sustained the children of Israel in the wilderness wandering, and a eucharistic reference, but may even be a eucharistic formula for the delivery of the bread.[71] We might also have paid further attention to the messianic and eschatological implications of the miracle meals in the synoptics, and to the radically compassionate meals to which Jesus invited the publicans and sinners, itself a revision of the concept of the Messiah.[72]

However, what we have discussed in this chapter has made clear that, while the past and present tenses of understanding the Eucharist are important, the future tense is also profoundly important, for it guarantees a happy issue from all the afflictions of the faithful and, equally significant, it points to the goal of history, when God shall establish his Kingdom in its fullness as well as encourage the church in its far-flung, wide-ranging, and historic mission. Within Protestantism, at least, the emphasis on the Eucharist has been mainly retrospective, so the correction was needed. In traditional Western liturgies the sense of a meal

70. *The Paschal Liturgy and the Apocalypse* (Richmond, VA: The John Knox Press, 1960), p. 77.

71. Otto Betz, *Die Eucharistie in der Zeit der griechischen Väter,* II/I, pp. 181ff.; and C. H. Dodd, *Historical Tradition in the Fourth Gospel* (Cambridge: Cambridge University Press, 1963), pp. 58ff.

72. The relevant references are Luke 22:14-23; cf. Mark 6:52, to be read in the light of Mark 8:17-21. See also Luke 22:30: ". . . that you may eat and drink at my table in the Kingdom." See also C. H. Dodd, *The Parables of the Kingdom* (London: Nisbet, 1935), pp. 55f. and 120-22.

was almost eliminated in favor of a sacrifice renewed, and it is the Eastern Orthodox Eucharist that has most faithfully preserved its eschatological reference. As Alexander Schmemann interprets it: "In the liturgy, which we have been commanded to celebrate 'until he comes,' we do not *repeat* and we do not *represent* — we *ascend* into the mystery of salvation and new life which has been accomplished once, but is granted to us 'always, now and forever and unto ages of ages.' And in this heavenly, eternal and otherworldly Eucharist, Christ does not come down to us, rather we ascend to him."[73] In this way the more recent liturgies have, in greater or lesser ways, restored the importance of hope to its proper place in the triad of theological virtues along with love and faith.

We have seen that each of the three elements in the eschatological banquet is of deep importance. Christ is the patient, suffering, expiatory Lamb sacrificed for our sins and a combination of many virtues including gentleness and peace, recalled in the Liturgy in the plea:

> O Lamb of God, that takes away the sins of the world,
> O Lamb of God, that takes away the sins of the world,
> Grant us your peace.

The second element, the Marriage, reflects the deep unity of love between Christ and his bridal community, the church. And the third element is the exulting sense of joy in this feast, and the everlasting joy it proclaims and promises. But for the impenitent we saw that there is the threat of judgment at the great assize at the end of history. The rejoicing is born of gratitude for Christ's gifts of forgiveness and eternal life, presaged in his own resurrection and ascension as a striking victory over the powers of evil, death, and darkness.

Finally, we examined the sense of eschatology in the recent liturgies of the Eucharist in several denominations. Unquestion-

---

73. Schmemann, *The Eucharist: Sacrament of the Kingdom* (Crestwood, NY: St. Vladimir's Seminary Press, 1988), p. 221.

ably there has been a recovery of this sense, but it is far from being fully and adequately expressed. In all liturgies it is exhibited in the seasonal prefaces at Easter, at the Ascension, and at All Saints. It is also seen in the acclamations in the prayers of thanksgiving that lead to the *Sanctus* and *Benedictus.* Some prayers refer to the benefit of the Eucharist as a promise of eternal life in this rather vague manner, but the number that refer specifically to the marriage feast of the Lamb are far too few, considering the allegorical richness of the conception. What is required as a minimum is the mention of the eschatological banquet in heaven, the marvelous communion of saints, and the joy that will characterize the marriage feast of the Lamb.

It is interesting that what the liturgies of the Eucharist have often omitted has been stressed by evangelical hymnody. A striking example is Charles Wesley's verse:

> Yet onward I haste
> To the heavenly feast:
> That, that is the fullness; but this is the taste;
> And this I shall prove,
> Till with joy I remove
> To the heaven of heavens in Jesus's love.

Horatius Bonar of the Church of Scotland has also caught the spirit splendidly in the verses of another hymn:

> This is the hour of banquet and of song;
> This is the heavenly table spread for me;
> Here let me feast, and, feasting, still prolong
> The brief, bright hour of fellowship with thee.

*   *   *

> Feast after feast thus comes and passes by,
> Yet, passing, points to the glad feast above,
> Giving sweet foretastes of the festal joy,
> The Lamb's great bridal feast of bliss and love.

Finally, Franz J. Leenhardt offers a practical suggestion to make clear within Protestant communions at least that commemoration and eschatological promise can be distinguished by applying the former to the bread and the latter to the cup, as the words that Jesus used at the institution of the Lord's Supper clearly indicate.[74] This would provide a valuable clarification of eucharistic practice.

The Roman Catholic *Constitution on the Liturgy* sums it all up: "In the earthly liturgy we receive a foretaste of that heavenly liturgy, which is celebrated in the holy city of Jerusalem towards which we journey as pilgrims . . ." (No. 8).

74. Cf. Leenhardt's *Parole Visible* (Paris: Delachaux & Niestlé, 1971). Here, on p. 86 in my translation: "The restitution of the eschatological sayings to the liturgy of the supper oblige one to fill a gap in our actual practice. The bread and the cup have been confused in the same theological and liturgical movement, by referring them both to the coming death. But we have previously noted that the cup of the new covenant inaugurated by the death of Jesus is a new rendezvous given to the communicants, the assurance of their participation in the Messianic feast. Liturgically it must be marked that the two perspectives should be distinguished: that of the cross and that of glory: that is to say to separate the distribution of the bread and the circulation of the cup. Each of these acts, reattached to the words of Jesus which supports it and nourishes the sense, should liturgically be a whole."

FIVE   The Eucharist as Communion: Joyful Meal of Unity

THE COMMON Anglican name for the Eucharist is *Holy Communion*. This conveys still another important facet of the meaning of this sacrament. It suggests the unity between God and humanity won by the reconciliation achieved on the cross by Christ, and the unity of the body of Christ effected by Christ in the Eucharist. Furthermore, the sense of unity of Christians — past, present, and future — is also manifested in the service of Holy Communion. What this sacred meal is intended to exhibit is the profound fellowship and sharing of Christians with Christ.

Both St. Paul and the synoptic writers demonstrate how important meals are either in breaking down barriers, or, negatively, where there is greed, in creating barriers. St. Paul insisted on the positive necessity of unity at the Lord's Supper in the statement: "The bread which we break, is it not a participation [communion] in the body of Christ? Because there is one bread, we who are many are one body, for we all partake of the one bread."[1]

The same apostle denounces the fracture of unity caused by the greediness of the rich who rush to eat the sacred meal or are drunk. He writes: "When you meet together, it is not the Lord's supper that you eat. For in eating, each one goes ahead with his own meal, and one is hungry and another is drunk. What! Do

1. I Corinthians 10:16b-17.

117

you not have houses to eat and drink in? Or do you despise the
church of God and humiliate those who have nothing?"[2] This
disunity could have occurred in the days when the *agape* preceded
the Eucharist. In any case, it shows the well-to-do having contempt for the poor and destroying the unity that should characterize fellow-members of the body of Christ.

It is also significant that the writers of the synoptic gospels
made the eating and drinking at table characteristic of the way
Jesus made outsiders feel at home in his company. The attitude
of Jesus was so striking that his enemies called him a glutton
and a wine-bibber. As David Cairns rightly says, "Eating and
drinking together at table is one of the great central human
symbols. It is, indeed, more than a symbol of fellowship; it
creates fellowship between the host and those who sit with him
at his table, and it binds them also to each other."[3] When Jesus
declared at the meal at Caesarea Philippi that he was indeed the
Messiah, every subsequent meal with the disciples would seem
to them to be pointing toward the messianic banquet at the end
of the age.[4] Luke particularly stresses the importance of meals
as a *mise-en-scène* for Christ's teaching, and especially of the
Lord's compassion for the poor, the beggars, the crippled, the
lame, and the blind.[5] It is also Luke who emphasizes how Christ
welcomed the disreputable tax collector Zacchaeus and the supposed prostitute Mary Magdalene, while the fourth gospel records Jesus speaking to the Samaritan woman who had five
husbands.[6] Nor should it be forgotten that the most famous
parable of Jesus — that of the prodigal son — ends with the
reconciliation with his father symbolized by a joyful welcome
feast.

2. I Corinthians 11:20-22.

3. *In Remembrance of Me* (London: Geoffrey Bles, 1967), p. 46.

4. J. Jeremias, *The Eucharistic Words of Jesus*, 3rd edn. transl. from the
German by Noel Perrin (New York: Scribner's, 1966), p. 205.

5. See Luke 14:21, part of a parable.

6. See Mary Magdalene in Luke 8:2 and 24:10, and Zacchaeus in Luke
19:2.

It is also important to notice that <u>the post-Resurrection</u> <u>appearances of Jesus often show that he ate and drank with the</u> <u>disciples.</u> The two disciples who met the risen Christ on the road to Emmaus knew the stranger to be the Christ when he broke and blessed the bread at table in the inn. After the same two joined the other disciples in Jerusalem, Jesus again appeared and ate with them. John also reported that the disciples on another occasion had breakfast with the risen Jesus beside the lake. And Peter witnessed to Christ before Cornelius the centurion: "God raised him on the third day and made him manifest, not to all the people but to us who were chosen by God as witnesses, who ate and drank with him after he rose from the dead."[7] Thus, whether we consider the meals at which Christ was host during his incarnate life, or his institution of the Lord's Supper, or the prior meals shared with his disciples, or the joyful nature of the Holy Communion shared in the primitive church,[8] we have to conclude that <u>a dominant characteristic of all these meals was a</u> <u>fellowship of profound unity.</u>

It is interesting that Louis Bouyer suggests that there is a double significance in the term *communio sanctorum* as applied to the experience of unitive fellowship in the Eucharist. *Communio sanctorum* (taking *sanctorum* as masculine) would mean communion among the saints or the sanctified, whereas *sanctorum* taken as neuter means communion *in* the holy things. Thus, he concludes: "the element of 'Communion' means that the Eucharist is a meal, a community meal, in which all the participants are brought together to have a common share in common goods, these common goods being first of all the bread and the wine of a real human meal, whatever their deeper significance."[9] This meaning, as we shall see, will be strongly stressed by the liberation theologians. In addition, however, there

7. Acts 10:40-41.
8. Acts 2:46b.
9. *Liturgical Piety* (Notre Dame, IN: Notre Dame University Press, 1955), p. 76. This literal meaning led the church in the Acts of the Apostles to share their goods as an expression of *agape* (divine love).

is the deeper meaning that in this holy meal we are united by the Holy Spirit with the presence of Christ in the worshiping community. It is especially here that Christ's promise to all of his future disciples is fulfilled, "Lo, I am with you always, to the close of the age."[10]

Even though the memorial aspect of the meal, with its potent reminder of the death of the Lord, is an essential facet, yet the reality of the divine vindication in the Resurrection and Ascension of Christ and the fulfillment of his promise to send the Holy Spirit at Pentecost, together with the recognition that the gifts of forgiveness and the promise of eternal life are the consequences of the cross, lift the minds and hearts of the participants in the Eucharist to the heights of joy. This, too, must be stressed in our interpretation of this unitive meal.

If there were time, it would be fascinating to explore the festal element in salvation and the way it topples self-importance and fear, and leads to holy hilarity — so appropriate for a happy family meal among Christians. Suggestions for its application to the Eucharist are found in Harvey Cox's highly original book *The Feast of Fools: A Theological Essay on Festivity and Fantasy.* Christ's overturning of the solemnity of the Sadducees and Pharisees, and Paul's sense that Christians must be fools for Christ's sake, are expressed in the sense of Christ as harlequin and jester. Cox claims: "Like the jester, Christ defies custom and scorns crowned heads. Like a wandering troubadour he has no place to lay his head. Like the clown in the circus parade, he satirizes existing authority, by riding into town replete with regal pageantry when he has no earthly power. Like a minstrel he frequents dinners and parties. At the end he is costumed by his enemies in a mocking caricature of royal paraphernalia. He is crucified amidst sniggers and taunts with a sign over his head that lampoons his laughable claim."[11] Cox also points out that in Christianity we have an irrepressible radical hope, and that

10. Matthew 28:20.

11. *The Feast of Fools* (Cambridge, MA: Harvard University Press, 1970), pp. 140-141.

laughter is hope's last weapon: "Its Christ is the painted jester whose foolishness is wiser than wisdom. Its church meets wherever men lift festive bowls to toast joys remembered or anticipated. Its liturgy is the exuberant enactment of fantasy before the eyes of a prosaic world. Its God is the often unspoken ground for refusing to be cowed into timidity or resignation by mere facts."[12] It is also the foundation of faith, hope, and charity created by the mighty acts of God in Christ celebrated in the Eucharist. Andrew Greeley confirms our view of the appropriateness and the source of religious humor: "It is the humor rooted in the gaiety and joy that comes from faith, hope, confidence and compassion. One laughs because one knows that no matter how desperate things are they are never serious in the ultimate sense." He further defines it as laughter "that rocks the walls of hollow tombs. The force of it can roll back stones from these tombs, and the conviction of it assures resurrection."[13]

There is no question that our Western worship at the Eucharist has become far too dolorous, dominated by the cross rather than the Resurrection. It is the Pentecostals and those in Catholicism and Anglicanism who have included a charismatic element in their worship who express the joy of salvation in a way that the early church did. Its source is their lively sense of heaven. As Daniel Hardy and David Ford see it: "One of the signs of it is the freedom of laughter in worship. In Pentecostal services it is often not laughter at a joke or anything in particular; it is simply an overwhelming liberation in God's presence. The laughter rings out, spreads through the congregation, and faces beam to God. . . . It is a foretaste of the complete praise of God in the infinitely good environment of his presence 'at home.'"[14] It is the equivalent of what Luther called the *risus paschalis*.

It is "Easter laughter" because God's last word is not condem-

12. *Ibid.*, p. 157.
13. In J. B. Metz and J. P. Jossua, eds., *Theology of Joy*, in *Concilium*, vol. 95 (New York: Herder and Herder, 1964), p. 139.
14. *Jubilate: Theology in Praise* (London: Darton, Longman and Todd, 1984), p. 68.

nation, suffering, or death, but the joy of resurrection and eternal life with all the friends of God united in gratitude and praise, as dimly glimpsed in the service of Holy Communion. Yet, J. J. von Allmen, recalling the dominating element of confession of sins in many eucharists, in a renowned witticism observed that "Christian worship is normally celebrated in a banqueting hall rather than in a laundry."[15] The dominating characteristic of the Eucharist should be abundant joy, exultation, jubilation.

The New Testament Conception of *Koinonia* (Communion)

We shall recover the true sense of "communion" as we trace its roots in the New Testament term *koinonia*. Paul uses the term to indicate that the nature of the Lord's Supper is essentially fellow-ship with the person of Christ. "To Paul," writes F. Hauck, "the exalted Christ is identical with the earthly and historical Christ who had body and blood. . . . This is for Paul the important thing in the celebration. It is self-evident that for Paul real union with the exalted Lord should include the blessing of forgiveness which He won by His death."[16] Fellowship with Christ also means for Paul that sharing in humility and suffering, as the historical Christ did, assures us of sharing the glory he attained. The Christian commu-nity as a whole is expected to share in the sufferings of Christ, but, of course, only in part, such as in facing obloquy or persecution.[17] In I John "communion" means an inner bond with the Father and the Son in the believer and its consequence is the brotherly fellowship of believers.[18] It is worth observing that in Acts 2:42

15. Von Allmen, *Worship: Its Theory and Practice* (New York: Oxford University Press, 1965), p. 162.

16. In G. Kittel and G. Friedrich, eds., *Theological Dictionary of the New Testament*, vol. III, p. 805.

17. Pauline references are to Romans 6:8; II Corinthians 5:1-7; and Galatians 2:19.

18. I John 1:3, 6, 7.

"communion" or "community" does not yet denote the concrete community of Christians since it had not yet separated itself cultically or legally from the Jewish community. Nor does it represent a community of goods (see 2:44). Rather, it is a term of spiritual significance indicating the high decree of concord among the first Christians.[19]

The best summary that I know of the meanings of *koinonia* is that provided by William Barclay in his *A New Testament Word Book*. It reads as follows:

> In the New Testament *koinonia* occurs some eighteen times. When we examine the connections in which it is used we come to see how wide and far-reaching is the fellowship which should characterize the Christian life.
>
> In the Christian life there is a *koinonia* which means "a sharing of friendship" and an abiding in the company of others (Acts 2:42; 2 Cor. 6:14). It is very interesting to note that the friendship is based on common Christian knowledge (1 John 1:3). Only those who are friends with Christ can really be friends with each other.
>
> In the Christian life there is a *koinonia* which means "practical sharing" with those less fortunate. Paul three times uses the word in connection with the collection he took from his churches for the poor saints at Jerusalem (Rom. 15:26; 2 Cor. 8:4; 2 Cor. 9:13; cf. Heb. 13:16). The Christian fellowship is a *practical* thing.
>
> In the Christian life there is a *koinonia* which is a "partnership in the work of Christ" (Phil. 1:5). Paul gives thanks for the partnership of the Philippians in the work of the gospel.
>
> In the Christian life there is a *koinonia* "in the faith." The Christian is never an isolated unit; he is one of a believing company (Eph. 3:9).

19. *Theological Dictionary of the New Testament*, vol. III, p. 809.

In the Christian life there is a "fellowship" *(koinonia)* "in the Spirit" (2 Cor. 13:14; Phil. 2:1). The Christian lives in the presence, the company, the help and the guidance of the Spirit.

In the Christian life there is a *koinonia* "with Christ." Christians are called to the *koinonia* of Jesus Christ, the Son of God (1 Cor. 1:9). That fellowship is found specially through the sacrament (1 Cor. 10:16). The cup and the bread are supremely the *koinonia* of the body and blood of Christ. In the sacrament above all Christians find Christ and find each other. Further, that fellowship with Christ is fellowship with his sufferings (Phil. 3:10). When the Christian suffers he has, amidst the pain, the joy of knowing that he is sharing things with Christ.

In the Christian life there is *koinonia* "with God" (1 John 1:3). But it is to be noted that that fellowship is ethically conditioned, for it is not for those who have chosen to walk in darkness (1 John 1:6).

The Christian *koinonia* is that bond which binds Christians to each other, to Christ and to God.[20]

Markus Barth's book *Rediscovering the Lord's Supper* stresses fellowship and has an interesting subtitle: *Communion with Israel, with Christ, and Among the Guests.* He sees three meanings implicit in the term *koinonia* as employed by St. Paul in I Corinthians 10:16b-17: "(1) to give, in and as a community, thanks to God for the gift of Christ, (2) to comfort and strengthen brothers and sisters in demonstrating that Christ's death has created the bond of mutual love, and (3) to signal to all the world that God's work embraces all creatures and that the number of God's people is not yet complete."[21]

---

20. William Barclay, *A New Testament Word Book* (London: SCM Press, 1955), pp. 71-72.

21. *Rediscovering the Lord's Supper* (Atlanta: John Knox Press, 1988), p. 48.

Fellowship at the Eucharist in Early Church History

The same striking quality of friendship that crosses all class and ethnic barriers is honored in the eucharistic liturgy of the church. The *Didache* includes the following prayers for the unity of the church:

> As this broken bread was scattered on the mountains, and gathered together into one, so let your Church be gathered together from the ends of the earth into the kingdom, for yours is the glory and the power through Jesus Christ for ever.

> Remember, Lord, the Church to deliver her from all evil and perfect her in love, and gather together the hallowed from the four winds into your kingdom which you have prepared, for the power and glory is yours for ever.[22]

Book VII, Chapter 25 of *The Apostolic Constitutions* repeats the same images in its prayer:

> Almighty Lord and everlasting God, gather your church from the ends of the earth into your kingdom, as this corn was scattered and is now made one loaf.[23]

Similarly, the eucharistic prayer of the *Testament of the Lord* beseeches God to sustain the unity of the church amid the diversities of its gifts:

> Sustain to the end those who have prophetic gifts, confirm gifts of healing. . . . Keep straight the way of those who carry the word of doctrine. Ever care for those who always do your will. Visit the widows. Help the orphans. Remember those who sleep in the faith. Give us an inheritance with the saints and grant us the power to satisfy you as they did. . . . Sanctify us all, O God, and grant that they who partake of these holy things

22. George Every, *Basic Liturgy* (London: The Faith Press, 1961), p. 72.
23. *Ibid.*

may be made one in you, that they may be filled with the Holy
Spirit to confirm their faith in the truth, that they may always
lift up the same doxology to you and to your beloved Son Jesus
Christ, by whom all praise and honour and might be to you,
with the Holy Spirit, for ever and ever.[24]

There is a strong sense of the communion of saints in the fourth-
century prayer of Serapion:

> We entreat you for them that sleep, whose names are in our
> remembrance. Hallow their souls, for you know them all. Hal-
> low all that sleep in the Lord. Let them be numbered with the
> holy powers and give them place and a part in your kingdom.
> Receive the eucharist of the people and bless them that bring
> offerings and eucharists, and grant health, happiness, and ad-
> vancement in soul and body to all this people through your
> Only-begotten Jesus Christ in the Holy Spirit, as it was and is
> and shall be from generation to generation and to ages of ages.
> Amen.[25]

The earliest Church Father, Ignatius, took special notice of
the unitive function of the Eucharist in advising the Christians
at Ephesus "that ye all by name come together in common in
the faith and in Jesus Christ . . . breaking the bread which is the
medicine of immortality." He also refers to the Eucharist as "one
flesh of our Lord and one cup for union with his blood."[26] As
Christ had forgiven the sins of the members of his body, so they
were forbidden to come to Communion if they had a dispute
with any member. The *Didache* is quite explicit on this matter:
"And let no one who has a dispute with his companion come
with you until they are reconciled, that our sacrifice may not be
defiled."[27]

24. *Ibid.*, p. 73.
25. *Ibid.*, p. 81.
26. Cited by Harold Fey in *The Lord's Supper: seven meanings* (New
York: Harper, 1948), p. 63.
27. *Ibid.*

Theologians historically divided as St. Augustine and Bernard Häring still see the Eucharist as the sacrament of love that demands complete unity between Christ and his disciples. St. Augustine in Sermon 227 wrote:

> If now you have received aright, you are what you have received: and so the Apostle expounds the Sacrament of the Lord's Table: *We who are many are one bread and one body.* This bread signifies to you how you ought to love unity. It was made out of many grains of wheat, which were separate, but were united by application of water, by a kind of rubbing together *(contritio)*, and baked with fire. So have you been ground together by the fast and the exorcism, wetted in Baptism, and baked by the fire of Christ and the mystery of the Holy Spirit. . . . Notice how at Pentecost the Holy Spirit comes: He comes in fiery tongues, to inspire the love whereby we are to burn towards God and despise the world, and our chaff be burnt away, and our heart refined like gold. So the Holy Spirit comes — after the water the fire — and you are made bread, which is the Body of Christ: and here is the symbol of unity.[28]

Bernard Häring insists that "When we are gathered together about one altar, eat of *one* bread and draw life from the love of the one Lord, the love that was ready to suffer death, then the meaning and the urgency of the mystery of our unity and responsibility for each other's salvation, into which we have been brought by baptism and confirmation, becomes even clearer to us." Häring continues by arguing that Christ at each celebration of the love that went to the cross brings his new commandment: "This is my commandment, that you love one another as I have loved you." As we receive his body sacrificed for us, Häring adds, we hear the words of Christ: "Father, I made known to them thy name, and I will make it known, that the love with which thou hast loved me may be in them, and I in them."[29]

28. Cited by A. G. Hebert in *Liturgy and Society* (London: Faber and Faber, 1961), p. 85.
29. John 17:26.

Häring concludes, "Before all else, the Eucharist teaches us the meaning and gives us the gift of concord."[30]

One who learned much from St. Augustine was the Reformer, John Calvin. He, too, had a vivid and reliable sense of the unity of Christ's followers, which is itself demanded and created by the presence of Christ in the Eucharist. His magisterial interpretation is as follows:

> The Lord in such wise communicates to us his body, that he becomes one with us and we with him. And since he has but one body, in which he gives us all a part, it follows that we through this participation become one body. This unity is symbolized by the bread which is brought forth for the sacrament; as it is baked out of many small grains so blended together that one cannot be separated from another, so likewise it happens to us, that we are united and bound together in such a unity of souls that no dissention or quarrel may divide us. [Then follows a reference to I Corinthians 10:16-17.] Verily we shall have gained a wonderful benefit from communion, if this thought is thereby impressed and engraved into our souls: that none of our brethren can be insulted, mocked, laughed at, despised, or in any way dishonoured, but that we at the same time insult, mock, laugh at, and despise Christ; that we cannot separate ourselves from the brethren without separating ourselves from Christ; and that Christ cannot be loved by us unless we love him in the brethren. . . . Thus it is that Augustine so often calls the Sacrament the bond of love — *caritatis vinculum*.[31]

It is clear from the New Testament, as from the early liturgical prayers, and from both Catholic and Protestant theologians, that in the Eucharist the important concept of communion means

30. The citations are from an article by Häring in *The Catholic Tradition: Mass and the Sacraments*, vol. 2, *A Consortium Book* (1979), pp. 216f.

31. *Corpus Reformatorum*, I, 126; also in *Opera Selecta*, I, 146, and the *Institutes*.

unity with Christ, unity in the body of Christ that is the church, and unity with Christians of all the ages in the so-called "communion of saints."

The Present-Day Significance of Communion

Curiously enough Anglicans and Roman Catholics value the term "Communion" very differently. Anglicans have never restricted it to mean that the individual's relationship to Christ is sufficient because their liturgies have always stressed its corporate sense. For Catholics, on the other hand, the term is often associated with a subjective piety — what can I gain for myself from the Eucharist?

In the twentieth century, however, there is a growing concern for the development of greater unity among the Christian churches. From the beginning the World Council of Churches was supported by the Church of England and the entire Anglican Communion, along with the Protestant Communions, such as the Lutherans, Presbyterians, Congregationalists, Methodists, Baptists, and the Disciples of Christ. Later, the Orthodox churches sent delegates to the Faith and Order meetings and most parts of the Roman Catholic Church sent official representatives. Some surprising unions have taken place, such as the United Church of South India, which united Anglicans, Methodists, and Congregationalists. Apparently, they have "lived happily ever after." But what is more important is that in the ecumenical liturgical discussions the great gap between Catholics and Protestants has begun to close. Catholics have returned to biblical studies and biblical preaching, while Protestants, who in the recent past seemed to regard the Eucharist as mere angel cake for the pious who had already received a meal of sirloin steak in the sermon, have begun to place more value on the Eucharist. Revaluation of worship is the order of the day in many Christian communities, and, as we have already seen and will see even more clearly later, this is particularly the case in the revaluation of the chief sacrament, the Eucharist.[32]

It can be generally stated that on the Roman Catholic side there has been rigid opposition on the part of the hierarchy to allowing Protestants to be admitted to the Eucharist in Catholic churches. Indeed, they would consider it lax and irresponsible of Protestants to admit all and sundry to Christ's table. As a matter of fact, the actual celebration of Communion on the part of several Protestant churches has been casual, brief, apparently hurried, not always deeply reverent, and too retrospective in its character. The gap does exist.

Even more objectionably individualistic to both Catholics and Orthodox are the tiny individual communion glasses used in many Protestant denominations. As early as 1965 J. J. von Allmen asked: "Need we remind the reader that to the one loaf should correspond the one cup (I Cor. 10:16ff.), and that there-

---

32. Significant volumes that exhibit this growing together and revaluation of the Eucharist are (to list only a few) Dom Gregory Dix, *The Shape of the Liturgy* (London: Dacre Press, 1945); Max Thurian and Geoffrey Wainwright, eds., *Baptism and Eucharist: Ecumenical Convergence in Celebration* (Geneva: World Council of Churches, and Grand Rapids: Wm. B. Eerdmans, 1983); E. Schillebeeckx, *Christ the Sacrament* (London and New York: Sheed and Ward, 1963); Y. Brilioth, *Eucharistic Faith and Practice: Evangelical and Catholic* (London: S.P.C.K., 1930); J. J. von Allmen, *Essai sur le Répas du Seigneur* (Neuchâtel: Delachaux & Niestlé, 1966); F. J. Leenhardt, *Ceci est Mon Corps* (Neuchatel: Delachaux & Niestlé, 1955); A. Schmemann, *Sacraments and Orthodoxy* (New York: Herder, 1965); J.-M. R. Tillard, *L'eucharistie, Paques de L'église* (Paris: du Cerf, 1964); M. Thurian, *Le Mystère Eucharistique* (Paris: Centurion-Taize, 1981); J. Jeremias, *Die Abendmahlsworte Jesu* (Göttingen: Vandenhoeck & Ruprecht: third edn., 1960); H. J. Schultz, *Ökumenische Glaubenseinheit aus eucharistischer Überlieferung* (Paderborn: Bonifacius, 1976). Also valuable are the reports of the various churches (e.g., the Lutheran–Roman Catholic exchange on the Eucharist and its meaning is most enlightening and promising), and the evidence they show on reciprocity in understanding the Eucharist. An early book on the growing convergence in worship was written by a Methodist minister and a Jesuit father, namely, Romey P. Marshall and Michael J. Taylor, S.J., entitled *Liturgy and Christian Unity* (Englewood Cliffs, NJ: Prentice-Hall, 1968), while the Anglican A. M. Allchin wrote an ecumenical eucharistic article for the first volume of *Studia Liturgica* (Amsterdam), pp. 61-68, in 1962.

fore the acquisition or use of individual cups is inadvisable as especially injurious to the communal character of the communion?" After this advice the Protestant professor added: "Fortunately, it is hardly necessary, because of the evident renewed awareness of the corporate aspect of eucharistic life."[33] Admirable theologian, he is not, alas, as good a prophet! One could, of course, equally criticize the refusal of the bread to communicants by the Roman Catholic Church, and take strong exception to the use of wafers in the Roman Catholic and Anglican Churches, which are as detrimental as individual glasses in denying the corporate celebration in Holy Communion. (There is much to be said for the mode of administration of Communion in the Church of Scotland, where each communicant takes a small piece of the common loaf and passes it to his or her neighbor.) Unless these elements of individualism are removed, the desirable unitive character of the Eucharist will be seriously weakened. If the sacredness of the meal and stress on unity are to be renewed, individual glasses, so reminiscent of cocktails, must be removed, and chalices and loaves must be substituted. Both are also important symbolically as expressions of Christian unity.

Among those who have been most concerned for a convergence between Roman Catholicism and Protestantism in the understanding of the Eucharist have been members of the Taizé Community in Burgundy, France, and three French-speaking Protestant theologians: Von Allmen, Leenhardt, and Bénoît. Among the many Catholics who have been leading the convergence it is difficult to choose, but the Dutch have been prominent, especially Schillebeeckx. Also contributing are the American Powers, the Frenchman Tillard, and the English Catholic Lash. Among the Anglicans, important liturgical studies with ecumenical implications have been undertaken by Dix, Cuming, Couratin, Every, Hebert, Jasper, Ratcliff, and Shepherd. Presby-

---

33. J. J. von Allmen, *Worship: Its Theology and Practice* (New York: Oxford University Press, 1965), p. 301.

terians include such scholars as M'Millan and Maxwell, while the
Methodists have Rattenbury, Wainwright, and White. Among
Baptists the chief names are Clark, Payne, and Winward. The
ecumenically minded Congregational scholars in the field of
worship were N. Micklem, Marsh, Todd, and Whale, along with
the hymnologist Routley. The two scholars of the century who
have caused the most thorough revaluation of the historical
changes in the interpretation of the Eucharist are Dom Gregory
Dix in *The Shape of the Eucharist* and the Swedish Lutheran
scholar Yngve Brilioth in his earlier work *Eucharistic Faith and
Practice: Evangelical and Catholic* (1930).

The fact remains, however, that the Eucharist, supposedly
the unitive meal, is not only closed to the world outside by some
denominations, but even refused to other Christians not of their
own church. This is increasingly perceived as a scandal, and a
betrayal of the plea of Christ for his followers, "that they may
all be one; even as thou, Father, art in me, and I in thee, that
they also may be in us, so that the world may believe that thou
hast sent me" (John 17:21). This is a further reason why the
emphasis on unity in the chief sacrament is being stressed in
recent prayers in the liturgy, and even in hymnody.

An outstanding example of a hymn written to celebrate unity
is the composition of Dr. Brian Wren:

> Lord Christ, the Father's mighty Son,
> Whose work upon the Cross was done,
> All men to receive,
> Make all our scattered churches one,
> That the world may believe.
>
> To make us one your prayers were said.
> To make us one you broke the bread,
> Its pieces scattered us instead,
> How can others believe?
>
> O Christ, forgive us, make us new!
> We know the best that we can do

Will nothing achieve,
And, humbled, bring our prayers to you
That the world may believe.

We will not question or refuse,
The way you work, the means you choose,
The pattern you weave;
But reconcile our warring views,
That the world may believe![34]

Meal of Unity and Its Meaning for Today

An initial meaning must be the scandal that Christians should feel that the meal that looks forward to the full establishment of the Kingdom of God at the second coming of Christ is the subject of argument as to its significance, and more disturbing, that Christians cannot agree to allow all other Christians of whatever denomination to be present at it. This is, as we have seen, so different from the meals at which the Lord invited the unrespectable and the marginalized, not to mention the fact that even his betrayer Judas was present at the Last Supper.

We should rejoice at the extraordinary ethnic variety of people coming from many different social classes who yet sense a fraternity and sorority in the festive meal of unity. Bishop Stephen Bayne was particularly impressed by this facet of the Communion when he was a choirboy. This is how he recalled the experience:

> I remember one Sunday morning when my eyes turned to the long row of people kneeling at the Communion rail. For some reason I had been looking at the soles of their shoes. And it was an extraordinarily moving sight, to me even then. These

34. Brian Wren, *Dunblane Hymns,* obtainable from the Warden, Scottish Churches' House, Dunblane. It is cited on p. 54 of David Cairns, *In Remembrance of Me* (London: Bles, 1967).

people, so many of whom I knew as giants and moguls in the congregation, were amazingly and secretly different, when you saw the soles of their shoes. There was a sort of anonymity about it for one thing. But the moving reflection came as I noticed the differences. A pair of new shoes would be revealed next to an old worn pair. There were holes in some soles, and some others had patches, and some were still of the color of new leather. Some were large and some were small. Some were stylishly narrow — others were broad and heavy.

And all this simple fraternity of the shoes seemed suddenly to be a religious thing. Here was a moment when earthly differences didn't seem to matter. Here was a place where people came quite without regard to their differences, brought together in an astonishing unity around something bigger than any of them.[35]

The liberation theologians would believe that this was a false egalitarianism, but union with Christ and with each other transcends the social and ethnic differences.

Perhaps in understanding the communal aspect of the Eucharist we should consider that the first disciples and all who followed them would, in this corporate action, reassert their identity with Christ and thus be recalled to their true selves again. When we reconsider the cross and the Eucharist that it recalls, we may feel ourselves transfigured and transformed. For in our union with the Lord in the Eucharist we visualize God's idea of what we should be like, as well as experiencing anew the forgiving love of God, demanding that we forgive all others.

It should also be for us an experience of the vast community of the friends of God spanning the centuries and all the continents. In a time of secularism, this should be a stimulus to exuberant joy and gratitude.

Finally, we cannot escape the imperative of communion with Christ, and our brothers and sisters must require us to translate

35. Bayne, *Mindful of the Love: The Holy Communion and Daily Life* (Greenwich, CT: Seabury Press, 1959), pp. 115-16.

communion into community in mission and in greater social service. As Miles Lowell Yates puts it, the toughest obligation of Communion is "to do, as my Lord has told me to do; to try to express communion in community; to let his sanctifying touch make me a serviceable and creative force . . . in the creation of what the Church is meant to be." He adds further: "We may remember that the holy instruments of the Upper Room, and hence the full communion of a man with God, were on the one hand the chalice and paten, but on the other the basin and towel."[36] Thus another of the benefits of union with Christ is that it should increase both our humility and our desire to serve others in his name.

The Expression of Unity in Modern Eucharists

One of the four alternate prayers of the modern Roman Rite, Eucharistic Prayer IV, has a profound sense of union and communion. Here is a part of it:

> Lord, look upon this sacrifice which you have given to your Church; and by your Holy Spirit, gather all who share this one bread and one cup into the one body of Christ, a living sacrifice of praise. Lord, remember those for whom we offer this sacrifice, especially N. our Pope, N. our bishop, and bishops and clergy everywhere. Remember those who take part in this offering, those here present and all your people, and all who seek you with a sincere heart.
>
> Remember those who have died in the peace of Christ and all the dead whose faith is known to you alone.
>
> Father, in your mercy grant also to us, your children, to enter into our heavenly inheritance in the company of the Virgin Mary, the Mother of God, and your apostles and saints. Then, in your kingdom, freed from the corruption of sin and death,

36. From A. Norman Pittenger and W. H. Ralston, Jr., eds., *God in Us* (Greenwich, CT: Seabury Press, 1959), pp. 115-16.

we shall sing your glory with every creature through Christ our
Lord, through whom you give us everything that is good.[37]

Eucharistic Prayer II has felicitous references to the unity
created by the Holy Spirit, with intercession for the church, and a
plea for unity with the saints. The relevant sections are as follows:

May all of us who share in the body and blood of Christ be
brought together in unity by the Holy Spirit.

Lord, remember your Church throughout the world;
make us grow in love, together with N. our Pope,
N. our bishop and all the clergy.

Remember our brothers and sisters
who have gone to their rest
in the hope of rising again;
bring them and all the departed
into the light of your presence.

Have mercy on us all;
make us worthy to share eternal life
with Mary, the virgin mother of God,
with the apostles, and with all the saints
who have done your will throughout the ages.
May we praise you in union with them,
and give you glory
through your Son, Jesus Christ.[38]

The modern German Lutheran Eucharistic Prayers are
briefer in reference to unity in Christ. Two examples are these:

And as all of us are one body in Christ through the fellowship
of his body and blood, so gather your faithful people from the

37. *Baptism and Eucharist: Ecumenical Convergence in Celebration*
(Geneva: World Council of Churches; Grand Rapids, MI: Wm. B. Eerdmans, 1983). All four Eucharistic Prayers can be found in English in *The
Sunday Missal: A New Edition* (London: Collins, 1984), pp. 37-63.
38. *The Sunday Missal*, pp. 46-47.

ends of the earth, that together with all the faithful we may celebrate in his kingdom the marriage feast of the Lamb.

Through this bread which we share with one another give us fellowship with Jesus Christ. Through this cup from which we drink unite us with him. Remember your church scattered throughout the world, and bring us together into your kingdom.[39]

The American *Lutheran Book of Worship* (1978) assumes rather than states that Christ creates the unity of the Church, but is clear and concise in its expression of the communion of saints:

Join our prayers with those of your servants of every time and every place and unite them with the ceaseless petitions of our great high priest until he comes as victorious Lord of all.[40]

The Reformed Church of France in its additional prayers of 1982 includes the following petitions in its Eucharistic Prayer II:

We humbly ask for your Holy Spirit,
to make us partakers of
Christ's body and blood
and unite us in a single body.
We pray for your goodness upon us all:
grant that we, too, with the witnesses of your people,
with Peter, Paul and the other apostles,
with Mary and the faithful of all times,
may have a share in eternal life
and sing your praises
through Jesus Christ, your beloved Son. . . .[41]

The Church of England's *Alternative Service Book* of 1980 has four Eucharistic Prayers. From the first we cite the following excerpt:

39. Thurian and Wainwright, eds., *Baptism and Eucharist,* pp. 137, 140.
40. *Ibid.,* p. 143.
41. *Ibid.,* p. 153.

> Accept through him, our great high priest,
> this our sacrifice of thanks and praise;
> and as we eat and drink these holy gifts
> in the presence of your divine majesty,
> renew us by your spirit,
> inspire us with your love,
> and unite us in the body of your Son,
> Jesus Christ our Lord.[42]

The Second Eucharistic Prayer not only insists on the union between Christ and his followers, but also asks for transformation:

> . . . fill us with your grace and heavenly blessing;
> nourish us with the body and blood of your Son,
> that we may grow into his likeness
> and, made one by your Spirit,
> become a living temple to your glory.[43]

And a final post-Communion prayer combines the thought of us all as forgiven prodigals, looking forward to eternity, and committed to bring life and light to others:

> Father of all, we give you thanks and praise, that when we were still far off you met us in your Son and brought us home. Dying and living, He declared your love, gave us grace, and opened the gate of glory. May we who share Christ's body live his risen life; we who drink his cup bring life to others; we whom the Spirit lights give light to the world. Keep us firm in the hope you have set before us, so we and all your children shall be free, and the whole earth live to praise your name; through Christ our Lord.[44]

The Episcopal Church of the U.S.A. in its *Book of Common Prayer* has several alternative forms of "The Great Thanksgiving."

---

42. *The Alternative Service Book, 1980, With the Psalter* (published jointly by Clowes, S.P.C.K., Cambridge University Press, Hodder & Stoughton, Oxford University Press, and Mowbrays), p. 132.

43. *Ibid.*, p. 135.

44. *Ibid.*, p. 144.

In Rite II's Eucharistic Prayer A, the *epiclesis* on the gifts continues thus:

> Sanctify us also that we may faithfully receive this holy Sacrament, and serve you in unity, constancy, and peace; and at the last day bring us with all your saints into the joy of your eternal kingdom.[45]

In Eucharistic Prayer B, the *epiclesis* continues as follows:

> Unite us to your Son in his sacrifice, that we may be acceptable through Him, being sanctified by the Holy Spirit. In the fullness of time put all things in subjection under your Christ, and bring us to that heavenly country where, with [_____] and all your saints, we may enter the everlasting heritage of your sons and daughters; through Jesus Christ our Lord, the firstborn of all creation, the head of the Church, and the author of our salvation.[46]

Furthermore, Alternative Great Thanksgiving D, which includes petitions for the whole church, its ministers and people, as well as for the departed, and recalling the communion of saints, also has a powerful plea for unity:

> Grant that all who share this bread and cup may become one body and one spirit, a living sacrifice in Christ, to the praise of your Name.[47]

The *Book of Common Order* of the Church of Scotland published in 1979 has one of the rare liturgies to use the term "communion" for the intimate union of Christ with his church in its Eucharistic Prayer. It is part of the *epiclesis*:

45. *The Book of Common Prayer and Administration of the Sacraments and Other Rites and Ceremonies of the Church . . . According to the Use of The Episcopal Church* (New York: The Church Hymnal Corporation, 1979), p. 363.
46. *Ibid.,* p. 369.
47. *Ibid.,* p. 375.

Send down thy Holy Spirit to sanctify both us and these thine
own gifts of bread and wine which we set before three; that the
bread which we break may be the communion of the body of
Christ, and the cup which we bless the communion of the blood
of Christ; that we may receive them to our spiritual nourishment
and growth in grace, and to the glory of thy most holy name.[48]

The Service of Word and Sacrament I of the United Church
of Christ in the U.S.A. (1969) has a parallel *epiclesis,* but the
theme of unity is stressed from the outset:

Beloved, this is the joyful feast of the people of God. Come
from the East and the West, and from the North and the South,
and gather about the table of the Lord.

Behold how good and pleasant it is when brothers dwell in
unity.[49]

The *epiclesis* reads:

Bless and sanctify by your Holy Spirit both us and these your
gifts of bread and wine, that in this holy communion of the
body and blood of Christ we may be made one with him and
he with us, and that we may remain faithful members of his
body until we feast with him in your heavenly kingdom.[50]

A Book of Services (1980) of the United Reformed Church
in the United Kingdom has three Eucharistic Thanksgivings.
The first expresses its concern for unity in the words:

Accept our sacrifice of praise;
and as we eat and drink
at his command
unite us to Christ
as one body in him,

48. Thurian and Wainwright, eds., *Baptism and Eucharist,* p. 157.
49. *Ibid.,* p. 155.
50. *Ibid.,* p. 156.

and give us strength
to serve you in the world.[51]

The Second Thanksgiving includes the vivid petition:

Father, accept through Christ
our sacrifice of thanks and praise;
and as we eat and drink these holy gifts,
kindle in us the fire of your Spirit
that with the whole Church on earth and in heaven
we may be made one in him.[52]

The Third Thanksgiving has this original *epiclesis:*

We beseech you
send among us your Holy Spirit
and give a new face
to this earth that is dear to us.
Let there be peace
wherever people live,
the peace that we cannot make ourselves
and that is more powerful than all violence,
your peace like a bond,
a new covenant between us all,
the power of Jesus Christ
here among us.[53]

The British *Methodist Service Book* (1975) in "The Sunday
Service" has a very direct and straightforward *epiclesis,* brief but
comprehensive:

Grant that by the power of the Holy Spirit
we who receive your gifts of bread and wine
may share in the body and blood of Christ.

51. *A Book of Services* (Edinburgh: The Saint Andrew Press, 1980),
p. 31.
52. *Ibid.,* pp. 36-37.
53. *Ibid.,* p. 37.

Make us one body with him.

Accept us as we offer ourselves to be a living sacrifice, and bring
us with the whole creation to your heavenly kingdom.[54]

The United Methodist Church of the U.S.A. has produced
an alternative Communion rite and published it in a volume
titled *We Gather Together* (1980). It also has a strong expression
of unity, as seen in the following prayer:

We experience anew, most merciful God,
the suffering and death,
the resurrection and ascension of your Son,
asking you to accept this our sacrifice of praise and
    thanksgiving,
which we offer in union with Christ's offering for us,
as a living and holy surrender of ourselves.

Send the power of your Holy Spirit on us,
gathered here out of love for you, and on these gifts.
May the Spirit help us to know in the breaking of this bread
and the drinking of this wine the presence of Christ
who gave his body and blood for all.
And may the Spirit make us one with Christ,
one with each other, and one in service to all the world.[55]

Ecumenical Eucharistic Rites

The Eucharist of the Community of Taizé, France, is celebrated
with seven different orders. Eucharistic Prayer VII, which includes a section combining an *epiclesis* and a sense of the functions

54. *The Methodist Service Book* (London: Methodist Publishing House,
1975), p. 58.
55. The fuller title is: *We Gather Together: services for public worship* . . .
(Nashville: Parthenon Press, 1980). The revised Communion Order's canon
is published by Thurian and Wainwright, eds., *op. cit.,* pp. 171-72.

of the Holy Spirit as the bond of unity, also links believers on earth with the saints in heaven. This is praying with theological fidelity, clarity, and concision:

> Sanctify your Church as on the day of Pentecost; let the Spirit of holiness lead her into all truth, strengthen her in her mission to the ends of the earth, and prepare her for your eternal kingdom, where we shall share the inheritance of your saints in light, with the Virgin Mary, with the apostles, prophets and martyrs, [with Saint N.]; all of us together await the return of your beloved Son: "Come, Lord Jesus!"

The appropriate response of the congregation is "Maranatha, the Lord is coming!"[56]

The British Joint Liturgical Group produced in 1983 a eucharistic canon intended to be used mainly for ecumenical occasions. It stresses unity both before and after the *Benedictus:*

> You send us your Holy Spirit to guide us into the truth,
> to bring us reconciliation and peace, and to renew in us the
> Body of your Son.
>
> Father, accept through Christ our sacrifice of thanks and praise:
> and as we eat and drink these holy gifts, kindle in us the fire
> of your Spirit that with the whole Church on earth and in
> heaven we may be made one with him.[57]

The Consultation on Church Union in the U.S.A., a multidenominational group, produced an ecumenical canon, which was published in 1979. Our citation follows the institution narrative just before the *epiclesis:*

56. Thurian and Wainwright, *op. cit.*, p. 182. The six previous eucharistic orders are found in *Eucharist at Taizé* (1962). For a description see my "Worship at Taizé: A Protestant Monastic Servant Community," in *Worship,* vol. 49, no. 1 (January 1975), pp. 23-34.

57. Thurian and Wainwright, *op. cit.*, p. 183. The prayer cited was prepared in 1978.

Through him you bestow the gift of your Spirit, uniting your
Church, empowering its mission, and leading us into the new
creation you have promised.

Grant that we may be for the world the body of Christ, redeemed through his blood, serving and reconciling all people
to you.

Remember your Church, scattered upon the face of the earth,
gather it in unity and preserve it in truth. Remember the saints
who have gone before us [especially _____ and
_____ (here may occur special names)].

In communion with them and with all creation, we worship
and adore you always. . . .[58]

The Eucharistic Liturgy of Lima was prepared for the plenary
session of the Faith and Order Commission of the World Council
of Churches by Brother Max Thurian of Taizé. It was celebrated
for the first time in 1972. Its comprehensiveness is its most striking
and valuable characteristic, and it presorts several references to
unity. The Prayer of Intercession has three pleas for unity:

That the churches may discover again their visible unity in the
one baptism which incorporates them in Christ, let us pray for
the love of Christ.

That the churches may attain communion in the eucharist
around one table, let us pray for the strength of Christ.

That the churches may recognize each other's ministries in the
service of their one Lord, let us pray for the strength of Christ.[59]

---

58. The Consultation on Church Union in the U.S.A., a multidenominational group, has produced several orders of worship that were published
in *Word, Bread, Cup* (Cincinnati: Forward Movement Publications, 1978).
Thurian and Wainwright have reproduced the eucharistic canon, *op. cit.,* pp.
184, 185.

59. Thurian and Wainwright, *op. cit.,* p. 251.

In the second *epiclesis* we find another:

> As we partake of Christ's body and blood, fill us with the Holy Spirit that we may be one single body and one single spirit in Christ, a living sacrifice for the praise of your glory.[60]

In the Commemorations we read:

> Remember, Lord, your one, holy, catholic and apostolic Church, redeemed by the blood of Christ. Reveal its unity, guard its faith. . . .

> Remember also all our brothers and sisters who have died in the peace of Christ, and those whose faith is known to you alone; guide them to the joyful feast prepared for all peoples in your presence, with the blessed Virgin Mary, with the patriarchs and prophets, the apostles and martyrs . . . and all the saints for whom your friendship was life. With all these we sing your praise and await the happiness of your Kingdom where with the whole creation, finally delivered from sin and death, we shall be enabled to glorify you through Christ our Lord.[61]

The Lord's Prayer is prefaced by the words:

> United by one baptism in the same Holy Spirit and the same Body of Christ, we pray as God's sons and daughters:[62]

The final Thanksgiving Prayer also emphasizes unity:

> In peace let us pray to the Lord: O Lord our God, we give you thanks for uniting us by baptism in the Body of Christ and for filling us with joy in the Eucharist. Lead us towards the full visible unity of your Church and help us to treasure all the signs of reconciliation you have granted us. Now that we have tasted of the banquet you have prepared for us in the world to come,

60. *Ibid.*, p. 253.
61. *Ibid.*, pp. 253-54.
62. *Ibid.*, p. 254.

may we all one day share together the inheritance of the saints
in the life of your heavenly city. . . .[63]

It seemed appropriate to end this chapter by considering the
unitive thrust of the Lima Liturgy because it is so comprehensive
in using the liturgical research and the ecumenical insights of
several Christian denominations, such as the Roman Catholic,
the Eastern Orthodox, the Byzantine, the Lutheran, and the
dominantly Protestant work of the American Consultation on
Church Union, and weaving them so expertly together in the
finest of ecumenical liturgies available.

In addition, it emphasizes the triple union in Holy Communion: the union of the individual with Christ that began at
baptism and was strengthened at confirmation and reaches its
peak in the Eucharist where the individual becomes a part of the
body of Christ. That company transcends the boundaries of
space and time, being both as transcontinental as the worldwide
church on earth and as transtemporal as the congregation of all
the saints gathered in the everlasting joys of heaven.

63. *Ibid.*

SIX The Eucharist as Mystery

THE TERM "mystery" or the plural "mysteries" has always been the primary designation for the Eucharist among the Eastern Orthodox churches since the patristic age. According to Ernst Benz, "The Eucharist in its present Orthodox form differs very little from the Eucharistic celebration used in the primitive Church. It is an elaborate, complicated mystery play."[1] Even today the liturgy is divided into two parts, the first for catechumens, or learners, and the second for believers. This division comes from the time of Constantine when the church required its new pagans to be instructed in Christian doctrine and practice before admission to baptism and the Eucharist. Hence catechumens were admitted only to the first part of the liturgy comprising prayers and the sermon. They left immediately after the sermon, and so the first part of the service ends with the triple cry, "Catechumens, leave!"

The stress on the mystery of the Eucharist continues when the presiding priest calls out: "The doors, the doors!" prior to the singing of the Creed, so that the doorkeepers exclude all except the initiates, for the Creed was considered a secret formula. And just prior to the breaking of the bread the priest calls: "Holiness to the holy" — a warning for worthy reception. Finally, in the Communion prayer, or *anaphora*, the mystery is

1. *The Eastern Orthodox Church, Its Thought and Life* (Chicago: Aldine Publishing Company, 1983), p. 34.

147

again emphasized in these words: "As partaker in Thy mysterious Communion take me up today, O Son of God, for I will not betray Thy secret to thine enemies, nor give Thee a kiss like Judas." Moreover, before receiving Communion, the believer renews his vow not to betray the mystery to the enemies of God.

Professor John Meyendorff points out the basic changes in the character of the Orthodox Eucharist consequent on the closure of the last pagan temples and the schools by the Emperor Justinian in the sixth century. The Christian liturgy, originally conceived as the cult of small persecuted communities, came to be celebrated in the vast and glorious basilica of Hagia Sophia, built by Justinian, in the presence of thousands of worshipers.

St. John Chrysostom (literally the "golden-mouthed" orator) preached to these many nominal Christians, advising them to prepare for the reception of the Eucharist by rigorous self-examination and fasting, and he also emphasized the mysterious and eschatological characteristics of the Eucharist. Two and three centuries later saw such additions as the iconostasis-screen between the sanctuary and the congregation, and the use of the communion spoon as a way of avoiding the placing of the sacramental elements in the hands of laity. The result was that "All these developments were aimed at protecting the mystery, but they resulted in separating the clergy from the faithful and in giving to the liturgy the aspect of a performance rather than of a common action of the entire people of God."[2]

Meyendorff also says that the writings of pseudo-Dionysius shaped liturgical forms he thought of only as symbols revealing the mysteries to the eyes of the faithful. This issued in "appearances and disappearances of the celebrant, veiling and unveiling of the elements, opening and closing of the doors, and various gestures connected with the sacraments. . . ."[3] These views were eagerly accepted by a church wanting to preserve the mysterious

2. *Byzantine Theology: Historical Trends and Doctrinal Themes* (New York: Fordham University Press, 3rd printing, 1987), p. 29.

3. *Ibid.*

character of the Eucharist from profanation by the masses now filling the churches.

The central emphasis on the mystery is still maintained by the theologians of the Eastern Orthodox Church. Alexander Schmemann, for example, criticizes the Western Church for having rejected the *mysterion,* which he defines as "the holding together, in a mystical and existential, rather than rational, synthesis of both the total *transcendence* of God and His genuine *presence*. But this mystery is precisely that of the Kingdom of God, the faith and piety of the Church being rooted in the experience *now* of that which is *to come,* in the communion by means of 'this world' with Him who is always 'beyond,' in truly partaking of 'the joy and peace of the Holy Spirit.'"[4] We may note the necessary use of paradox to maintain the description (*not* a definition) of the mystery. Schmemann comes closer to an explanation of the experience of the liturgical mystery in declaring that "the Kingdom of God [is] a reality to be experienced now as the new life in the Holy Spirit, as real anticipation of the new creation."[5]

The important Etchmiadzin Consultation of the Orthodox Churches of 1975 contains this definition of the Eucharist: "Truly, the Eucharistic Liturgy is the climax of the church's life, the event in which the people of God are celebrating the incarnation, the death and the resurrection of Jesus Christ, sharing his glorified body and blood, tasting the Kingdom to come."[6] That very definition suggests the driving eschatological character of the Eucharist and its cosmic conviction that an all-inclusive Kingdom is begun, continued, and fully to-be-established by the glorified Christ at his second coming.

---

4. *Church, World, Mission: Reflections on Orthodoxy in the West* (Crestwood, NY: St. Vladimir's Press, 1979), p. 60.

5. *Ibid.*

6. "The Liturgy after the Liturgy" can be found in Ion Bria, ed., *Martyria/Mission: The Witness of the Orthodox Churches Today* (Geneva: The World Council of Churches, 1980). It is reprinted in Thurian and Wainwright, eds., *Baptism and Eucharist: Ecumenical Convergence in Celebration* (Geneva: World Council of Churches, and Grand Rapids: Wm. B. Eerdmans, 1983), pp. 213-18. The citation comes from p. 214.

Mystery Theology

In the liturgical movement in the West, patristic theology has
had a significant rebirth of interest. This has come partly
through the witness of the Eastern Orthodox Church in ecumenical gatherings — a church that has become familiar in
France with many Russian refugees and in the United States
as well with the establishment of several Orthodox national
churches. There are two other important reasons for an increasing familiarity with a mystery theology. One is the important analysis and exposition of the *Mysterientheologie* associated with the German Benedictine abbey of Maria Laach.
The second highly significant reason for the importance of the
mystery theology is that it appears to have had a profound
impact on the chief liturgical document to emerge from the
Second Vatican Council in Rome. This was the *Constitution
on the Sacred Liturgy*, promulgated on December 4, 1963. For
these reasons the mystery theology itself and its influence on
the *Constitution on the Sacred Liturgy* will receive our immediate
attention.

Maria Laach and its associated Benedictine monasteries
exhibit many of the dominant aspects of the liturgical movement. These include a return to the biblical and Christ-
centered tradition of the early church; recognition of the importance of the vivifying Word proclaimed in the lections and
sermons of the synaxis as well as in the *verbum visibile* of the
Eucharist; the need for an objective and corporate, as con-
trasted with a subjective and individualistic, liturgical piety; an
emphasis on the *communal* offering of the eucharistic sacrifice;
and a complementary stress on the Holy Communion as a
commemorative repast. Other aspects are the strongly social
implications of the Eucharist for the healing of class and ethnic
divisions and its potential contribution to Christian art. But
Maria Laach Abbey's chief contribution to the understanding
of the liturgy has been the systematic exposition of it as the
efficaciously sanctifying representation of the Christian mys-

tery of salvation. This is what the so-called *Mysterientheologie* is all about.[7]

Its chief exponent, Dom Odo Casel, distinguishes three correlated aspects of the *mysterium*.[8] First of all, the supreme Mystery is God in his own Being, the utterly Holy and Unapproachable One, Ineffable and Transcendent. Second, the revelation of God in Christ is the personal mystery of God the invisible revealed in the flesh; in his humiliation, Incarnation, sacrificial death upon the cross, as in his Resurrection and Ascension, God marvelously reveals himself in a way that far surpasses all human capacities. The third mystery is that of the cult, which is defined as a liturgical action "in which the redemptive act is rendered in the rite,"[9] and "since the cultic community accomplishes the rite, it shares the saving rite and through it attains redemption."[10]

It must, however, be insisted on that for Casel, not only the Passion of Christ, but the entire work of redemption is made present again in the liturgy, from his first to his second advent. Moreover, this is declared and believed to be not a psychological or subjective reality, but an ontological and objective reality, which, though veiled in symbol or image, actually shares in the reality of God's redemptive action of grace for his people.

Related to "mystery" is the term "transfiguration," another seminal term for the Eastern Church as for Maria Laach. The purpose of the liturgy, as of the Christian religion, is to sanctify, even to deify, mankind, bringing transfigured Christians to the Christ of the Transfiguration. Through the bestowal of grace in

7. See the overenthusiastic evaluation of the mystery theology in the article by Alphonse Heitz in *La Maison-Dieu*, VII (1946), where he describes as mere "tidbits" *(amorces)* the contribution of predecessors of the Maria Laach school. See the sober and well-argued study of it in Louis Bouyer, *The Liturgy Revived: A Doctrinal Commentary of the Conciliar Constitution on the Liturgy* (Notre Dame, IN: The University of Notre Dame Press, 1964).

8. See *Das christliche Kultmysterium* (Regensburg, 3rd edn., 1938).

9. The technical terms used are *Repraesentatio* and *Gegenwartigsetzung*.

10. *Das christliche Kultmysterium*, p. 121.

the liturgy, humanity is raised to the supernatural order and therefore into sharing the divine existence, light, and glory. Maria Laach is not interested in any individual meditations on the crucified Christ or devotions to the Christ "imprisoned" in the Tabernacle, but only in a proleptic sharing in the life of the glorified Christ. The focal center is Christ in glory, but with the constant remembrance that this Christ went "from God to God" by the route of humiliation and the *via dolorosa*.

Abbot Herwegen in *Kirche und Seele* made a sharp distinction between the sentimental, subjective, and individualistic piety of the later medieval and post-Tridentine Mass and the objective and corporate liturgical piety of the Fathers both in the East and the West. In the same book he also argued that medieval romanticism had shifted the emphasis in the Eucharist from the union of the whole church to a concentration on individual benefits to be derived from the Mass. By such a misplaced emphasis, Herwegen maintained that a Christocentric action of the church had degenerated into a pious or moralistic passivity of the laity as individual spectators who were no longer participants in the eucharistic action. It is clear that the mystery theology and its practical implications in the liturgy at Maria Laach was as much a revolution as it was a restoration.

Some indication of the importance of this theology and its influence may be found in the number of eminent Roman Catholic theologians who have endorsed or partly endorsed the theological and practical insights of Maria Laach. Among these should be mentioned Dom Anscar Vonier, O.S.B., Henri de Lubac, S.J., Jean Daniélou, S.J., P. Doncoeur, S.J., Pie Duployé, O.P., Eugène Masure, and the Oratorian Louis Bouyer, all of whom expound the *Mysterientheologie*. It is accepted with some reservations by François Diekamp, J. Butler, Karl Adam, and G. Söhngen. It is, however, severely criticized by the distinguished liturgical historian Joseph Jungmann, S.J., and by Theodore Klauser.

Mystery theology has been attacked for denigrating the scholastic and medieval interpretations of the Mass as rank

Greek antiquarianism, and as denying the once-for-allness of history in claiming the reenactment of the crucial historic event in the liturgy. A more serious criticism, perhaps, is that in asserting the primacy of the corporate and objective piety of the Eucharist it has underplayed the importance of the personal and individual appropriation of the grace of the Eucharist. Louis Bouyer suggests that the attempt to explain the Christian mystery "mainly in the context of the pagan mysteries of the first centuries was more or less unfortunate, because it tended, contrary to the hopes of its own promoters . . . to obscure our appreciation of the creative originality, and therefore, everlasting validity, of the great vision of Christianity."[11]

The ecumenical significance of the mystery theology is profound, for not only does it provide a bridge between Eastern Orthodox and western Catholic theology and liturgiology, but it offers a third alternative to medieval scholastic and post-Tridentine eucharistic interpretations, and this has met with an interested response on the part of Protestant theologians. Its most impressive fruit has been the revivification of parish life through emphasis on the divine initiative and the action of transforming grace in the Eucharist.

The *Mysterientheologie* has many other important implications. Faith, in its view, is more than assent to intellectual propositions, since it requires the commitment of the whole life of the entire person to God. Humanity is no longer regarded in atomistic fashion, but as part of the people of God, mystically incorporated into the *corpus Christi* in the action of the Eucharist, sharing the life, purposes, and divine energy of God. This theology, furthermore, views daily work as worship, the offering that the Christian in the world brings to the company of the transfigured, to be presented in the Offertory of the liturgy, together with the perfect offering of the Atonement renewed. The Eucharist itself is transformed as well: it is no longer merely a hierarchical offering in which the laity are passively present,

11. *The Liturgy Revived,* p. 15.

but an action of grace in which the general priesthood of the people of God is exercised in response to the gracious offering and sacrifice of the great High Priest, Christ himself.[12]

Mystery Theology in the
Constitution on the Sacred Liturgy

Louis Bouyer states that the Conciliar Constitution begins with a proclamation that endorses and "represents the best fruit of what has been achieved in the work of pioneers like Dom Odo Casel and the whole Maria Laach school which now receives its due recognition."[13] It is the understanding that the liturgy is to be understood essentially as "the Paschal Mystery."[14]

Paragraph 5 of the *Constitution on the Sacred Liturgy* gives as the foundation of its teaching on the liturgy the assertion that Christ achieved his task principally by the paschal mystery of his blessed passion, resurrection from the dead, and glorious ascension, whereby dying, he destroyed our death, and rising, he restored our life. For it was from the side of Christ as he slept the sleep of death upon the cross that there came forth the wondrous sacrament of the whole church. The fifth paragraph concludes: "From that time onward, the church has never failed to come together to celebrate the Paschal Mystery: reading these things 'which were in all the Scriptures concerning Him' (Luke 24:27), celebrating the Eucharist in which 'the victory and triumph of His

12. See the present author's *Worship and Theology in England: The Ecumenical Century* (Princeton: Princeton University Press, 1965), p. 29, for a brief consideration of the contributions of the Augustinian canons of Klosterneuberg, Austria, and the *Centre de Pastorale Liturgique* in France, in spreading and supplementing the work of Maria Laach Abbey.

13. *The Liturgy Revived*, p. 11.

14. "The Paschal Mystery" is essentially the recognition of the Eucharist as the Christian Passover effected through the cross and Resurrection of Christ, as described in our second chapter, "The Eucharist as Memorial," giving Christian slaves redemption as the Passover freed Jewish slaves in Egypt.

death are made again present,' and at the same time giving thanks 'to God for His unspeakable gift' (II Cor. 9:15) in Christ Jesus, 'in praise of His glory' (Eph. 1:12) through the power of the Holy Spirit." As Louis Bouyer rightly says, this restores "a view of Christianity possessed by the Fathers of the Church both Greek and Latin, Eastern and Western."[15] The Council therefore restored to the church again in its liturgy the true sense of mystery as the great secret of God's design for the salvation of the world, which is made known in preaching the Word of God and in the Eucharist, which transforms us into living members of the body of Christ, reconciled to God through the cross and living in hope of everlasting life through the Resurrection. In the Christian celebration the mystery of Christ is proclaimed, but the work of salvation is accomplished as well, as a prayer of the Leonine Sacramentary affirms, *opus redemptionis exercetur* — the work of redemption is effected. The best commentary is St. Paul's, for two sayings of his are combined in the Constitution's statement "Thus by baptism men are plunged into the paschal mystery of Christ: they die with Him, are buried with Him, and rise with Him. . . . In like manner, as often as they eat the Supper of the Lord, they proclaim the death of the Lord until He comes. . . ."[16]

As Bouyer rightly says, the apostle Paul expounded the cross as the true Pasch, not because it happened on the day of the Jewish celebration of the Passover, but because the Pasch "prepared, sketched, promised to the faithful people of God: 'Christ, our Passover, has been immolated! . . .' (I Corinthians 5:7)."[17] Just as in the first Passover only the houses containing faithful Israelites, where the blood of the Lamb was visible on the lintel of the door, indicated who would be spared, the effusion of the blood of the cross indicates those in Christ whose sins are forgiven and redeemed from slavery into the freedom of adopted sons and daughters of God.

15. *The Liturgy Revived*, p. 13.
16. Paragraph 6 of the *Constitution on the Sacred Liturgy*.
17. *The Liturgy Revived*, p. 20.

It will be remembered that critics of the mystery theology argued that it was derived from the mystery religions current in the period of the early church and centuries before. It may be worth raising the question, if only to answer it briefly, whether the Christian church derived its ideas of salvation from the mystery religions.

Dean Inge, himself a considerable mystic, claimed that Catholicism owed to the mysteries "the notions of secrecy, of symbolism, of mystical brotherhood, of sacramental grace, and, above all, the three stages in the spiritual life: ascetic purification, illumination, and *epopteia* [supreme bliss] as the crown."[18] That judgment makes much of similarities, but takes no account at all of the radical differences between Christianity and the mystery religions. S. Angus, who has made a thorough study of mystery religions and of early Christianity, acknowledges the likenesses, citing Farnell on the Eleusinian mysteries: "To understand the quality and intensity of the impression we should borrow something from the modern experiences of the Christian Communion Service, Mass, and Passion Play, and bear in mind also the extraordinary susceptibility of the Greek mind to an artistically impressive pageant."[19] Such a judgment says nothing about the weaknesses of the mystery religions, such as their combination in many cases of astrology and magic. This makes all the more relevant the warning of St. Paul: "For we have to struggle, not with blood and flesh, but with the angelic Rulers and angelic Authorities, the potentates of the dark present, the spirit forces of evil in the heavenly sphere,"[20] and his triumphant claim that "I am persuaded that neither the Powers, nor the Ascension of the stars nor their Declinations shall be able to separate us from the love of God in Christ Jesus our Lord."[21]

The mystery religions appealed to feelings rather than to

18. R. W. Inge, *Christian Mysticism* (London: Methuen, 1899), p. 354.
19. "Mysticism," in *Encyclopedia Britannica*, 11th edn., vol. XIX, p. 121b.
20. Moffatt's translation of Ephesians 6:12.
21. Moffatt's translation of Romans 8:38-40.

"moral loyalties and spiritual perceptions," said Angus.[22] Certainly what Clement of Alexandria affirmed could not be said of the mystery religions: "Philosophy was to the Greeks the preparatory discipline for the Gospel which the Law provided to the Jews."[23] The mysteries lacked intellectual apologists.

There were other striking differences between Christianity and the mystery religions. Christianity was based dominantly upon history — the life of Jesus of Nazareth and his teaching, but the mystery religions were founded exclusively on myths. Christianity was a universal religion and found a means of satisfying the social and individual instincts and desires of humans, while the social and economic aspects of life were totally ignored by the mystery religions, which catered only to secret societies of individuals who had no concern to rejuvenate society.

Furthermore, Christianity, like Judaism, had a sacred scripture, and was ready to accept, as Judaism was not, Jew and Greek, rich and poor, slave and free, men and women. Even St. Paul, in whom some have detected mysticism like that of the mystery religions, has a mysticism that, in two important respects, differs from the mystery religions: "first, as regards the human factor, there is a conspicuous absence of any idea of absorption in the deity. . . . Secondly, as regards the Divine factor, in the mystic fellowship the faith-mysticism of Paul is faith grounded in a historic Personality to whose love faith is the necessary response. . . . The Christian . . . becomes like Christ, but never Christ."[24] Furthermore, as Angus asserts, "Christian enthusiasm was awakened and sustained not by an ideal, but by a Person."[25] On the other hand, one can imagine that a member of one of the mystery religions might well find

---

22. S. Angus, *The Mystery-Religions and Christianity: A Study in the Religious Background of Early Christianity* (New York: Scribner's, 1925), p. 262.

23. *Stromateis* 6.17; see also 1.5 and 1.16.

24. Angus, *op. cit.*, p. 296.

25. *Ibid.*, p. 305.

some aspects of Christianity very attractive, for this gospel brought a sustaining comfort to the sufferers of the Greco-Roman world, for its "Lord of Glory" had been "The Man of Sorrows" in an earthly life of conflict culminating in an agonizing death and as the *passibilis Christus* sublimely portrays the redemptive aspects of suffering and expects in return both self-sacrifice and loyalty — demands far higher than those of the mystery religions.[26] Our conclusion must be that the probability of mystery religions influencing Christianity is small, but that the superiority of Christianity over the mystery religions is striking both theologically and ethically, while historically its superiority is proved by its survival and spread.

"Mystery" in Scripture and the Early Church

The value of the term "mystery" for the Eucharist must be determined in part by whether and how it has been used biblically and in the early history of the church, which will be our next concern.

While rabbinic Judaism in its apocalyptic condemned any secret doctrines, an exception was made for the Book of Daniel, where it signifies an eschatological mystery, a concealed intimation of divinely ordained future events whose disclosure and interpretation are reserved for God alone and for those inspired by his Spirit.

In the synoptic gospels there is reference to the mystery of the divine lordship of Christ in Mark 4:11ff. and parallels, distinguishing between the disciples and the masses who hear him uncomprehendingly in his parables. The implication is that the disciples understand the mystery of the divine rule, but not others. They, according to Matthew 13:16-17, know that they are witnessing the dawn of the messianic time and kingdom.

26. Daniel 2:28, 29 and 4:9. The citation is from G. Bornkamm's valuable article *"musterion"* (mystery), in G. Kittel, ed., *The Theological Dictionary of the New Testament,* transl. Geoffrey W. Bromiley (Grand Rapids: Wm. B. Eerdmans, 1967), vol. IV, pp. 802-28. I am much indebted to this article.

In the Pauline corpus the term *musterion* refers to Christ as the mystery of God (see Col. 2:2; also 1:27 and 4:3). In I Corinthians 2:6-16, St. Paul is clearly countering the gnostics of that city who looked for a wisdom that exceeded that of the cross, which the apostle insists must be openly proclaimed. The mysterious wisdom of God, as Bornkamm analyzes it, was prepared before the world existed (I Cor. 2:7), was concealed from the aeons (I Cor. 2:8; Eph. 3:9), and was hidden in God, the Creator of all things (Eph. 3:9). But on the cross, which was set up by the rulers of this world, the Lord of glory dies, and through the divine vindication of the resurrection of Christ, this mystery of God, hitherto secret, is now revealed to those who are in Christ and have believed the gospel preached to them.[27] The marvel is the joining of the Gentiles in the inheritance of salvation in Christ, as Ephesians 3:4ff. indicates. It is a cosmic eschatological event, for it reveals the mystery of understanding the whole created world in terms of God's revelation in Christ (Eph. 1:9-10). It is divine revelation on the part of God that discloses this mystery to those chosen by him. St. Paul sums up his desires for his converts in the words "that their hearts may be encouraged as they are knit together in love, to have all the riches of assured understanding and the knowledge of God's mystery, of Christ, in whom are hid all the treasures of wisdom and knowledge."[28] All references to "mystery" elsewhere in the New Testament refer to secret knowledge with apocalyptic significance. In Revelation 17:5 and 7, for example, the mystery of the harlot Babylon is the hidden significance of her appearing and her Satanic power, which will be destroyed in the future. Bornkamm concludes: "In sum, *musterion* is a rare expression in the New Testament which betrays no relation to the mystery cults"; thus "there are serious objections against bringing Jesus or Paul under the category of the mystagogue."[29]

27. I Corinthians 2:6-8.
28. Colossians 2:2-3.
29. *The Theological Dictionary of the New Testament,* vol. IV, p. 824.

Louis Bouyer clarifies the meaning of the term "mystery" in Scripture by a series of negations that avoid possible confusion. The term does not mean any truth that we may accept but find inexplicable, nor is it a secret discipline hidden from the common herd (the explanation of the parable of the sower in the synoptics is a striking exception). Nor can mystery be discoverable by the highest human wisdom; in fact, it even seems folly to the wise. It is the special revelation of God and a communication of the Holy Spirit, as the first and second chapters of the First Epistle to the Corinthians make abundantly clear. It is, then, in Christ alone, and especially in his passion and resurrection, that the wisdom of God is carried to its final realization in both his words and actions.[30]

According to Bornkamm, the term "mystery" is used unreflectingly in apologetic writers but in the struggle with gnosticism and the mystery religions it comes to be a central concept, especially when figuratively applied to Christianity, for the basic facts of salvation, for Old Testament figures and events believed to have typological significance, as when Justin Martyr calls the Old Testament a veiled prophecy of Christ, and as when the outstretched arms of Moses are seen as a proleptic reference to the cross.[31] Alexandrian theology, following gnostic and neo-Platonic ideas, considers the truths of the Christian religion as mysteries, which are taught only by stages to initiates, and in veiled form.[32] For our purposes, it is the use of *musterion* for the sacraments in the early church that is of the greatest interest and relevance.

For Justin Martyr and Tertullian, the pagan mysteries are a devilish imitation of the Christian sacraments. It is only in the fourth century that the term "mystery" is applied to the Christian sacraments as a cultic repetition and re-presentation of Christ's self-sacrifice, but in symbolical concealment. The saving acts and their cultic representation are both called *musterion*, and Eusebius

30. *The Liturgy Revived,* pp. 16-18.
31. *Dialogue with Trypho* 44 and 111.
32. Cf. Clement of Alexandria, *Stromateis* 4 and 5.57.2.

of Caesarea writes: "The Lord and Saviour Himself, and the priests who go out from Him . . . present in veiled form in the bread and wine the mysteries of His body and saving blood."[33] The term "mysteries" has an even wider reference in worship, since it means not only Christ's passion and resurrection, but also his Incarnation and his enthronement in glory. G. Bornkamm points out the interesting fact that the Latin equivalent for "mystery" is *sacramentum,* and asks how this can be when its natural meaning is a soldier's oath. This, he declares, is because an oath had originally the character of an initiation; and the secondary sense of *sacramentum* for the Christian would be the rule of faith to which he is engaged at baptism.[34] In Latin theological writings *sacramentum* and *musterion* are equivalents.[35]

The term "mystery" does not easily lend itself to precise definitions, and this must have seemed appropriate in describing the dealings of God with humanity. As A. M. Ramsey summarizes the situation:

> But of the mystery there were, in the Church of the first five centuries, several explanations all held in the Church's tolerant embrace. Thus some patristic writers simply assert that Christ feeds the souls of men, without explaining how; some use language of "type" and "symbol" and "representation"; some emphasize a change wrought in the elements by consecration so that they are the body and blood of Jesus while still remaining also bread and wine. The Church was content that these theories should be held side by side. But whatsoever theory is adopted the mystery calls forth awe and worship from those who share in the Liturgy.[36]

---

33. *Demonstratio Evangelica* 5.3.19. Eusebius, the church historian, says that the memorial of Christ takes place "according to the mysteries handed down by Him" (*op. cit.,* 1.10.38).

34. *The Theological Dictionary of the New Testament,* vol. IV, p. 827.

35. For example, St. Ambrose in *De Mysteriis* 27 writes: *ubi est ecclesia, ubi mysteria sua sunt, ibi dignatur suam impertire praesentiam.*

36. *The Gospel and the Catholic Church* (London: Longmans, Green and Co., 1936), pp. 111-12.

The Permanent Value of the Concept of "Mystery"

After reflecting on the meanings of the term "mystery" as applied to the Eucharist in both the New Testament and the early church, we must now consider the permanent values of designating the Eucharist as a mystery or as mysteries.

First among such values must be the recognition of the element of divine transcendence in all God's dealings with humanity, and especially in the self-giving of his eternal Son. For us it should lead to a very suitable humility. So argues Stephen F. Bayne, Jr., who defines a "mystery" as "an act of God which we can use and share, without understanding it or seeing it as God sees and understands it," commenting: "There is a healthy humility about this word."[37] The cross still staggers us because of the transcendence of *agape* — a love for those who are apparently unlovable or undeserving of love, as in Romans 5:8, "God shows his love for us in that *while we were yet sinners Christ died for us.*" The Eucharist is the proof of the enduring love of the crucified and risen and glorified Christ for his undeserving people.

There have, of course, been standard Western, often rationalistic objections, which implied that mystery was only an equivalent for our ignorance or unwillingness to be guided by reason. Paul Verghese writes thoughtfully about these objections in *The Joy of Freedom: Eastern Worship and Modern Man.* He points out that Western critics are suspicious of mysticism because of its anti-rational tendencies, its supposedly unmediated access to God, its drift toward religious syncretism, the fear of the loss of individual identity in the divine, as well as the philosophical problem of "ineffability."[38] His reply is that "In the relentless pursuit of clarity, these philosophies hope to reduce all mysteries to problems or puzzles, originating either in lack of knowledge or unclear thinking," and he wishes to affirm the necessary transcendence of the

37. *Mindful of the Love: The Holy Communion in Daily Life* (New York: Oxford University Press, 1962), p. 6.
38. *The Joy of Freedom* (London: Lutterworth Press, 1967), p. 26.

living God. He is satisfied with the following definition: ". . . union with Christ as an experience in the Body of Christ, through the Holy Spirit, is what constitutes the Christian life. At the heart of that life is the great mystery of the eucharist."[39] God, he insists, is not limited by language or by knowledge. Here we have recourse to the *via negativa*, or negative theology, which affirms that God transcends all that we can know about his essence, and the so-called "apophatic" limitations on human knowledge of God that recommend silence. The famous theologian Gregory of Nyssa, expounding Ecclesiastes 3:7 — "a time to keep silence, and a time to speak" — suggests to the theologian:

> In speaking of God, when there is a question of his essence, then is *the time to keep silence.* When, however, it is a question of His operation, a knowledge of which can come down even to us, that is *the time to speak* of His omnipotence by telling of His works and explaining His deeds, and to use words to this extent. In matters which go beyond this, however, the creature must not exceed the bounds of its nature, but must be content to know itself. For, indeed, in my view, if the creature never comes to know itself, never understands the essence of the soul or the nature of the body, the cause of being . . . , if the creature does not know itself, how can it ever explain things which are beyond it? Of such things it is the *time to keep silence;* here silence is surely better. There is, however, a *time to speak* of those things by which we can in our lives make progress in virtue.[40]

Certainly negative theology is a medicine for the treatment of arrogance, and Orthodoxy has always insisted upon the primacy of love in the divine-human encounter.

Furthermore, in dealing with the relationship of the Creator with the creature, and of the union of God and humanity, we

39. *Ibid.,* pp. 35-36.
40. Gregory of Nyssa, *Commentary on Ecclesiastes,* Sermon 7, *Patrologia Graeca,* XLIV, col. 732 D, transl. H. Musurillo in *From Glory to Glory: Texts from Gregory of Nyssa's Mystical Writings* (New York: Scribner's, 1961), p. 129, cited in John Meyendorff's *Byzantine Theology,* p. 14.

often have to use paradox or be silent. The Benedictine scholar, Professor Aidan Kavanagh, has a sublime definition of Christian worship and of the Eucharist that ends with a string of paradoxes that are pearls of illumination:

> It is the world seen in the light of Christ's gospel as a marriage feast, a table fellowship, in which God is the host, His Son the bridegroom, and we are the Spirited bride whose dowry is the life of the bridegroom himself. About the table all are gathered in free and equal association with the Source and Origin of all that is. And this is so not just in spite of our sin, but somehow, and mysteriously, because of that sin, that *felix culpa* which required so great a Redeemer.

He continues his account of this mystery:

> It eased us down into unfamiliar and portentous thoughts on matters such as God's gracious illiberality, on our own sin's capacity for being called *felix,* on death's proclivity to be less an end than a beginning, and on the curiousness of banqueting with joy upon the body and blood of one's host.[41]

A second value that the emphasis on mystery makes clear is that *lex orandi* is *lex credendi,* and that it is in the surrender of the human will in worship and union with God that he is best known. The real danger is that theology may become a rationalizing process utterly distinct from the experience of the knowledge of God. The Orthodox Church has always insisted that the soul of dogma is found in the Christian liturgy and particularly in the mystery of the Eucharist, which is dominated by rejoicing. Paul Verghese insists that God can be known but never exhaustively, and then only in love and surrender, and that "controlling knowledge of God has not been given to man."[42] Hence God

41. "Liturgy and Ecclesial Consciousness: a Dialectic of Change," in *Studia Liturgica* (Rotterdam), vol. 15, pp. 2-17. The citation comes from p. 17.

42. *The Joy of Freedom,* p. 35.

is revealed in worship and prayer rather than in conceptual or descriptive formulas abstracted from experience. This conviction also preserves the sense of revelation as a mystery unveiled by the triune God, never a full disclosure of his inmost Being, for that is beyond man's capacity to receive.

The third value of mystery in the Eucharist is that it emphasizes the dominant eschatological experience. This is the leading characteristic of the patristic and Orthodox experience of the Eucharist. This is briefly defined by Alexander Schmemann as "her very nature as *passage* and ascension into the Kingdom of God."[43] The Eastern church recognized the basis of the Eucharist less in the Last Supper than in the encounters of the disciples with the risen Christ and the commencement of the Kingdom of God. For them, as the successors of the disciples, the celestial wedding supper has already begun, and they share the climax of the process of redemption in the vision of John in Revelation, who heard the voice of a great multitude, crying: "Hallelujah! For the Lord our God the Almighty reigns. Let us rejoice and exult and give him the glory, for the marriage of the Lamb has come, and his Bride has made herself ready. . . ."[44] As Ernst Benz observes: "The Orthodox liturgy has preserved unchanged this early Christian mood of rejoicing and spiritual gladness. In this its character is quite different from the Eucharist in, say, Reformed Christianity, where the early Christian spirit of gladness is clouded over and obscured by the spirit of penitence."[45] The same author encapsulates the joyful, charismatic experience of the Orthodox Church at the Eucharist in the following description: "The miracle — that in breaking bread with Christ in accordance with a ritual taught them by Jesus Himself at the Messianic wedding supper the

---

43. *Church, World, Mission*, p. 139.
44. Revelation 19:6-7.
45. *The Eastern Orthodox Church*, p. 23. The very early Christian rejoicing is recorded in Acts 2:46, where we are informed: "And breaking bread in their homes, they partook of food with glad and generous hearts, praising God."

fellowship of the baptized are once again in the presence of the Redeemer — is the real creative core of the Orthodox liturgy. And the congregation feel it to be so, feel that they themselves are witnessing the epiphanies of the resurrected Christ."[46] Again, we have to acknowledge that the mystery drama of the Eucharist reenacts the whole mystery of salvation, the Incarnation, the death and resurrection of the Logos, his glorification, and the outpouring of the Holy Spirit, and its climax is the descent, the appearance, and the divine presence of the resurrected Christ, who enters the congregation as "King of the universe borne invisibly over their spears by the angelic hosts." The congregation is not allowed to forget this epiphany of the resurrected Christ, for the celebrating priest after the great eucharistic prayer cries: "Christ is in the midst of us!" and the assisting priest responds, "He is with us and will be." The same cry is repeated after the communion of the priests, is made again while the communion is given to the believers, and the choir reiterates the claim as it exults: "Blessed is He who comes in the name of the Lord, God is the Lord and has appeared to us." After the distribution the choir sings:

> We have seen the true light;
> We have received the Holy Spirit;
> We have found the true faith.
> Let us worship the inseparable Trinity,
>   for it has redeemed us.

Such rejoicing is far from the Western relegation of eternal life to the indefinite future: it is an immediate entry into the life of heaven shared proleptically and mystically, as well as mysteriously, on earth.

The fourth value of the concept of mystery is that it rightly necessitates a catechumenate, a period of instruction after baptism to prepare believers for the privilege of the Eucharist. If this great mystery is to be kept the privilege of believers, such

46. *Ibid.,* p. 24.

instruction is a necessity, not, as in some Protestant churches, an optional extra. The sense of mystery keeps alive the recognition that attendance at the Eucharist is the supreme privilege of the members of the body of Christ.

The Expression of the Mystery in Contemporary Liturgies

The final part of this chapter will be devoted to tracing the concept of mystery in modern eucharistic liturgies. It goes without saying that it is supremely expressed in the liturgies of the Eastern Orthodox Church. In the Russian Orthodox Liturgy, in both the Divine Liturgy of St. John Chrysostom and that of St. Basil the Great, including the Office of Preparation, there are no less than seventeen references to "the mysteries": four are in the Office of Preparation, and thirteen in the Liturgies. Of these seven are in Chrysostom's Liturgy, and five in Basil's. In Basil's Liturgy there is a prayer expressing a powerful sense of the divine transcendence that goes as follows: "O Master of all, . . . invisible, unsearchable, uncircumscribed, immutable, the unbegotten Father of our Lord Jesus Christ."[47] And in Chrysostom's Liturgy there is a prayer that proceeds: "count us worthy to partake of Thine appalling and heavenly mysteries . . . with a pure conscience, unto the remission of sins, the forgiveness of offences, the participation of the Holy Spirit, the inheritance of the Kingdom of heaven, and unto boldness towards Thee, not unto judgment, nor unto condemnation."[48] It clearly enunciates the privileges of the great sacrament. The references to the mysteries in St. John Chrysostom's rite make prominent the adjectives "divine," "holy," "appalling," "life-giving," "heavenly," and "pure." The references to the mysteries in

47. All references in this paragraph are to the English translation of the Russian Orthodox Liturgy published as *The Orthodox Liturgy being the Divine Liturgy of S. John Chrysostom and S. Basil the Great according to the Use of the Church of Russia* (London: S.P.C.K. for the Fellowship of SS. Alban and Sergius, 1939). The prayer is cited on p. 67.

48. *Ibid.*, p. 83.

St. Basil's Liturgy employ the description "this great mystery of salvation"[49] and the adjectives "holy," "heavenly," "pure," and "life-giving."

Perhaps the greatest tribute paid to the Orthodox sense of "the mysteries" is that the Second Vatican Council decided that its Eucharistic Prayer IV in the Missal was to be modeled on the Eastern Eucharist. Its preface has a hint of transcendence: "Through all eternity you live in unapproachable light" and "lead all men to the joyful vision of your light." Among the *mirabilia Christi* it declares, "he sent the Holy Spirit from you, Father, as his first gift to those who believe," and it employs a different Invocation of the Holy Spirit *(epiclesis)* as the formula of consecration:

> Father, may this Holy Spirit sanctify these offerings.
> Let them become the body and blood of Jesus Christ our
> Lord as we celebrate the great mystery
> which he left us as an everlasting covenant.

The memorial acclamation of the people is prefaced by the words:

> Let us proclaim the mystery of faith:

The people respond:

> Christ has died,
> Christ is risen,
> Christ will come again.

> Dying you destroyed our death,
> rising you restored our life,
> Lord Jesus, come in glory.

> When we eat this bread and drink this cup,
> we proclaim your death, Lord Jesus,
> until you come in glory.

49. *Ibid.,* p. 53.

Lord, by your cross and resurrection
you have set us free.
You are the Saviour of the world.[50]

The General Preface of the modern German Lutheran Rite of 1955/77 has a preface reminiscent of the Orthodox parallel: "Through Him [Christ] the angels praise your majesty, the heavenly hosts adore you, and the powers tremble; together with the blessed Seraphim all the citizens of heaven praise you in brilliant jubilation. Unite our voices with theirs and let us sing in endless adoration. . . ."[51] Its use of the *epiclesis* has by now become a commonplace in modern eucharistic liturgies. On the other hand, its strong eschatological emphasis is outstanding, as is its metaphor of the nuptial feast, "that together with all the faithful we may celebrate in his kingdom the marriage feast of the Lamb," which is a very early imitation of the Orthodox mystery.[52]

The American *Lutheran Book of Worship* of 1978 expresses the eschatological stress in its first *epiclesis,* thus:

Send now, we pray, your Holy Spirit, the spirit of our Lord and of his resurrection, that we who receive the Lord's body and blood may live to the praise of your glory and receive our inheritance with all your saints in light.[53]

The *epiclesis* of the English *Alternative Service Book, 1980* in its Third Eucharistic Prayer has a strong eschatological thrust that should delight the Orthodox. It reads as follows:

50. *The Sunday Missal: A New Edition* (London: Collins, 1984). Eucharistic Prayer IV is on pp. 52-55.
51. From the *Agende für evangelisch-lutherische Kirchen und Gemeinden,* I, translated and borrowed from the Lutheran/Roman Catholic Joint Commission, *The Eucharist* (Geneva: Lutheran World Federation, 1980). Our citation is taken from Thurian and Wainwright, eds., *Baptism and Eucharist: Ecumenical Convergence in Celebration* (Geneva: World Council of Churches, and Grand Rapids: Wm. B. Eerdmans, 1983), p. 136.
52. *Ibid.,* p. 137.
53. *Ibid.,* p. 143.

> Send the Holy Spirit on your people
> and gather into one in your kingdom
> all who share this one bread and one cup,
> so that we, in the company of all the saints,
> may praise and glorify you for ever. . . .[54]

The sense of the presence of the Holy Spirit is powerfully stated
in the opening words of the Fourth Eucharistic Prayer:

> *President:* The Lord is here
> *All:* His Spirit is with us.[55]

Furthermore, an alternative formula at the distribution of the
elements is:

> The body (blood) of Christ keep you in eternal life.[56]

The Book of Common Prayer of the American Episcopal
Church has in the preface of Eucharistic Prayer D a fine sense
of the angels that surround God:

> Fountain of life and source of all goodness, you made all things
> and fill them with your blessing; you created them to rejoice
> in the splendor of your radiance.
>
> Countless throngs of angels stand before you to serve you night
> and day; and, beholding the glory of your presence, they offer
> you unceasing praise. Joining with them, and giving voice to
> every creature under heaven, we acclaim you, and glorify your
> Name, as we sing (say). . . .

After the *Sanctus* and the *Benedictus* the celebrant continues:

> We acclaim you, holy Lord, glorious in power. Your mighty
> works reveal your wisdom and love.[57]

---

54. *Ibid.,* p. 138.
55. *Ibid.,* p. 139.
56. *Ibid.,* p. 143.
57. *The Book of Common Prayer,* p. 373.

Eucharistic Prayer B finely expresses the purpose of creation:

> In the fullness of time, put all things in subjection under your Christ, and bring us to that heavenly country where, with [_____] and all your saints, we may enter the everlasting heritage of your sons and daughters. . . .[58]

While the eschatology is there, curiously there is no mention of the nuptial joy in heaven, nor of the mystery in the Holy Communion.

The Presbyterian Churches in the U.S.A. have both *The Worship Service Book* of 1970 and since 1984 *The Service Book for the Lord's Day: Supplemental Resources, I.* The former has a worthy *epiclesis:*

> Great God: give your Holy Spirit in the breaking of bread so that we may be drawn together, and joined to Christ the Lord, receive new life, and remain His glad and faithful people until we feast with Him in glory.[59]

The Service Book for the Lord's Day, containing *Supplemental Resources, I,* has no less than eight Great Prayers of Thanksgiving for use in the Lord's Supper. It is one of the rare Protestant communions to use the term "holy mysteries of the Lord's Supper." Eucharistic Prayer D has the following *epiclesis:*

> We ask you to send your Holy Spirit upon the offering of the holy church, gathering into one all who share these holy mysteries. . . .[60]

The preface to Eucharistic Prayer A has a sense of transcendence:

> How wonderful are your ways, almighty God,
> How marvelous is your Name, O Holy One.
> You alone are God.[61]

---

58. *Ibid.,* p. 369.
59. *The Worship Service Book* (Philadelphia: The Westminster Press, 1970), p. 36.
60. *Ibid.,* p. 107.
61. *Ibid.,* p. 96.

In addition, on a few occasions the celebrant invites the congregation:

> Let us proclaim the mystery of faith

which receives the response:

> Christ has died,
> Christ has risen,
> Christ will come again.[62]

Eucharistic Prayer G includes in the preface:

> Almighty Father, Creator and Sustainer of life,
> your majesty and power, your continued blessings,
> and your great goodness fill us with wonder.[63]

Thus, the American Presbyterians maintain a due sense of the wonders of God, the mystery, not only of faith but of the Eucharist itself, and the proleptic joy anticipating heaven.

The Book of Common Order of the Church of Scotland (1979) also uses the term "mystery" in reference to the Holy Communion, for its Eucharistic Prayer contains the Thanksgiving:

> Thrice holy and blessed is thy Son Jesus Christ, blessed in all his gifts, blessed in that Holy mystery which he did institute. . . .[64]

The other petitions have a strong sense of Christ's resurrection, the life everlasting, and the communion of saints.

A Book of Service of the United Reformed Church of the United Kingdom has prayers that are simple, clear, relevant, and profoundly biblical. "Thanksgiving I" immediately after the dialogue proceeds:

62. *Ibid.*, p. 97.
63. *Ibid.*, p. 116.
64. Thurian and Wainwright, *op. cit.*, p. 157.

> With joy we give you thanks and praise,
> Almighty God, Source of all life and love,
> that we live in your world,
> that you are always
> creating and sustaining it by your power,
> and that you have so made us
> that we can know and love you,
> trust and serve you.[65]

In the Third Thanksgiving there is a fresh *epiclesis:*

> We beseech you
> send among us your Holy Spirit
> and give a new face
> to this earth that is dear to us.
> Let there be peace
> wherever people live,
> the peace that we cannot make ourselves
> and that is more powerful than all violence,
> your peace like a bond,
> a new covenant between us all,
> the power of Jesus Christ
> here among us.[66]

There is also an effective nonseasonal part of the Great Thanksgiving, with a strong eschatological emphasis:

> We thank you that Jesus was born among us;
> that he lived our common life on earth;
> that he suffered and died for us;
> that he rose again;
> and that he is always present
> through the Holy Spirit.

---

65. *A Book of Services: The United Reformed Church in the United Kingdom* (Edinburgh: The Saint Andrews Press, 1980), p. 28.
66. *Ibid.,* pp. 36-37.

We thank you that we can live in the faith
that your kingdom will come,
and that in life, in death
and beyond death you are with us.[67]

Yet for all the clarity of these prayers there is little sense of
sheer wonder or mystery, and only the slightest suggestion of
paradox.

The Methodist Servicebook of England, which appeared in 1975,
precedes the *Sanctus* and *Benedictus* with high praise for God:

Father, all-powerful and ever-living God,
It is indeed right, it is our joy and our salvation,
always and everywhere to give you thanks and praise
through Jesus Christ your Son our Lord.
You created all things and made us in your own image.
When we had fallen into sin, you gave your only Son to be
our Saviour.
He shared our human nature, and died on the cross.
You raised him from the dead, and exalted him to your
right hand in glory, where he lives for ever to pray for us.
Through him you have sent your holy and life-giving Spirit
and made us your people, a royal priesthood,
to stand before you to proclaim your glory and celebrate
your mighty acts.
And so with the company of heaven we join in
the unending hymn of praise:

After the Acclamation, the prayer continues:

We praise you, Lord God, king of the universe. . . .[68]

That prayer concentrates on Creation, Redemption, Resurrection, Christ's perpetual intercession, the gift of the Holy Spirit,

67. *Ibid.,* p. 28.
68. *The Methodist Servicebook* (London: Methodist Publishing House,
1975), pp. 56, 57.

and the priesthood of all believers in an admirable economy of words combined with fidelity to the mighty acts of God.

The American Methodist equivalent rite for the Eucharist stresses the living presence of Christ:

> We experience anew, most merciful God,
> the suffering and death,
> the resurrection and ascension of your Son,
> asking you to accept this our sacrifice of praise and thanksgiving,
> which we offer in union with Christ's offering for us,
> as a living and holy surrender of ourselves.

This is followed immediately by the *epiclesis:*

> Send the power of your Holy Spirit on us,
> gathered here out of love for you, and on these gifts.
> May the Spirit help us know in the breaking of this bread
> and the drinking of this wine the presence of Christ
> who gave his body and blood for all.
> And may the Spirit make us one with Christ,
> one with each other, and one in service to all the world.[69]

The emphasis on the realized presence of Christ is admirable, but it seems odd that shortly after this is affirmed the Holy Spirit is called up to effect it; furthermore, one would hope that the Holy Spirit would be appealed to for the gift of sanctification. On the other hand, the request for strength for service to the world is admirable and a guard against ingrowing and individualistic piety.

This chapter will close with a glance at the ecumenical liturgies of Taizé, of the British Joint Liturgical Group, and the World Council of Churches' Lima Liturgy.

The Liturgy of the Taizé Community precedes the record of the Institution with the *epiclesis:*

69. The prayer comes from the "alternative rite" of the United Methodist Church in the U.S.A. as revised in *We Gather Together* (1980) and is reproduced in Thurian and Wainwright, *op. cit.,* p. 172.

May that Spirit of power today consecrate our eucharist and thus fulfill the word of your beloved Son who wills to give us his body and blood.

The congregation responds to the reading of the Institution Narrative thus:

Great is the mystery of the faith. We proclaim your death, Lord Jesus, we celebrate your resurrection, we await your coming in glory. . . .

As the prayer continues we sense overwhelmingly the power of the presence of the Holy Spirit:

Sanctify your Church as on the day of Pentecost: let the Spirit of holiness lead her into all truth, strengthen her in her mission to the ends of the earth, and prepare her for your eternal kingdom, where we shall share the inheritance of your saints in light, with the Virgin Mary, with the apostles, prophets and martyrs, (with Saint N.); all of us together await the return of your beloved Son: "Come, Lord Jesus!"

All: Maranatha, the Lord is coming![70]

The eucharistic canon of the rite formulated by the British Joint Liturgical Group ends, as it begins, in adoration, and, immediately after the Institution Narrative, proceeds as follows:

Therefore, heavenly Father, obeying the command of your dear Son, and looking for his coming again in glory, we celebrate the perfect sacrifice of his death upon the cross, his mighty resurrection and his glorious ascension.

All: Christ is Victor. Christ is King. Christ is Lord of all.

Father, accept through Christ our sacrifice of thanks and praise:

---

70. The entire prayer is a revision of 1972 made of *The Eucharist of Taizé* (1962) and is reproduced in Thurian and Wainwright, *op. cit.,* p. 182.

and as we eat and drink these holy gifts, kindle in us the fire of your Spirit that with the whole Church on earth and in heaven we may be made one in him. Count us worthy to stand before you as your people and to offer without ceasing our adoration and service, through Jesus Christ our Lord. Through him, with him, and in him, in the unity of the Holy Spirit, all honour and glory are yours, Father Almighty, now and forever.

All: Amen.[71]

The reference to the Holy Spirit as "the fire of your Spirit" is a vivid way of recalling Acts 2:3-5: "And there appeared to them [that is, the apostles at Pentecost] tongues as of fire, distributed and resting on each one of them. And they were all filled with the Holy Spirit and began to speak in other tongues, as the Spirit gave them utterance." Old spooky images of the "Holy Ghost" die hard, and the warmth of the Holy Spirit and its power is better imaged as fire.

The ecumenical Lima Liturgy has many qualities, particularly of many different liturgical strands of many times and countries in an apparently seamless robe. In an admirable *epiclesis,* derived in part from the fourth-century Liturgy of St. James, it reminds us of the work of the Holy Spirit in other than usual aspects of our salvation, and warrants citation:

O God, Lord of the universe, you are holy and your glory is beyond measure. Upon your eucharist send the life-giving Spirit, who spoke by Moses and the Prophets, who overshadowed the Virgin Mary with grace, who descended upon Jesus in the river Jordan and upon the Apostles on the day of

71. See Thurian and Wainwright, *op. cit.,* pp. 182-83. The Group provides two interesting notes. One points out that "as far as possible the mighty acts of God are expressed in terms of present activity rather than as past events," presumably to make them seem more immediately relevant. The second note indicates that the acclamation (which we have cited) is placed after the narrative, not to imply that this is the consecration formula, but to place the acclamation at the end of the *anamnesis,* thus "providing congregational endorsement of what has just been said."

Pentecost. May the outpouring of this Spirit of Fire transfigure this thanksgiving meal that this bread and wine may become for us the body and blood of Christ.

To which the response is:

Veni Creator Spiritus![72]

That is an *epiclesis* that should delight liturgists of the Orthodox Church who insist that the true effect of the presence of the Holy Spirit is to "transfigure" the faithful. The Orthodox Church would also, one may guess, rejoice in the closing Prayer of Thanksgiving, which claims that at the Eucharist the church already tastes — as it were — the *hors d'oeuvres* of the eschatological banquet:

> O Lord, we give you thanks for uniting us by baptism in the Body of Christ and for filling us with joy in the eucharist. Lead us towards the full visible unity of your Church and help us to treasure all the signs of reconciliation you have granted us. Now that we have tasted of the banquet you have prepared for us in the life to come, may we all one day share together the inheritance of the saints in the life of your heavenly city, through Jesus Christ, your Son, our Lord, who lives and reigns with you in the unity of the Holy Spirit, ever one God, world without end.[73]

In concluding this search through the various modern liturgies to see how far they have incorporated the sense of the Eucharist as a profound mystery, the result — if we compare their liturgies with those of the Eastern Orthodox churches — is rather disappointing. But some progress has been achieved. All have prayers that glorify the God whom countless angels adore, ending in the *Sanctus* and *Benedictus,* but few suggest the ineffable nature of God in his Essential Being. There is little of the apophatic in these liturgies. But, and this is some compensation, there is an increasing

72. The first *epiclesis* of two, which we have cited, appears in Thurian and Wainwright, *op. cit.,* p. 253. Thurian is the compiler.
73. *Ibid.,* p. 254.

sense of grateful wonder at the marvelous works of God concentrated in Christ, and in the wonderful preparation God has readied for his own in eternity, though often the threat of the great judgment of Christ is forgotten in modern communion services. But the growth in the celebration of the eschatological is important, and increasingly the appreciation for the role of the Holy Spirit in the Eucharist as the Spirit of Truth, the Sanctifier, the Reconciler and Creator of Peace, and, of course, in the *epiclesis* that has been so frequently copied, the Spirit of Unity and the one who takes the things of Christ and makes them ours — the Consecrator of the Eucharist.

One can only wish that the growing humility of the many churches will encourage in them the wondering recognition of the amazing mystery of our redemption and our celebration of it in the Eucharist. Some of that sense of mystery has been caught in the following poem of John Betjeman, a devout Anglican and English Poet Laureate, which is called "A Lincolnshire Church."

> There, where the white light flickers
> By the white and silver veil,
> A wafer dipped in a wine-drop
> Is the Presence the angels hail,
> Is God who created the Heavens
> And the wide green marsh as well,
> Who sings in the sky with the skylark,
> Who calls in the evening bell,
> Is God who prepared His coming
> With fruit of the earth for His food,
> With stone for building His churches
> And trees for making His rood.[74]

Finally, we must affirm with Schillebeeckx that <u>God is "an identified mystery, which still remains a mystery."</u>[75]

---

74. Cited on p. 85 of Edward Knapp-Fisher, *Eucharist, Many-sided Mystery* (Worthing, Eng.: Churchman Publishing, 1988).

75. Edward Schillebeeckx, *The Understanding of Faith* (New York: Seabury Press, 1974), p. 16.

SEVEN   The Eucharist as Liberation
and Social Justice

THIS ASPECT and interpretation of the Eucharist scandal-
izes both impenitent traditionalists and conservative capitalists. The so-called "liberation theology" unsurprisingly origi-
nated in Central and South America where colonialism, coupled
with violent military dictatorship, has kept the gap yawning
between the rich and the poor most obvious and violently maintained, and is least forgivable. Its pioneering theologian is
Gustavo Gutiérrez, whose book appeared in an English translation in 1973 with the title *A Theology of Liberation* and the subtitle
History, Politics and Salvation.[1]

Gutiérrez correlates the Eucharist with human brotherhood.
He sees the life of Christ as a total self-giving for others, vividly
recalled in the chief sacrament. He also views the Eucharist as
a feast of joy that the church shares and wishes others to share.
Its very reason for existence is to create brotherhood and sisterhood, and its background is the Jewish Passover that celebrates
the liberation from Egypt and the covenant established by God
on Sinai. Furthermore, Gutiérrez acknowledges that liberation
from sin is at the very root of the need for political liberation
and socio-economic justice. Finally, he argues that true communion with God and others presupposes the abolition of all injustice and exploitation.[2]

1. Published by Orbis Books, Maryknoll, New York, which has since
published many similar books of Hispanic theological reflections.
2. Gutiérrez summarizes his views on the Eucharist on pp. 262-65 of
his *The Theology of Liberation*.

180

Gutiérrez states unflinchingly the case that charity is not enough, and that true compassion demands revolutionary action. And he sees all this as a legitimate consequence of a true understanding of *koinonia*.[3] This term, translated "community," has a triple sense. It signifies the common ownership of the goods necessary for human existence, and is backed by the citation: "Never forget to show kindness and to share what you have with others, for such are the sacrifices which God approves" (Heb. 13:16; cf. Acts 2:44 and 4:32). It is exemplified as "a concrete gesture of fraternal charity," for St. Paul uses this term to denote the collection made for the poor Christians of Jerusalem (2 Cor. 9:13; cf. 2 Cor. 8:3-4 and Rom. 15:26-27). Because of this collection the Corinthian Christians are said to give glory to God through their "liberal contribution to their need and to the general Good" (2 Cor. 9:13; cf. 2 Cor. 8:3-4; Rom. 15:26-37). Second, *koinonia* signifies the union of the faithful with Christ in the Eucharist: "When we bless 'the cup of blessing,' is it not a means of sharing in the blood of Christ? When we break the bread, is it not a means of sharing in the body of Christ?" (I Cor. 10:16). Thirdly, *koinonia* means the union of Christians with the Holy Trinity: "The grace of the Lord Jesus Christ, and the love of God, and fellowship in the Holy Spirit, be with you all" (2 Cor. 13:14; cf. Phil. 2:1).[4] Finally, Gutiérrez warns: "Without a real commitment against exploitation and alienation and for a society of solidarity and justice, the Eucharistic celebration is an empty action, lacking any genuine endorsement by those who participate in it."[5]

Now we must recognize as a fundamental characteristic of liberation theology its emphasis on *praxis,* a term that is borrowed from Marx. It demands that reflection on the socio-

---

3. He borrows from Yves Congar, with acknowledgment, the threefold implication of the New Testament term *koinonia*.

4. Gutiérrez also uses the following New Testament references: for union with God the Father — I John 1:6; for union with God the Son — I Cor. 1:9; cf. I John 1:3; and for union with the Holy Spirit — II Corinthians 13:14 (the Trinitarian Blessing).

5. *Op. cit.,* p. 265.

economic situation of the wretched poor calls for revolutionary action. Furthermore, it stresses that the poor themselves, as well as the priests who serve them for Christ's sake, must be involved in challenging the political *status quo* so that it does not remain *ante*, but improved, often at the cost of great sacrifice. This sometimes involves "protest masses" and often requires prophetical sermons.

This emphasis on action is admirably expounded in the third chapter, "How Liberation Theology is Done," of a book written by Leonardo and Clodovis Boff, *Introducing Liberation Theology* (1987). The first stage requires a living commitment to the poor, and at its highest level means living "*permanently* with the people, making [one's] home among the people, living and working alongside the people."[6]

The analysis of the situation of the poor requires attempts to find out not only why the poor are oppressed and what God's plans are for the poor, but also what is the appropriate form of action. The poor are "the dispossessed masses on the peripheries of cities and in rural areas" in the third world. Liberationists reject the empirical explanation that sees poverty as vice, the result of laziness, ignorance, or sheer evil, and they reject the suggestion that the answer is aid because that merely treats the poor as pitiable and postpones a radical solution. Liberationists also reject the functional explanation that poverty is due to backwardness and requires reform interpreted as an improvement of the present system, because this is a mere palliative. Instead, Liberationists accept the dialectical explanation that interprets poverty as oppression, since it is "the product of the economic organization of society itself, which *exploits* some — the workers — and *excludes* others from the production process — the underemployed, and all those marginalized in one way or another."[7] This envisages

6. *Introducing Liberation Theology,* translated from the Portuguese by Paul Burns (Maryknoll, NY: Orbis Books, 1987), is the work of Franciscans, Leonardo and Clodovis Boff. The reference is to p. 23.

7. *Ibid.,* pp. 26-27. At this point the Boffs refer to chapter 3 of Pope Paul II's encyclical *Laborem Exercens,* where the Pontiff defines the root of

poverty as both a collective and conflictive phenomenon, requiring an alternative system. It asserts that the way out of the present system is revolution, radical change of such a nature that the poor are no longer objects but stand up as subjects.[8]

The Boffs openly acknowledge that liberation theology "uses Marxism purely as an *instrument*." But they add immediately: "It does not venerate it as it venerates the gospel."[9] Liberationists also include in their conception of "the poor" those who are penalized by the present system, such as blacks, indigenous peoples, and women in a patriarchal society. They feel acutely all the disadvantages the poor are experiencing, including debt, dependence, exposure, anonymity, contempt, and humiliation.

Where then does the theological component enter into their thinking? The Boffs insist that the poor are rightly to be seen as "the Disfigured Son of God," by which they mean that the poor are the disfigured image of God. Furthermore, they empathize with the Son of God made the suffering servant and rejected, as well as with the memorial of the poor and persecuted Nazarene. Finally, they enter profoundly into the sacrament of the Lord and Judge of history.[10]

This means that liberation hermeneutics consciously looks at the Bible as a way of seeing the oppression/liberation process with the illumination of faith. This, they admit, is not the only way of interpreting the Bible, but they insist that it is the appropriate and relevant way of interpretation in the third world. To quote the Boffs: "From the heart of the great revelation in the Bible, it draws the most enlightening and eloquent themes that speak to the poor; God the father of life and advocate of the oppressed, liberation from the house of bondage, the prophecy of a new world, the kingdom given to the poor, the church as total sharing."[11]

---

the situation as the supremacy of capital — enjoyed by the few — over labor — practiced by the many.

8. *Ibid.*, p. 27.

9. *Ibid.*, p. 31.

10. *Ibid.*

11. *Ibid.*, p. 32.

In a book written in 1989, Leonardo Boff expounded more fully his Christology and his interpretation of the Resurrection. Its title is *Faith on the Edge,* and its subtitle is *Religion and Marginalized Existence.* He projects a view of Christ as the liberator, not Christ as the celestial monarch, nor the defeated, suffering Christ of popular piety:

> All of the deeds, words, and attitudes of Jesus implying a call to conversion and a change in relationships — his position vis-a-vis the marginalized of the Palestinian Society of his time, his preference for the poor, his conflicts with the religious and social status quo of his place and time, the political content of his proclamation of the Reign of God, the reasons for his execution — acquire a special relevance and make up the image of a Jesus who is liberator.[12]

In the same book, Boff's interpretation of the Resurrection also stresses its relevance for the marginalized, for it manifests that to die for others and for God, as Jesus did, is not without significance, for the anonymous deaths of the defeated who gave their lives for the sake of justice find their explanation in Jesus' vindication by the Father. It is the proof, to cite M. Horkheimer, that "the hangman does not triumph over the victim."[13]

One of the most recent statements of the pioneer of liberation theology, Gustavo Gutiérrez, sums up his thought two decades after his first theology.[14] This essay rejoices in the fact that theology is being done outside the customary European and North American confines, and thus Amerindian, Black, and Hispanic theologians are examining the "preferential option for the poor" and oppression, including the reduced status of women. Thus, there are liberation theologians in the United

12. *Faith on the Edge* (San Francisco: Harper & Row, 1989), p. 125.
13. *Ibid.,* p. 141. Boff, with acknowledgment, cites M. Horkheimer, *Die Sehnsucht dem ganz Anderen* (Hamburg, 1972), p. 62.
14. The opening essay of Marc H. Ellis and Otto Maduro, eds., *Expanding the View: Gustavo Gutiérrez and the Future of Liberation Theology* (Maryknoll, NY: Orbis Books, 1989).

States as well as in Africa, Asia, and the South Pacific. Gutiérrez insists that from the beginning the term "preferential option for the poor" was intended to deny all exclusiveness and to express solidarity with those whom we should first seek out. In his own words, "I insisted that the great challenge was to maintain both the universality of God's love and God's predilection for those on the lowest rung of the ladder of history."[15]

Then Gutiérrez develops three levels of liberation: first, liberation from social situations of oppression and marginalization; second, a personal transformation by which we live with profound inner freedom in the face of every kind of servitude; and third and last, "there is the liberation from sin, which attacks the deepest root of servitude; for sin is the breaking of friendship with God and with other human beings, and therefore cannot be eradicated except by the unmerited redemptive love of God whom we receive by faith and in communion with one another."[16] In the same volume Leonardo Boff writes of the deep spirituality of Gutiérrez, and of the drastic opposition he has faced from conservatives in the Vatican, who are characterized by a clerical and hierarchical view of the church that separates the church from the world, the sacred from the profane, and the supernatural from the natural, and that emphasizes the church as mystery rather than as the people of God. He shows how poor yet how profoundly spiritual his friend's life is: "He shares the hardships of the area he belongs to and out of which he develops his theological reflection. . . . In the midst of immense historical and social challenges he has been able to confront personal challenges: the hostility of his own brothers in the faith [Franciscan friars] and persecution by sectors of the church in his own country, Peru, and by the doctrinal authorities of the Vatican."[17] The book closes with an essay by Pablo Richard, who speaks of the new "ecclesial base communities"

15. *Ibid.*, p. 15.
16. *Ibid.*, p. 25.
17. *Ibid.*, p. 47.

that enable the poor to participate in a new language, a new symbolism, a new rhythm, new liturgical forms, and a new reading of the Bible. The essay ends by making the proud claim: "Liberation theology is perhaps the most mature product of the process of decolonization and de-Westernization in the church. Liberation theology's future is also linked to this process."[18]

Our concern will eventually be to offer both appreciation and criticism of liberation theology, especially as it refers to the Eucharist, which the brilliant liberationist theologian of Sri Lanka, Tissa Balasuriya, has expounded so illuminatingly.[19] In the meantime, one cannot pass by the apparent strength of the liberation insistence upon Christian compassion, and, as we shall shortly see, the strong biblical elements in their theology, the courage of the priests who defend and support the poor against the defiance and often violence of the rich, and their insistence on the central aspect of sharing in Holy Communion. At the same time the demurrers among the conservatives also have shown their mettle in complaining that the political has overwhelmed the transcendental aspects of the Christian faith, neglected the fact that Christ has already redeemed the world although his Kingdom has indeed yet to come in its fullness, and "kenoticized" (emptied) the human Jesus of Nazareth to such a degree that his Incarnation is virtually ignored, making him merely the rebel of Nazareth. They note that the sacrifice of the cross is merely an example of gross injustice, bravely faced, and the Resurrection a more just verdict on his life, without any accompanying assurance of everlasting life for the faithful of every social class who are penitent and compassionate.

In what follows we shall examine the biblical and patristic foundations, or at least supports, claimed to undergird the liberation theology, and look at the same time for both exegesis and eisegesis, for every theology has the possible pitfall before

18. *Op. cit.*, conclusion of Section 50.
19. Balasuriya's book is *The Eucharist and Human Liberation* (Maryknoll, NY: Orbis Books, 1979).

it of reading into the text what was not intended by its writer or redactor.

Biblical and Patristic Support for Liberation Theology

At the outset one would expect little support for so political an expression of Christianity, since its Master declared before Pilate: "My kingdom does not belong to this world. If it did, my followers would be fighting to save me from arrest from the Jews; my kingly authority comes from elsewhere."[20] In fact, however, there is much in support of the concern for social justice and the demand to assist the poor, the sick, the lame, the blind, and all social misfits as an expression of love for the neighbor, which is the test of true love for God.

God's concern for his people miserably dragged down and defeated in body and spirit is found in his magisterial delivery of them from slavery under their Egyptian taskmasters into the freedom of the great trek to the promised land, celebrated each year in the commemoration of the Passover.

Balasuriya insists that the liberation of the Jews from Egypt prefigures the liberation of mankind in Christ. In *The Eucharist and Human Liberation* he highlights God's judgment on irrelevant sacrifices in Isaiah 1:11-17 and Isaiah 58:4-8, connects it with the blindness to justice cited in Micah 3:1-3 and 6:9-11, and sums it up in the striking words of the prophet Micah in 6:7-8.

> "What shall I bring when I approach the LORD?
> How shall I stoop before God on high?
> Am I to approach him with whole-offerings or yearling
>   calves?
> Will the LORD accept thousands of rams or ten thousand
>   rivers of oil?

20. John 18:36. For a sense of the striking relevance of the Bible for the liberationists, see Robert McAfee Brown, *Unexpected News: Reading the Bible with Third World Eyes* (Philadelphia: Westminster Press, 1984).

Shall I offer my eldest son for my own wrong-doing?
   my children for my own sin?

God has told you what is good;
   and what is it that the LORD asks of you?
Only to act justly, to love loyalty,
   and to walk wisely before your God."

The prophetic denunciations of unethical or hypocritical forms of worship were renewed by Jesus when, for example, he overturned the tables of the money-changers in the Temple and charged them with turning his Father's house into a den of thieves.

Balasuriya insists that Jesus contested male domination in religion. Far from having no contact with women, Jesus was friendly with them, included them among his followers, and even befriended women of ill repute such as the Samaritan woman who had had five husbands and Mary Magdalene, supposedly a former prostitute, who were among the first to evangelize others. Moreover, Christ's injunction against divorce was in fact a defense of the rights of women, who earlier could be easily repudiated by their husbands. Furthermore, it was to faithful women who stood by the cross that Jesus first revealed himself after his resurrection.[21]

Moreover, it is a proof of the communitarianism of Jesus that he told the Parable of the Good Samaritan, for Samaritans were looked down upon by the Jews as inferior, and yet it is the Samaritan who shows genuine charity by bandaging the wounds of the robbed and stricken man, lifting him on his own horse and paying for him at the inn, while the Jewish priest simply passed by on the other side.[22] Clearly, it is the undesirable man who is our neighbor in Christ's understanding.

While Jewish prayers taught the devout to think of God in august terms as Lord, Creator, King, and Sovereign Master,

21. *The Eucharist and Human Liberation,* pp. 56 and 54.
22. Luke 10:25-37.

Christ taught his followers to think of him in filial terms so that God, as in the Lord's Prayer, was acknowledged to be their Father and the Father of all humanity, rejecting all discrimination in the form of race, gender, or status. It was this combination of universality and intimacy of approach that was so new. If God's holiness is to be acknowledged more and more, that includes his justice to all, for he is against all victimization of the poor and weak. As for the plea for the coming of God's kingdom, this can mean the final eschatological consummation of all things in God, but since the prayer includes the petitions "Thy kingdom come" and "Thy will be done on earth as it is is in heaven," it also asks for the values revealed by Jesus to be actualized here on earth. Balasuriya sees a radical mystique in the Lord's Prayer, for here is a "fine combination of revolutionary commitment and love for all. . . . Forgiveness has to be a liberation of both oppressor and oppressed in a transformed relationship."[23] The strange petition "Do not lead us to the test but deliver us from evil" is interpreted as a prayer like that of Jesus on the Mount of Olives, since "we can so easily succumb to the selfishness of seeking special privileges of all types: of race, creed, color, class, sex, position." Finally, Balasuriya sees the Lord's Prayer as it is, a "masterpiece of Jesus' revelation of the fatherhood of God and of human solidarity. It explains why Jesus contested all forms of evil prevailing in his day and helped in the integral liberation of persons." The same author then relates the death of Christ to the Eucharist by adding, "That is why he was killed. His body and blood were given for others in this cause. It is what he invites us to do when we meet him in the Eucharist. 'Do this in remembrance of me.'"[24] Balasuriya concludes his chapter on the Lord's Prayer by quoting the prayer of Kim Chi Ha, a well-known Christian poet, from his Declaration of Conscience smuggled out of prison:

23. *The Eucharist and Human Liberation*, p. 71.
24. *Ibid.*

As you cannot go to heaven alone,
Food is to be shared. . . .
As all share the light of the heavenly stars,
So food is something that must be shared. . . .
Ah, food is something that must be shared.

As for the petition "Give us this day our daily bread," this is clearly communitarian, whether it is interpreted as "Give us today the food we need" or "Give us the bread today we need tomorrow," for it stresses the need for *our*, not *my*, daily bread. And the liberation theologian is constrained to add: "Food cannot be ensured for all persons regularly . . . unless the socio-economic and political structures of our societies have a minimum of efficiency and justice."[25]

Furthermore, in Matthew 25:31-46 Jesus makes it plain that it is compassion for the hungry, or thirsty, or strangers, or sick or those in prison that will determine one's destiny in the divine judgment at the end of history, and Luke's entire gospel concentrates on Christ's compassion and his challenge to the socio-economic and political values and attitudes of his time. His communitarian spirit is admirably expressed in the many invitations to the poor and the socially and economically despised to join him in table-fellowship.

We reach some cloudier exegesis when we consider their treatment of the death of Jesus, for they view it not as a reconciliation between God the Father and humanity and as an act of redemption for the sins of the world, but exclusively, it appears, as an example of radical social injustice in Pilate's willingness to have Christ crucified in the place of a common murderer. Rafael Avila links crucifixion and resurrection in this unfamiliar manner: ". . . the Eucharist . . . is not the proclamation of the natural death of Christ but of the socio-political injustice by which Christ was put to death." For this interpretation he employs Acts 3:13 and 15, and his conclusion is: "To celebrate the Eucharist, therefore, is

25. *Ibid.*, p. 169.

to affirm the act by which the Father radically negated the injustice resulting from the sin of the world, and to proclaim publicly the injustice committed against the Just One, not simply that it may be exposed and denounced, but primarily to collaborate with the Father in the resurrection (affirmation) of those affected by injustice (negation)."[26] One senses here that a political interpretation has completely overshadowed and therefore obscured any theological interpretation of the central event of the Christic saga.

The profound concern of the liberationists for *sharing* is better grounded in the life of the apostolic church, where there is much less text-straining. Clearly, the cheerful community was a genuine *koinonia*, a community where everybody had everything in common; indeed, theirs was an utopian Christian communalism. Acts 2:44-47 record the following: "And all who believed were together and had all things in common; and they sold their possessions and goods and distributed them to all, as any had need. And day by day, attending the temple together and breaking bread in their homes, they partook of food with glad and generous hearts, praising God and having favor with all the people. And the Lord added to their number day by day those who were being saved." Communalism it was, and utopian, but it was not long before the unitive and generous spirit was broken.

Perhaps communalism was never fully established in Corinth because it is there that St. Paul excoriates the greedy wealthy members of the church because they rush to eat their own food and do not divide and share it with the poor. Avila claims that the unavoidable conclusion is that "if the bread is not shared, the supper of the Lord is not celebrated." He adds, almost savagely, "A church that refuses to share the bread is — rather than the body of the Lord — a 'den of thieves.' It nullifies, therefore, its verbal witness by its actions."[27]

Clearly, the Eucharist was more than a devotional action, and certainly not an act of individual piety; it was community

26. Rafael Avila, *Worship and Politics* (Maryknoll, NY: Orbis Books, 1981), p. 48.
27. *Ibid.*, p. 57.

devotion. Thus any division among believers was systematically denounced, as in the early prayer:

> Just as this loaf was previously scattered on the mountains, and when it was gathered together it became an unity, so may your church be gathered from the end of the earth into your kingdom.[28]

St. Justin Martyr signaled that an important part of the Eucharist was the Offertory, when Christians brought offerings, each as generously as he or she could, in order to assist "the orphans and widows, and those who are in want because of sickness or other cause, and those who are in bonds [prisoners], and, in short, . . . all those in need."[29]

The Eucharist in the mid-second century was a devotional communal act with a strong social component in which Christians shared their possessions with the needy, and this was an act central to the celebration, not an optional extra. Like St. Paul, St. Cyprian, bishop of Carthage, who was beheaded in 258 for his fidelity to the faith, denounced the rich for their insensitivity and meanness toward the poor, denying them the right to Holy Communion unless they made an offering for the poor: "Do you rich and wealthy," he cried, "think that you celebrate the Lord's feast, you who do not at all consider the offering, who come to the Lord's feast without a sacrifice, who take part in the sacrifice that the poor person has offered?"[30] Moreover, bishops like St. Ambrose of Milan and St. Basil of Caesarea rejected the offerings of the high and mighty if they had murdered citizens, however brutal their threats against the clergy might be, because only the penitent are invited to Christ's table. The Eucharist, it was constantly stressed, was the mark of liberty, the offering made, not by slaves, but by the free. Furthermore,

---

28. *The Didache* 9.4.

29. *Apology* 1.67.6.

30. The Cyprian citation comes from Treatise 8.15, *On Works and Almsgiving,* and the Chrysostom citation from *Homilies on 2 Corinthians,* 20.

one can hardly overstress the extraordinary fraternity and sorority expressed by these ancient Christians as they transcended in their membership barriers of race, nationality, class, economy, and gender. It was not sarcasm, but a tribute that fair-minded observers remarked: "How these Christians love one another!"

Much as there is to endorse and imitate in insisting on the demand for social justice on the part of Christians and making it an essential part of the understanding of the Eucharist, it seems to this writer to be going too far to interpret the resurrection of Christ in exclusively socio-political terms. Avila's interpretation is a case in point:

> Returning Jesus to life, which the powerful of his time had taken from him, the Father "topples the powerful from their throne," annihilating the worst they could do to the struggle for justice. The annihilation (negation) thus placed in the hands of all those who had been wronged the most powerful weapon to continue the struggle. The resurrection is, therefore, the ultimate basis for rebellion.[31]

Such a statement indeed seems to make a shadow of sense for those critics who claim that the extreme theological liberationists make Jesus into the John the Baptist of Karl Marx and turn the Gospel of Mark into the Gospel of Marx — *Das Kapital*.

On the whole, however, apart from the last example of eisegesis, the liberation theologians interpret fairly their sense of the relevant portions of the Old and New Testaments, as well as apt passages from the early fathers.

Occasionally, as we might have guessed from the proud claim of Pablo Richard, the liberation theologians exaggerate in claiming that their theology is totally unique and wholly different from the theologies of Europe and North America. Therefore, for the next section we have deliberately chosen a modest title, "Glimpses," to indicate that these European or American theologians who emphasize the social and often the socio-economic

31. Avila, *Worship and Politics,* p. 71.

implications of Christianity were their ancestors, whether they like it or not. But few previous theologians have emulated them in using the analysis of Marx so dialectically in conjunction with a Christian social application lacking in the Communist analysis.

Western Glimpses of the Social
Implications of the Eucharist

Liberation theology is generally associated with the prophetic priests of third world countries, especially in Central and South America, so that it is often forgotten that they had their predecessors not only in the Bible and in the early fathers of the church, but also in nineteenth-century theologians in both Britain and the United States, as well as elsewhere in Europe.

It is worth remembering who some of them were. In the Anglican Broad Church there were the "Christian socialists," including their leader, Frederick Denison Maurice, who insisted that the Eucharist should summon not mere individuals, but would-be sharers of this common Holy Communion meal. Hence he wrote, inviting them to join the Christian family:

> Come, then, brother man, not as a fine, dainty, selfish epicure, to seek some special and solitary blessings for yourself; but come as one of a family, to seize a common food which is given to all, a sacrifice which has been offered for all. Come, and eat it in haste, with your shoes on your feet and your staff in your hand, as a man who has a journey before him and work in hand, as a pilgrim, not as a philosopher. But again: eat it, all of you, as risen men, as spiritual creatures; not as those who are peeping into the ground and muttering, to ask the aid of some familiar spirit; not as those who come with cowardly prostration before a daemon whose favour they are bribing; but as those who have their habitation and their polity with Christ, their Representative and Intercessor.[32]

32. F. D. Maurice, *Theological Essays* (originally published in 1853; the

The Tractarians, too, combined their sacramental views with a deep sense of commitment to the poor and oppressed in industrial cities of England such as Leeds, where Edward Pusey, after John Henry Newman left Oxford for Rome, exercised a ministry acutely aware of and compassionate toward the marginalized folk. Their successors, the Anglo-Catholics, wore themselves down to the bone for the oppressed and underprivileged in the East End of London. One of the most famous Anglo-Catholics, Frank Weston, Bishop of Zanzibar, raised the roof in his plea to the Congress of 1923 with the following searing words: "And it is folly — it is madness — to suppose that you can worship Jesus in the Sacraments and Jesus on the throne of glory, when you are sweating him in the souls and bodies of his children. It cannot be done. . . . Go out and look for Jesus in the ragged, in the naked, in the oppressed and sweated, in those who have lost hope, in those who are struggling to make good. Look for Jesus. And when you see him, gird yourselves with his towel and try to wash their feet."[33] He, surely, belongs to the company of Mother Teresa of Calcutta!

Not many years later the Anglican Archbishop William Temple said that one might ask "whether cut-throat competition is not in the same category of disorder as the cutting of throats" and concluded that, according to Christian presuppositions, "in place of the conception of the Power-State we are led to that of the Welfare-State."[34]

---

reference is to the republication of 1957, introduced by S. C. Carpenter, p. 194).

33. "Our Present Duty," in *The Report of the Anglo-Catholic Congress* (London, 1923), pp. 185-86.

34. William Temple, *Citizen and Churchman* (London: Eyre and Spottiswoode, 1947). The citations are respectively from p. 32 and p. 30. See also chapter 3 of Dr. Karen Heetderks Strong's 1991 Drew University Ph.D. dissertation, "Redemption as a Key to the Nature of the Church and its Social Role in the Theology of Frederick Denison Maurice and William Temple." See also the Rev. Dr. David McIlhiney's admirable account of the Anglican Church's work in the East End of London, showing that Broad Churchmen and Evangelicals as well as High Churchmen were involved: *A Gentleman in Every Slum: Church of England Missions in East London, 1837-1914* (Allison Park, PA: Pickwick Publications, 1988).

Possibly the earliest English liberation theologian was Bishop J. A. T.

Nor should the contribution of the French worker-priests of the present century be forgotten as precursors of the liberation theologians. It was they who familiarized the worldwide Roman Catholic Church with a socio-economic emphasis that was formulated in the theology of the important Vatican II Council.

One can also point with admiration to the North American exponents of the "Social Gospel," including the Baptists Walter Rauschenbusch and Harry Emerson Fosdick, the Methodist Frank Mason North, the Congregationalist Washington Gladden, the Unitarian Francis Greenwood Peabody, and the memorable Benedictine Virgil Michel, to demonstrate that others beside Anglicans were aware of the social and economic implications of the gospel. Nonetheless, the fact remains that it is the martyrs of the American Hispanic world who are the most striking witnesses to liberation theology. They include Archbishop Ernesto Romero of El Salvador, assassinated while celebrating the Eucharist because he had urged the death squad soldiers to end the killing of their own people, the three Maryknoll nuns who ministered to orphaned, refugee children, who were tortured and killed for this service, and some years later the six Jesuits and their housekeeper, also in El Salvador, who were murdered by death squads. These are God's witnesses to the desperate need for a liberating theology that will create a more just social order and give freedom and life in place of slavery and slow death to the forgotten. We can anticipate the communion of saints when we learn that "when the names of those killed by the Contras were called out during the Eucharist in Nicaragua, the priest would call out 'Present at the altar.'"[35] These men and women who accept mortal risk are indeed determined to accept Christ's challenge to take up their cross and be worthy disciples of his (Matt. 10:38).

Robinson, as is manifested in his innovative book *Honest to God* (1963), where he declares: "The test of worship is how far it makes us *more sensitive* to the 'beyond in our midst', to the Christ in the hungry, the naked, the homeless, and the prisoner."

35. Reported during a sermon preached by the Rev. Professor Gibson Winter at Trinity Episcopal Church, Princeton, New Jersey, April 21, 1991.

The death of Christ, apart from its salvific and thus its dominant concern, is seen by liberation theologians as the grossest instance of injustice on Pilate's part, preferring, at the behest of the Jewish authorities, to spare a murderer and send an innocent, maligned man to crucifixion. But they also see the Resurrection as God's rectification of injustice. Their stress should make all comfortable Christians aware of the sacrificial nature of the Eucharist and its socio-economic implications for those who would be faithful to Christ's insistence that we love him in the deprived neighbor.

It must also be recognized that it is through the Roman Catholic theologians such as Gutiérrez and Avila, Leonardo Boff and Tissa Balasuriya, that the social, economic, and political implications of the Eucharist have been recognized. But there have been many others, theologians with a profound sense of practical compassion. They include, among Europeans, two Germans, Fr. Johann Baptist Metz,[36] with his insistence on "subversive memory" in the Eucharist, and Jürgen Moltmann,[37] the theologian of hope, as well as the French priest J.-R. M. Tillard[38] and the English Catholic Nicholas Lash.[39] The many American priests sensitive to liberation theology include the Franciscan Kenneth R. Himes,[40] the Je-

36. See his *Faith in History and Society* (New York: Seabury Press, 1984). In it he argues that the eucharistic *anamnesis* provides "a dangerous memory of freedom" calling into question the present social order and rekindling hope through Christ's Passion and Resurrection.
37. See his widely read *Theology of Hope* (London: S.P.C.K., 1967), which in part reflects the insights of Ernst Bloch, the so-called "warm Communist."
38. See his "la triple dimension du signe sacramental," in *Nouvelle Revue Theologique,* vol. 83 (1961), pp. 225-54.
39. See Lash's book *His Presence in the World: A Study in Eucharistic Worship and Theology* (London: Sheed and Ward, 1968).
40. See his "Eucharist and Justice: Assessing the Legacy of Virgil Michel," in *Worship,* vol. 62 (1988), pp. 201-24. The present author is immensely grateful to this Franciscan friar and friend for his recommendation of several significant books on liberation theology, and rejoices that both were contemporary researchers at Princeton's Center of Theological Inquiry in 1991.

suit Edward J. Kilmartin,[41] the coauthors Jesuit James L. Empereur and Dominican Christopher G. Kiesling,[42] and Fr. David N. Power.[43] Three remarkable women of the Catholic Church who have written books on almost the same theme are Mary Collins the Benedictine,[44] Monika Hellwig,[45] and the feminist Elisabeth Schüssler Fiorenza.[46] An important early backer of the liberationists was the American Presbyterian clergyman, Robert McAfee Brown.[47] Other Protestant writers emphasizing liberationist themes in their biblical exegesis are Walter Brueggemann of the United Church of Christ[48] and the Mennonite John Howard Yoder.[49]

41. See his chapter, "The Sacrifice of Thanksgiving and Social Justice," in Mark Searle, ed., *Liturgy and Social Justice* (Collegeville, MN: The Liturgical Press, 1980), and his "A Modern Approach to the Word of God and Sacraments of Christ: Perspectives and Principles," in F. A. Eigo, ed., *The Sacraments: God's Love and Mercy Actualized* (Villanova, PA: Villanova University Press, 1979), pp. 64ff.

42. Their joint book is *The Liturgy That Does Justice* (Collegeville, MN: The Liturgical Press, 1990).

43. See especially his *Unsearchable Riches: The Symbolic Nature of Liturgy* (New York: Pueblo Publishing Company, 1984), and the second item in footnote 44.

44. See "Eucharist and Justice," in *Worship: Renewal to Practise* (Washington, D.C.: The Pastoral, 1987). Sister Mary Collins, O.S.B., coedited with Father David Power, *Can We always Celebrate the Eucharist?* (*Concilium* 152; New York: Seabury Press, 1982).

45. See her book *The Eucharist and the Hunger of the World* (New York: Paulist Press, 1976).

46. Since feminism is a protest against male chauvinism in the churches as in the world, a form of long-standing oppression, a corrective was needed and is supplied by her book *In Memory of Her* (New York: Crossroad Publishing Co., 1983), which emphasizes the role of women, and points both to the mother of Christ and the first witnesses testifying to the Resurrection.

47. See his *Theology in a New Key: Responding to Liberation Themes* (Philadelphia: Westminster Press, 1978); *Gustavo Gutiérrez* (Richmond, VA: John Knox Press, 1980); and *Unexpected News: Reading the Bible with Third World Eyes* (Philadelphia: Westminster Press, 1984).

48. *The Prophetic Imagination* (Philadelphia: Fortress Press, 1978) is an admirable account of prophetic criticism and prophetic enablement.

49. *The Politics of Jesus* (Grand Rapids, MI: Wm. B. Eerdmans, 1972) is an unconventional approach to its theme and shows the radical attitude to debts and property dues forgiven in the Jubilee year, which occurred every fifty years in Israel.

Criticisms of Liberation Theology

It is hardly surprising that so radically social and economic an approach, which claims that it is the authentic gospel of Christ, has elicited acrimonious as well as occasionally thoughtful constructive criticism. One of the earliest critics bears the same surname as the founder of liberation theology: he is Fr. Juan Gutiérrez, author of *The New Liberation Gospel.*[50] Essentially, he argues that Gustavo Gutiérrez has virtually lost the vertical dimension in theology because of his dominant, if not exclusive, concern for the horizontal or sociological aspect, describing it as "an encounter between faith and sociology" more generously on page 36, but thirty pages later insisting that Marxism determines the other Gutiérrez's understanding of both the gospel and the Bible. A variation of the criticism is that the priest he criticizes makes charity more important than the Christian love of God.[51]

A whole coterie of critics of liberation theology combined to produce, under the editorship of Ronald Nash, a volume entitled *Liberation Theology.*[52] The editor insists that their choice of socialism for the intended economic betterment of the oppressed masses is mistaken, for "in promoting the violent means of exchange, they have taken a path that will not only deny their people bread but also deprive them of liberty," and it is ironic to call such a movement *liberation* theology.[53] Michael Novak echoes the same point: "Choosing the utopian road, they seem to imitate the Grand Inquisitor, who out of pity for the people promised bread, not liberty."[54] Carl F. H. Henry says that "God becomes merely a co-worker in an essentially man-centered program," but acknowledges that evangelicals must "stand firmly for a championing of the gospel's irreducible relevance for

50. Published by the Franciscan Herald Press of Chicago in 1977; its subtitle is *Pitfalls of the Theology of Liberation*.

51. These criticisms were made in the above order on pp. 36, 66ff., and 78.

52. Published by Mott Media in 1984.

53. *Liberation Theology*, p. 66.

54. *Ibid.*, p. 43.

oppressed multitudes, and in places of human exploitation and oppression we must actively identify evangelical Christianity with the justice that God demands." He concludes on a note of anxiety: "While the church of Christ may well be disconcerted that it took Christianity almost nineteen centuries to eradicate slavery, the whole world should be terrified, as missionary church historian Samuel H. Moffet notes, that it took communism only a single generation to bring it back."[55]

Richard John Neuhaus argues that "while Gutiérrez proposes the church as a recruitment office for the revolution" out of a pastoral concern for the poor, yet he might more wisely get an agreement among Christians to be rid of various forms of oppression. For Christians who differ as to the means of accomplishment would merely commit themselves to a revolutionary solution that could bring in another set of socialist rulers who would dominate the masses in a new form of slavery. Citing Galatians 3:28, Neuhaus affirms with Paul that in Christ Jesus "There is neither Jew nor Greek, there is neither slave nor free, there is neither male nor female," but adds "there is neither bourgeoisie nor proletariat." His conclusion is that it is the church's duty "not to be silent about injustice, nor to apotheosize particular manifestations of the revolutionary struggle." His reason for the decision is "the modesty appropriate to our placement in history, to absolutize any alternative to the kingdom [of God], anything short of the kingdom."[56]

---

55. *Ibid.;* both citations come from p. 202.
56. *Ibid.,* pp. 226, 235, and 232, in this order.
It is interesting that the Anglican Archbishop of Canterbury, William Temple, who believed strongly in protesting against injustice but supported the kind of justice that is approximated in a welfare state, who insisted that since Christians disagreed on policy and party lines, they shouldn't divide the Christian community by insisting that there is only one Christian solution, or Christian party policy. In defense of this view, he wrote that this is because it allows "plenty of room for honest difference of opinion as regards the best way to apply Christian principles to actual conditions" (quoted from *Personal Religion and the Life of Fellowship* [London: Longmans, Green and Co., 1926], p. 77). It is extremely doubtful that he would, in the Latin American situation, take the side of the military dictatorship since he was a convinced socialist, but definitely not a Marxist.

The substantial basis of all these criticisms is that while oppression must be overcome, it is not by accepting a single utopian and materialistic philosophy such as Marxist analysis, to which Christianity is added. Such a program cannot be identified with the Kingdom of God.

Two sympathetic yet balanced critics of liberation theology are Schubert M. Ogden, author of *Faith and Freedom: Toward a Theology of Liberation,* and Durwood Foster, who has a concise and impressive essay entitled "A Critical Reflection on the Theologies of Liberation" assessing their strengths and weaknesses.[57] Ogden's approach is philosophical and religious, as is appropriate for a process thinker, while Foster's is an almost exclusively theological approach. Their critiques will conclude this section of the chapter.

Ogden argues that liberationists produce testimonies rather than rounded systematic theologies, for they are rationalizations of socio-economic and political positions already adopted. He also maintains that these theologians do not consider the metaphysical being of God, but only God in relation to us. His hardest cut of all, however, is the assertion that they identify or confuse two entirely different kinds of liberation — *redemption* and *emancipation.* The former is liberation "from death, transience, and sin attested by the apostolic witness," while the latter is "emancipation from bondage called for by the various movements for human freedom — political, economic, cultural, racial, and sexual." Further, he asks: Which is primary in their theological methodology? His fourth criticism is that liberationists have typically "too restricted or provincial an understanding of the various forms of bondage from which men and women, as well as their fellow creatures, need to be emancipated." Finally, Ogden points out that to take the historical Jesus (not the apostolic witness to Christ) as the foundation of Christology is a mistaken theo-

57. Ogden's book was republished in a revised and enlarged edition by Abingdon Press, Nashville, Tennessee, in 1989, and Durwood Foster's concisely clarifying essay appeared in Deane William Ferm, ed., *Liberation Theology, North American Style* (New York: Vertizon, 1987), pp. 1-12.

logical foundation from which to build, and is typically liberal.[58]

Durwood Foster insists at the outset that the new theological
voices of our time are sounding Christ's declaration of his own
mission, namely, "to set at liberty those who are oppressed" (Luke
4:18), a theme that established theology had forgotten, despite the
"dehumanizing blight of racism, sexism, and economic exploitation." Liberation theology has raised the protest loud and clear, by
criticism of the *status quo ante* and its championing of "basic
biblical goals." He notes five strong and five dubious features in
many manifestations of the current rising trend. The first strength
is the direct link of liberation theology with Christ's action to
relieve the afflicted through righting of wrongs. "Over against the
whole matrix of injustice, Liberation Theology rightly summons
us in Christ's name to a committed praxis of resistance and
transformation."

Next, the liberationist theology involves "in its praxis sectors
of humanity hitherto almost completely excluded from the Christian theological enterprise, which is not merely about, but *of* the
poor, Blacks, Asians, Native Americans, and homosexuals."

In addition, liberation theology "emphatically endorses and
enlists human freedom in the outworking of ultimate purpose"
and interprets this as meaning that "Christ stands for God with
and through humanity — for the essential conjunctivity of divine
and human effort" — and thus it blocks out predestination in
claiming the primacy of religious freedom, as well as the end of
human slavery in other ways.

In the fourth place, the liberationists "target the worldly
here and now for salvific transformation"; thus the divine reign
will overcome fallen humanity that was still fundamentally good,
and it will come "on earth as it is in heaven." God's rule is not
for a remote future but for the here and now, because the present

58. These five criticisms are found in order in Ogden's *Faith and
Freedom* on pp. 31 (twice), 34, and 96-97. His fifth criticism is aimed directly
at Jon Sobrino's *Christology at the Crossroads: A Latin American Approach*
(Maryknoll, NY: Orbis Books, 1978).

age sees the divine judgment and experiences simultaneously the inbreaking of God's future. This is an "inaugurated eschatology," one in which the transformation aimed at embraces the social, economic, and political aspects of communal life.

Fifth and finally, the assets of liberation theology include a willingness to be informed theologically by external and secular sources and an openness to hear the dispossessed themselves tell how things are in depth, so that relevance is guaranteed.[59]

But Foster also has doubts about some of the emphases of liberation theologians. First, he asks "whether Liberation's obsession with Justice has not foreshortened the Gospel of healing love" as the basic will of love in Christ. This is also the basis of his righteous indignation, and he wonders whether this has been adequately expressed in liberation theology. Foster's answer is, "No."

Second, parallel to the virtue recognized in encouraging the poor to have a positive role, isn't there a tendency of each group separately to pursue its own self-interest rather than the salvation of the world, or even of the individual as desired by Christ? The answer, according to Foster, is that "the neighbor Christ commands we love as ourself is not as such our blood brother or our sister or our class comrade but the next person . . . whose patent need or essential help we encounter on life's way. Christ frees us for this neighbor and it would be ironic if 'liberation' theology should place boundaries between us and her or him."

Third, while liberationists affirm human responsibility on the one hand, on the other they have an utopian disposition "to exaggerate collective freedom while neglecting the need for grace and a concomitant tendency to curtail individual freedom for the sake of collective control." Isn't it possible that in asserting the role of freedom in religion, which is good, it has expressed it excessively so that in avoiding the classical Augustinian over-

59. Foster's approval of liberation theology is found on pp. 1-4 of his essay.

emphasis on dependence upon God, the liberationists have fallen into the opposite pit of Pelagianism? Further, the liberationists make much of sin, but this is largely the sin of foes — especially American capitalists. Where is there acknowledgment of one's own sin, the sin of one's group, and one's implication in universal sin? Or is this forgotten?

The fourth reservation of Foster is that "in its commendable attention to the secular here and now, Liberation Theology may tend to overshoot the mark and neglect, when it does not outrightly negate, the vertical and eternal dimension also integral to Biblical faith." Here Foster refers to Tillich's claim that there is the Kingdom within history, and there is also, inseparably conjoined therewith, the Kingdom beyond history.[60] In a further reference to Tillich, Foster points to his insistence that it is not Jesus' maleness or Jewishness that matters, for he is the Christ because all that is merely Jesus is sacrificed to his mission and this makes him the Christ, the bearer of universal justice and healing love.[61] Foster concludes: "The present question . . . is whether and to what extent Liberation Theology owns *that* Christ as its and our Lord and Savior."[62]

Again, the fundamental question is whether, in the concern for horizontal justice, which is important as an expression of genuine love, the vertical and transcendental aspects of the Christian faith have not been undervalued. That is what both Schubert Ogden and Durwood Foster rightly ask, as do many others who admire the social compassion and determination for socio-economic justice exhibited by the liberation theologians.

Two recent sympathetic but not uncritical books on liberation theology by North American Catholic writers are Arthur McGovern's *Liberation Theology and Its Critics: Toward an Assess-*

60. The reference is to Paul Tillich's *Systematic Theology,* vol. III (Chicago: The University of Chicago Press, 1963), pp. 363ff.

61. Tillich's *Systematic Theology,* vol. I (Chicago: The University of Chicago Press, 1951), pp. 3-8.

62. Foster's doubts are found on pp. 4-10 of his essay, while pp. 10-11 address the future of liberation theology.

ment and Paul E. Sigmund's *Liberation Theology at the Crossroads: Democracy or Revolution.* The former is a Jesuit professor of philosophy, and the latter is a professor of politics. Both recognize that there have been important changes in liberation theology since the sixties away from Marxism toward socialism, and a stronger emphasis on spirituality. The first book is valuable for reporting the different criticisms of liberationist writers in North America, Latin America, and Europe, and for the major modifications McGovern proposes. The second book, as its subtitle indicates, proposes that the liberation theologians make a shift away from supporting revolution and toward establishing democracy. Both authors consider liberation theology's emphasis on sharing to be theologically and politically highly significant.

Liberation Changes Needed in the Eucharist

Instead of trying to answer the criticisms made by moderate critics of the liberation theologians, we can let them do that for themselves. They have several highly competent exponents among them, and in some cases, especially in that of Gutiérrez, the criticisms have been rebutted. Gutiérrez, for example, has insisted that the transcendental dimensions of faith are necessary to correct the utopianism of the Marxist dialectic and the *superbia,* or arrogant pride, of all societies. Instead of more analysis of the debate, it seems both appropriate and useful for our purposes to imagine what changes a liberationist Eucharist would show.

In the first place, liberationists would insist on a return of prophetic preaching[63] to the Latin American churches, with scathing and searing criticisms of the indifference of the oppressors of the poor, the marginalized, the stranger, the prisoner, and

63. Or, there may be a place for group meditations as provided by Fr. Ernesto Cardenal in his two-volume collection entitled *El Evangelio un Solentiname* (San José, Costa Rica: Departmento Ecumenico de Investigaciones, 1979).

the sick, in order to awaken the dormant consciousness of the affluent and to raise the material hopes of the oppressed.

The actual character of the congregations gathered for the Mass or Lord's Supper would also have the forgotten members of society included as unembarrassed and welcome members of the body of Christ. The poor, the stranger, the ex-prisoner, and the newly healthy man, woman, or child would be back again in the Christian family to share in the meal of unity and friendship, peace and justice.

Justice, moreover, would be visibly recognized in the offertory, which would include not only the bread and wine to be shared anew in the imminent feast, but also monetary or other expressions of generosity (such as food or flowers or clothing and similar necessities) to illustrate most vividly the concept of justice.

Central to the whole emphasis of this joyful, unitary meal in which Christ is the Host (as on Calvary he was the victim), is the sharing of the bread and wine, after the consecratory prayer of thanksgiving. One hopes that it will not be long before women priests will also be vivid symbols of the egalitarian and communitarian thrust of the gospel of Christ, and as reminders of their friendship with the Incarnate Christ and their witness to both the cross and Resurrection celebrated at the Eucharist.

The symbolism of broken bread must remind the gathered Christians, as Joseph Grassi reminds us, that this is our spiritual nourishment at Christ's table, as well as a call for the desperately needed actual bread to feed the world's hungry.[64] Here there are two further symbolic reminders. The third is that as the whole loaf is broken into fragments, so was Christ's body on the cross a broken body — the cost of our redemption; and the fourth is the sign of divine and human cooperation in God's sending of the earth, the seed, the sun and the rain, and humanity's work in sowing and planting, raising both wheat and grapes, as well

64. Grassi, *Broken Bread and Broken Bodies: The Lord's Supper and World Hunger* (Maryknoll, NY: Orbis Books, 1985), pp. ix, 39, 51, 55, 57, 61, 87ff., 94, and 111.

as transporting, buying and selling, wrapping and bottling them, before they reach the holy table or our domestic tables. All these symbols should be emblems of our gratitude to God and to the human community, and an encouragement or, if need be, an admonition not to spoil or waste the gifts of God in nature. We are thus all invited or threatened (if wanting) to be Christian ecologists.

Some of the main concerns of liberation theology have already been related to the liturgy, but the seminal and central one has yet to be stated. This is the emphasis on a true *solidarity of sharing*. No longer can the church be satisfied with the handouts of charity, or the privatization of prayers, and least of all with the indifference with which any suggested change toward socio-economic justice was met. No longer may the suggestion of "the preferential option for the poor" be met with such a response as was offered by a self-made multi-millionaire publisher who was very generous to New York's Central Park installations. His attitude toward the poor was that they were either "lazy or dumb."[65] No consideration had been given to the education, the family support, the inherited characteristics, the health, or the moral and spiritual training of the poor. Nor is it sufficiently realized that indifference toward the poor is not neutrality but support for their oppressors. This was admirably expressed by the courageous black Anglican Archbishop of the Church of the Province of South Africa, Desmond Tutu, who said: "The neutral spectator who watches the huge and heavy foot of the elephant tread down the tail of the mouse gives no comfort to the mouse."[66] In the struggle for justice there are no neutrals.

If the Eucharist is the central sacrament of the God of love, so very compassionately and sacrificially revealed in Christ, then social justice is the minimal expression of love. Furthermore, if following Christ the man of peace is a central concern, as it should be, then it

---

65. Reported in the obituary columns, p. 46 of the *New York Times,* May 5, 1991.

66. Cited from *Unexpected News* by Robert McAfee Brown, p. 19.

is interesting that good men as far apart as Reinhold Niebuhr and Pope Paul VI (otherwise unlikely theological companions) are in agreement: "'If you want peace,' they said, 'work for justice.'"[67] And in the struggle for justice we may have to leap over the important boundary of patriotism, which Albert Camus recognized in writing: "I should like to love my country and still love justice."[68] The very heart and soul of justice is found in sharing. And the deepest kind of sharing is life-sharing, as taught by the liberation theologians and exemplified by people such as Sister Lorette, who has dedicated her life to working with the poor in New Jersey's capital, Trenton, a soiled industrial city, not only talking but walking with them, and expecting downward mobility for the rich so that for both poor and rich there may be forward mobility. The liberationists' motto is *Conocer a Dios es obrar la justicia:* to know God is to do justice.

The cross and Resurrection in all eucharists are signs of the redeeming and reconciling love of God in Christ, of the hope of everlasting life and the forgiveness of sins for every Christian, and of a universalism that includes even enemies. But it also includes the understanding that Christ the liberator himself suffered violent death as the oppressed, and yet he was vindicated in the Resurrection and Ascension, and with him all the oppressed, marginalized, and downtrodden for whom he had a special concern during his earthly ministry and whom he welcomed to his table. Finally, we must recall the judgment seat of Christ at the end of human history.

Present-Day Liturgical Expressions of Liberation Theology

The best expressions of liberation in the liturgy are to be found in the experimental masses prepared by liberation priests in the third world (which is two-thirds of the world, in fact), with the collaboration of the people whom they serve. The thrust for

67. *Ibid.,* p. 45.
68. *Ibid.,* p. 159, where Camus's epigram is cited.

solidarity, justice, peace, and unity is so recent a Christian concern that many church liturgies only faintly echo these demands in their liturgies. So the representation from Europe and North America will not be very impressive. But we can rest secure that future liturgies will reflect social justice more determinedly and vividly.

As a token of what may come, it is worth looking at the new Roman Catholic prayers and the proposals of a West German Kirchentag in Nuremberg. In *The Liturgy That Does Justice*, Empereur and Kiesling suggest that eucharistic prayers contain subtle pointers to social justice, and they cite the words of the president in Eucharistic Prayer II of the modern Roman Rite: "May all who share in the body and blood of Christ be brought together in unity by the Holy Spirit." In Eucharistic Prayer III they find another prayer for unity: "Grant that we, who are nourished by his body and blood, may be filled with the Holy Spirit and become one body and one spirit in Christ." The same authors cite the Great Thanksgiving in Rite II of the Episcopal Book of Common Prayer, which begs God to sanctify the faithful "to serve you in unity, constancy, and peace." This stress on unity they rightly derive from John 17:21-23, and they insist that the unity of Christ's followers is fundamental to the divine intent and to the fulfillment of the Eucharist. Then they go on to show that unity has several components: "It entails a certain equality among the disciples of Christ" (Gal. 3:2 is cited in proof of this). Further, the unity allows for a variety of gifts, as I Corinthians 12:4-6 teaches. Finally, "unity implies the harmonious interaction of these equal, but variously endowed, persons who constitute Christ's ecclesial body," as affirmed in Ephesians 4:6. In conclusion, they insist that ". . . without ecclesial social justice, the divine intent for the body of Christ and the fulfillment of the Eucharist will be frustrated," precisely because otherwise harmony will be fractured by favoritism, conflict, and smothering of some members' gifts.[69]

69. *The Liturgy That Does Justice* (Collegeville, MN: The Liturgical Press, 1990), pp. 117-18.

A direct debt to liberation theology is to be found in Roman Prayer IV (also of 1970), which echoes what might be their most frequently cited verse, one in which Christ defined his ministry. The prayer goes as follows:

> Conceived through the power of the Holy Spirit and born of the Virgin Mary, he became like us in all things but sin. To the poor he proclaimed the good news of salvation, to prisoners, freedom, and to those in sorrow, joy. In fulfillment of your will he gave himself up to death.

A forum meeting at the church of St. Lawrence, Nuremberg, in 1979 made a series of proposals for the improvement of the celebration of the Eucharist, to make it a meal of hope instead of a gloomy and impersonal celebration, with a concern to live differently and ecologically. The signs they intend the Eucharist to convey are these:

- Bringing to the table bread and wine, signs of God's goodness, becomes an action in its own right.
- We use real bread as a basic sign of our daily sustenance.
- We express our care for creation in prayers of thanksgiving and hymns.
- We look for visible expressions of our creaturely joy.
- We take seriously periods of fasting as initiation into a simpler life.
- We frame concrete intercessions and also confess the sins of our prosperity.

Acting in Solidarity

The bread and wine we receive at Jesus' table make us hunger and thirst for the coming of God's justice. We cannot be guests of the Crucified without living the solidarity he practiced. So the church is celebrating the meal unworthily if it does not live in solidarity; it is belying the hope offered to the hungry and the oppressed.

The following are the first signs of that solidarity in our celebrations of the Lord's Supper:

- We give space, as we have done at this Kirchentag, to remembering hunger and oppression.
- We express in concrete intercessions our hope for God's justice.
- We look for forms of a credible thank-offering and bring to the meal what we want to share.
- We invite strangers and aliens to the meal and take account of their presence in the forms of our celebration.
- We go to the sick and the lonely and celebrate the meal with them.
- We also use grape juice for the sake of alcoholics.[70]

The nearest we come to liberation theology in the Orthodox Church is in two petitions of the Liturgy of St. John Chrysostom. The president prays thus:

Remember, Lord, those at sea, those travelling, the sick, those in adversity, prisoners, and their salvation.

Remember, Lord, those who bring forth fruit and do good works in your holy churches and remember the poor; and send out your mercies upon us all.[71]

---

70. Thurian and Wainwright, eds., *Baptism and Eucharist: Ecumenical Convergence in Celebration* (Geneva: World Council of Churches and Grand Rapids: Wm. B. Eerdmans, 1983 reprint), pp. 235-36. The document continues by suggesting ways to think universally rather than merely locally so that other churches may be understood better and to arrange for shared visits. Further, it expresses a desire that congregations include the Lord's meal in family services and devise more suitable forms for such relatively informal services. It looks toward ways to make a more human celebration involving spontaneity, communal singing, and music-making, discovering festive decorations and ornaments, and making the family circle around the altar a comfortable possibility, not forgetting to provide a place for strangers, and earnestly desiring that they may naturally share each others' experiences of hopes and fears (*ibid.*, pp. 236-37).

71. *Ibid.*, p. 119.

It should be recognized that the Orthodox Church is seriously considering both "Liturgy after the Liturgy" and "Confessing Christ through the Liturgical Life," two documents incorporated in Ion Bria, ed., *Martyria/Mission: The Witness of the Orthodox Churches Today,* which was published by the World Council of Churches in Geneva in 1980.[72]

The German Lutheran Church has one prayer from its *Agende für evangelisch-lutherische Kirchen und Gemeinden,* I, of 1955, which was updated on a trial basis in 1976 and 1977. It faintly recalls the cooperation of God with humanity in work, thus: "Lord, our God, Ruler over all. We praise you for the wonder of your creation. You bless human labour and endow us with life and joy."[73] No doubt later trial uses will include bolder claims for social justice.

The Swedish Lutheran Church includes in its Liturgy of 1975 an *epiclesis* expressing more boldly the same point, as well as suggesting by implication the symbolism of bread and wine, as follows:

> Sanctify also through your Spirit this bread and wine, fruits of the earth and toil of people which we bear unto you, so that we, through them, partake of the true body and blood of our Lord Jesus Christ.[74]

The French Reformed Church includes in its Liturgy of 1982 a strong ecological emphasis in Eucharistic Prayer IV:

> O God of love and holiness, our Creator and our Father . . .

---

72. The first text was published by *The International Review of Missions,* vol. LXVII, no. 265 (January 1978). It also appears in Thurian and Wainwright, *op. cit.,* pp. 213-18, and contains the significant statement: "Since the Liturgy is the participation in the great event of liberation from the demonic powers . . . aim[ing] at liberating human persons from all structures of injustice, exploitation, agony, loneliness, and at creating real communion of persons in love" (p. 214).

73. Thurian and Wainwright, *op. cit.,* p. 141.

74. *Ibid.,* p. 152.

your universe you put in our care;
your creation you entrust to our hands
with all its wonders and its travail.
You make us partners in your labours
and invite us to share in your rest. . . .[75]

The Church of Scotland's *Book of Common Order* (1979)
ends the eucharistic prayer with reference to the communion of
saints, but immediately before this is a petition and rubric as
follows:

These things, O Lord, we seek not only for ourselves but for
all in the communion of thy Church and especially for . . .
[*here the minister may pray for the sick, and the poor, and for the
needs of particular persons; or a short period of silence may be
observed.*][76]

The United Reformed Church in the United Kingdom produced *A Book of Services* (1980), including petitions that emphasize ecology and the needs of the oppressed:

We pray for
*those in trade and industry
members of the professions
all who serve the community*

Grant that men and women in their various callings
may have grace to do their work well;
and may the resources of the earth be wisely used,
truth honoured and preserved,
and the quality of our life enriched.

We pray for
the sick and the suffering

75. *Ibid.,* p. 157.
76. See *A Book of Services* (Edinburgh: The Saint Andrew Press, 1980),
p. 24.

victims of injustice
the lonely and the bereaved

Comfort those in sorrow;
heal the sick in body or in mind;
and deliver the oppressed.
Give us active sympathy
for all who suffer; and help us
so to bear the burdens of others
that we may fulfill the law of Christ.[77]

The same volume contains a reaffirmation of Christ's self-proclaimed mission, in which gratitude is offered to God the Father

for Jesus Christ
your beloved son,
whom you called and sent
to serve us and give us light,
to bring your kingdom to the poor,
to bring redemption to captives. . . .[78]

and in which a reminder of the great judgment is tied to the theme of justice, "rejoicing that he who is exalted at your right hand will speak up for us and will come to do justice to the living and the dead on the day you have appointed." The same prayer pleads vividly for ecology and peace:

We beseech you
send among us your Holy Spirit
and give a new face
to this earth that is dear to us.
Let there be peace
wherever people live,

77. *Ibid.,* p. 35.
78. *Ibid.,* p. 36.
79. *Ibid.,* p. 37.

the peace that we cannot make ourselves
and that is more powerful than all violence. . . .[79]

The impact of the concerns of the liberationist theologians is clearly felt in these clear, concise, and beautifully natural prayers.

The Episcopal *Book of Common Prayer* (1979) includes a prayer that stresses creation and the failure to treat it as God's gift:

At your command all things came to be: the vast expanse of interstellar space, galaxies, suns, the planets in their courses, and this fragile earth, our island home.

By your will they were created and have their being.

From the primal elements you brought forth the human race, and blessed us with memory, reason, and skill. You made us rulers of creation. But we turned against you and betrayed your trust: and we turned against one another.

Have mercy, Lord, for we are sinners in your sight.[80]

The United Methodist Church of the U.S.A. in its Rite of 1980 stresses unity in its *epiclesis* in the following words:

And may the Spirit make us one with Christ,
one with each other, and one in service to all the world.

The after-Communion prayer strongly emphasizes service of others that reflects God's own self-giving generosity:

You have given yourself to us, Lord.
Now we give ourselves for others.
Your love has made us a new people:
As a people of love we will serve you with joy.[81]

80. This comes from Eucharistic Prayer C in Holy Eucharist Rite II.

81. Thurian and Wainwright, *op. cit.,* p. 172.

It is difficult to generalize about Baptists since they cherish a considerable degree of local autonomy ecclesiastically, and in recent years, after playing an important part in the liturgical movement, have come to reaffirm free prayers. However, similar to the Presbyterians in one aspect of their Communion services, they follow the prayer of thanksgiving with an interesting form of distribution of the elements. Dr. W. M. S. West, when Principal of Bristol Baptist College in England, reported: "After the prayer of thanksgiving, the bread (growingly one loaf) is broken in quarters and placed upon plates for distribution to the congregation where they sit. Each person breaks a piece off and then, where possible, holds the plate for his or her neighbour." This is a way of indicating egalitarianism and service at the Lord's table.[82]

The communitarian emphasis is strongly asserted in the Eucharist celebrated by the United Church of Christ in the Philippines during the Offertory Prayer:

Minister/Liturgist: Our Loving Father, we offer these gifts from our labor. We bring this money, part of our earnings. May it help advance the work of your Church, not only within her walls, but also to the larger community.

We bring these elements for the common meal we are about to partake of: they represent the fruit of the land you have loaned us to use; they remind us of our common need to nourish our bodies and to share with those who lack these necessities. They also symbolize the sanctity of common things which you can transform into a sacrament, a visible sign of an inward grace. Purify these tokens, O Father, for our use now in the sharing of these bread/camote/banana and wine/juice in this sacred meal of remembrance of him who shared his life with us. Through Jesus Christ our Lord. Amen.[83]

---

82. *Ibid.,* p. 173. The account of Dr. West occupies pp. 172-74.
83. *Ibid.,* p. 201.

Although the emphasis is strongly Zwinglian, it is also power-fully corporate.

The Offertory is also an important sign of communal care on the part of the body of Christ in the Zaire Rite for the Mass (1975). In the offertory procession the explanatory rubric reads:

Some members of the assembly bring the gifts to the altar, while a suitable song is sung. When the gift-bearers reach the sanctuary, where the celebrant is waiting, the singing stops. Firstly, the gifts intended for the needy of the community are offered while one of the bearers says: Priest of God, here is our offering, may it be a true sign of our unity.

The priest makes a sign of gratitude: for example, a slight clapping of his hands. He then takes the gifts, and with the help of his ministers, he places them in a suitable place. Then the bread and wine are presented by two people, who say together

O priest of God, here is bread, here is wine; gifts of God, fruits of the earth, they are also the work of man. May they become food and drink for the Kingdom of God.[84]

Finally, the Ecumenical Eucharistic Rite of Lima has several echoes of the concerns of the liberation theologians. One prayer, in the form of an *epiclesis* in the first part of the liturgy (that of the Word), asks: "pour out your spirit on us again that we may be faithful to our baptismal calling, ardently desire the commu-nion of Christ's body and blood, and serve the poor of your people, and all who need our love. . . ." The Intercessions in-cludes the petition:

84. This is reproduced from *Afer 17* (1975) and is an English translation of the *Rite Zairois de la Célébration Eucharistique,* which was prepared for trial use aiming to bring the Roman Rite more into accord with African tradition and mentality. Our citation is from Thurian and Wainwright, *op. cit.,* p. 207.

For the leaders of the nations, that they may establish and defend justice, let us pray for the wisdom of God.

Kyrie eleison.

The Preparation in the Liturgy of the Eucharist begins thus:

Blessed are you, Lord God of the universe, you are the giver of this bread, fruit of the earth and of human labour, let it become the bread of life *[a parallel petition is offered for the wine]*.

The Preface gives God the Father thanks for the gift of his Son, of whom it is said:

He accepted baptism and consecration as your Servant to announce the good news to the poor.

The second *epiclesis* begs:

As we partake of Christ's body and blood, fill us with the Holy Spirit that we may be one single body and one single spirit in Christ, a living sacrifice to the praise of your glory. . . .[85]

These changes in liturgy have all been very modest. As liberation theology extends its influence we can expect more dramatic change in the structure of the liturgy itself. Gutiérrez suggests the direction of these changes when he writes:

This is the Eucharist: a memorial and a thanks-giving. It is a memorial of Christ which presupposes an ever-renewed acceptance of the meaning of his life — a total giving to others. It is a thanksgiving for the love of God which is revealed in these events. The Eucharist is a feast, a celebration of the joy that the Church desires to share. . . . The Christian Passover takes on and reveals the full meaning of the Jewish Passover. Liberation

85. Produced from ecumenical sources in 1982, its editor was Max Thurian of the Taizé Community in Burgundy, France.

from sin is at the very root of political liberation. The former reveals what is really involved in the latter. But on the other hand, communion with God and others presupposes the abolition of all injustice and exploitation. . . . The objects used in the Eucharist themselves recall that brotherhood is rooted in God's will to give the goods of this earth to all people so that they might build a more human world. . . . The Eucharist rite in its essential elements is communitarian and oriented toward the constitution of human brotherhood. . . . Without a real commitment against exploitation and alienation and for a society of solidarity and justice, the Eucharistic celebration is an empty action, lacking any genuine endorsement by those who participate in it. . . . "To make a remembrance" of Christ is more than the performance of an act of worship; it is to accept living under the sign of the cross, and in hope of the resurrection. It is to accept the meaning of a life that was given over to death — at the hands of the powerful of this world — for love of others.[86]

86. From *The Theology of Liberation* (Maryknoll, NY: Orbis Books, 1973), pp. 262-63.

EIGHT

Transignification and
Eucharistic Symbols

ONE OF THE most interesting developments in eucharistic theology bears the awkward name "transignification." It is awkward because in some cases it is spelled with a double "s," and it is awkward to try to find an equivalent simple term to indicate that the bread and wine in the Eucharist have changed their significance in an act-sign that registers that they have become the body and blood of Christ.

This new way of looking at the "real presence" of Christ is preferred to the Tridentine and Aristotelian explanation of the mystery, which was termed "transubstantiation," affirming that what looked like bread and wine had, in its underlying substance, become the body and blood of Christ as the institution narrative was pronounced by the priest. Aristotelianism is no longer applied to our experience of the nature of objects, and the emphasis on the change effected by the priest smacks of a magical clericalism no longer thought to be valid, since it must be Christ himself who is the consecrator. The new term is drawn from social anthropology, and has been vigorously defended by two Dutch Dominican theologians, Schoonenberg and Schillebeeckx. It has been thoroughly expounded and evaluated for the English-speaking world by the American Jesuit Joseph M. Powers.[1]

1. Edward Schillebeeckx, O.P., expounds the "new approach" in *The Eucharist,* translated by N. D. Smith published in 1968 in New York by

Schoonenberg's views were expressed in a series of articles. His concern was to interpret Christ's presence in the Eucharist in a personalist, not a substantialist, manner. A spatial presence is either/or, because one is either there or not there; but personal presence permits a rich variety of degrees, depending upon the communicating power of the transmitter and the capacity of the recipient of the communication. If God is the transmitter, and a faithful human being the recipient, then the communication is maximized. "Thus, the presence of God to the 'graced' man is more personal than is His presence to the man who is not justified by faith. But this grace-presence is, concretely, in Christ and the bond of the Spirit who unites men to Christ. In faith, man takes Jesus to heart, the glorified Lord who is the source of salvation, together with the Father who is always with Him and the Spirit whom both give as their gift, the gift of oneness with God."[2]

This presence of Jesus is much more real than that of a friend who writes a letter from a distance. The paradox of Christianity after the Ascension is that through the presence of the Spirit, although Christ was physically absent to the disciples, he seemed closer than before. Of far greater significance is the fact that the sacraments are actions of which he is the principal agent in the community of the church. In short, Schoonenberg sees Christ in the Eucharist giving himself in the most intense way possible, as the gift of life to the church.[3]

Attractive as this new approach might seem, there were many opponents who thought the term "transignification," or its equivalent "transfinalization," was intended as a substitute for "transubstantiation." The critics affirmed that a change in

---

Sheed and Ward. Joseph M. Powers, S.J., offered a brief, concentrated explanation of transignification in an article entitled "Mysterium Fidei and the Theology of the Eucharist," published in *Worship,* vol. 40, no. 1 (1968), pp. 17-35. A fuller account had appeared the previous year in *Eucharistic Theology* (New York: Herder and Herder, 1967).

2. Powers, *Eucharistic Theology,* p. 122.
3. Cf. John 6:56ff.

meaning could not be equated with a change in substance, and thus the concepts are mutually exclusive ideas. Powers argues that "transfinalization" is seen not only in the Jewish celebration of the Passover, but in the Eucharist itself as the creative word of Christ changes the meaning of Passover, for "the meaning of eating and drinking in the Eucharist now centers around the body and blood of Christ, the organ of the sealing of the new covenant, the creation of a new people, a people whose unity is in the unique reality of the body of Christ."[4] Furthermore, Powers explains, "It is the 'body handed over for you' which is the perennial sacrificial reality which is God's gift of worship and sanctification to man."[5] "Transignification" does not mean that the believer thinks or feels differently about the bread and the cup. On the contrary, this bread and cup celebrate the covenant of Calvary and the deliverance of humanity from the slavery of sin. And "they celebrate this covenant and delivery in the very organ of their accomplishment: the real body of Christ, present under the appearance of bread and wine."[6] Theologians such as Schoonenberg and Schillebeeckx who have proposed the use of the term "transignification" do not mean to contradict the traditional belief in the change that takes place in the Eucharist. Their intention is to "remove this change and presence from a purely physical level to the specifically sacramental level, the level on which the inner meaning of ritual and liturgical language is the content of the power of the sacrament: the sacraments of the new law contain the grace *which they signify*."[7] Powers concludes: "In this presence and in the sacramental sharing in its meaning, sinners are made holy, mortal man shares in God's glorious immortality, fragmented and divided man is drawn into that oneness in which and toward which it was created:

4. Powers's article "The Theology of the Eucharist," in *Worship*, vol. 40, no. 1, p. 28.
5. *Ibid.*, p. 29.
6. *Ibid.*, p. 30.
7. *Ibid.*, p. 31.

the one-ness which is given to us as we grow into the full stature of Christ."[8]

This preliminary account of "transignification" needs to be clarified by a consideration of its meaning as expounded by Edward Schillebeeckx himself. He affirmed with B. Welte that the being of things changes with a change of relationship. For example, a colored cloth is purely decorative, but if a government declares that this is the national flag, its meaning has radically changed since it is the organ through which patriotism is expressed. Thus, a new meaning is given to the Eucharist, not by any man, but by the Son of God.[9] Schillebeeckx argues that bread and wine, already useful to humanity in that they nourish physical life, have a further meaning in human intercourse, for "bread is the symbol of life and wine is the symbol of the joy of life."[10]

Schillebeeckx finds the notion of a "visit" made by Christ to the elements quite alien to the Eucharist, for "What happens in the Eucharist is that the faithful share in Christ's rising to life and accomplish this with him in faith while giving thanks to God. . . . The really sacramental element, the *ratio sacramentalis,* is precisely our eucharistic accomplishment with Christ of, and salvific inclusion in, the life-giving death of the Lord."[11] In further reflection he adds: "In this commemorative meal, bread and wine become the subject of a new *establishment of meaning,* not by men, but by the living Lord in the church, through which they become the *sign* of the real presence of Christ giving himself to us."[12] Moreover, the Eucharist as an

8. *Ibid.,* p. 35. See also the "Anglo-Catholic" theologians of the Church of England such as Charles Gore and William Temple with their anticipations of transignification (the latter used the term "transvaluation"), as recorded by E. L. Mascall in his revised edition of *Corpus Christi* (London, 1965), pp. 227-45. Schillebeeckx also refers to this group in *The Eucharist,* p. 117.

9. *The Eucharist,* p. 113.

10. *Ibid.,* p. 130.

11. *Ibid.,* p. 136.

12. *Ibid.,* p. 137.

event is viewed as Christ's personal gift of himself to his fellowmen and, within this, to the Father.

Finally, Schillebeeckx tries to answer the question whether "transignification" and "transubstantiation" are identical. They are not, even though transignification is intimately connected with transubstantiation. He concludes: "In my reinterpretation of the Tridentine datum, then, I can never rest content simply with an appeal to a human *giving of meaning alone,* even if this is situated in faith. Of course, a transignification of this kind has a place in the Eucharist, but it is borne up and evoked by the re-creative activity of the Holy Spirit, the Spirit of Christ sent by the Father. God himself *acts* in the sphere of the actively believing, doing and celebrating Church, and the result of this divine saving activity is sacramentally a 'new creation' which perpetuates and deepens our eschatological relationship to the kingdom of God."[13] His very last words in this volume loyally cite those of *The Pastoral Constitution on the Church in the Modern World:* "The Lord left behind a pledge of his hope and strength for life's journey in that sacrament of faith where natural elements refined by man are changed into his glorified Body and Blood, providing a meal of brotherly solidarity and a foretaste of the heavenly banquet."[14]

There appears to be a contradiction in the presentation of the thought by Schillebeeckx in that, on the one hand, he says that it is better to have a personalistic view of the Eucharist than one that stresses only a physical change (as transubstantiation does), and yet, on the other hand, he finally concludes that transubstantiation cannot be omitted. This seems, at first glance, to be a bowing to authority rather than a steady maintenance of his own convictions. Unsympathetic critics could, of course, challenge Schillebeeckx with having changed an ecclesial law and

13. *Ibid.,* p. 151.
14. Part I, ch. III, para. 38 of *The Pastoral Constitution of the Church in the Modern World,* in Walter M. Abbott, S.J., ed., *The Documents of Vatican II* (New York: Guild Press, American Press, and Association Press, 1966), pp. 236-37.

heritage of the Roman Catholic Church for an existential or phenomenological human perception of its meaning, but that was countered in advance by the insistence that the change in the symbol-act had been authorized by the words of the Word of God himself, Christ.

This very criticism, to which we have just alluded, was made in the work of another Dominican, Fr. Colman O'Neill, in his volume *New Approaches to the Eucharist.* "It would seem obvious," he wrote, "that the new Eucharistic theory posits a purely anthropological change — one, that is, which depends solely on the use that man makes of things."[15] This criticism, however, fails to meet Schillebeeckx's point that it is not a human invention, but it is the intention of the God-man that is here authoritative. Fr. O'Neill finds the theory unsatisfactory for other reasons, mainly because it does not disclose how Christ can be fully present in the Eucharist as compared with the other sacraments. He adds that, while a friend's gift may incarnate a friendship, one can communicate with him in a direct corporeal contact that is personal. In the case of Christ, however, the Eucharist cannot procure such direct personal corporeal contact; at least it approaches it and transcends the order of mere gift-action. Here again, Schillebeeckx recognizes Christ as offering in his death the gift of life to all the faithful: that is not *mere* gift-action, but the ultimate gift.

A second criticism is that there is no clear sense of the eucharistic sacrifice in the transignification view of the Eucharist. O'Neill holds that Schillebeeckx and others maintain a Bonhoefferian view of Christ as "the man for others" in their interpretation of the Eucharist. It is an existential, not an ontological definition of the meaning of the Eucharist. The new theory is based upon "Christ-acting-in-the-Church-through-symbols," but, says Colman O'Neill, on the contrary, what we analyze is

15. Fr. O'Neill's book was published by Alba House, the Society of St. Paul, in Staten Island, New York, NY 10314. The first criticism cited appears on p. 114.

not actions initiated by Christ in the liturgical assembly, but the symbol-actions of men and women living in the church who through such actions express their faith in the saving mysteries of Christ. He sums up this criticism thus: "The fact that Christ himself enters the major symbol-actions of the Church is logically *subsequent* to this and takes place at another level of reality, the ontological level."[16]

The American Jesuit Joseph Powers is an admirable exponent of transignification. Powers recognized that there was a surge on the part of thoughtful Catholic theologians to find a better justification for the change in the Eucharist than the Tridentine explanation of transubstantiation. He finds five compelling reasons for this demand for change in the interpretation of the Eucharist. The first is the growing conflict between the Aristotelian philosophy of nature and that of contemporary physicists. The second is the recovery of the insight that a sacrament is in the category of a "sign" and that sacraments are essentially personal encounters with God. In the third place, there has been an attempt to revalue the Council of Trent's emphasis on the "substance of bread" from a new worldview. Fourth, the encouragement for a restatement of the interpretation of the Eucharist derived from Vatican II's *Constitution on the Sacred Liturgy*. Fifthly, and finally, the ecumenical encounter of Roman Catholic theologians with other Christian theologians also had its impact.[17]

The primary emphasis of the new approach was the acknowledgment that reality is not of man's making, resulting in the fact that the Eucharist is essentially "givenness" — the gift of Christ to humanity and to the Father, and that it is found in a meal proclaiming the death of the Lord that has been

16. *Ibid.*, p. 125. It should be noted, however, that these criticisms rely less on Schillebeeckx's exposition than that of Luchesius Smits, O.F.M., which raised "actual questions concerning Transubstantiation and the interpretation of the Lord's words in the Eucharist." Smits's work appeared in Dutch in 1965 in Roermond.

17. Powers, *Eucharistic Theology*, pp. 147ff.

constituted as the sacramental memorial of the death, resurrection, and glorification of Christ.[18] In addition, we can see in the Eucharist the sacramental visibility of Christ's self-giving, which is not only that of Calvary but a continuous characteristic of his earthly and heavenly life. Bread and wine are thus given a new meaning by the Lord of the church, and so the words of consecration are directed not simply to bread and wine, but to believers. And Christ is present sacramentally in an action that is the gift of himself.[19] Christ is present, therefore, in a sign-act (not a thing, but an action of self-communication to other persons). Powers uses the illustration of a diamond engagement ring, which at one level is merely two precious commodities, gold and a diamond, but at a higher level is the profound gift of love.[20] In the Eucharist the sign-action is not man's, but God's, the work of Christ and of the Holy Spirit through whom Christ gives himself in the sacrament of the Eucharist. It must be observed that the ritual does not charm grace out of heaven, for it is God's absolutely free gift — this is what "grace" means. It is the gift of his presence and power, saving, sanctifying, and redeeming man.[21]

Finally, Powers insists that transubstantiation takes place through transignification. Two citations will make this clear. The first explains:

> What takes place in the consecration, then, is not simply the change of bread into body, wine into blood. What takes place basically is Christ's gift of Himself in the Church. He gives Himself, the whole of His timeless sacrificial reality before the Father, to the worshipping community, as its offering, its sacrifice, its life. It is His word, not man's, which changes the bread and the cup into the signs of His giving. And the reality of the sign lies in the fact that in the totality of the action Christ is

18. *Ibid.,* p. 149.
19. *Ibid.,* p. 152.
20. *Ibid.,* pp. 166ff.
21. *Ibid.,* p. 168.

giving Himself with the community through the bond of His Spirit.[22]

The second citation tries to eliminate a possible misunderstanding:

> The reality is Christ's gift, not the action of man or the merely physical reality of bread and wine. And this reality is only available to man in another gift of Christ — faith. . . . This change is not a change in molecular structure. Christ is not "under" or "behind" or "inside" the physical realities involved. He gives Himself in His own way, in sovereign freedom, from all the conditions of material existence. He gives Himself, in short, in mystery.[23]

It is interesting that Powers comes to the same conclusion as Schillebeeckx, namely that in the mystery of Christ's real presence in the Eucharist, both transignification and transubstantiation must be held together. Schillebeeckx's reason for this decision is given at the conclusion of *The Eucharist,* and, in fairness to him, should be indicated:

> I have struggled with the interpretation of this *mysterium fidei* and, in faithful reverence for what the Catholic *confession* of faith has for centuries allowed Christians to experience in the celebration of the Eucharist, I cannot personally be satisfied with a *purely* phenomenological interpretation without metaphysical density. Reality is not man's handiwork — in this sense realism is essential to the Christian faith. In my reinterpretation of the Tridentine datum, then, I can never rest content simply with an appeal to a human *giving of meaning alone,* even if this is situated within faith. Of course, a transignification of this kind has a place in the Eucharist, but it is borne up and evoked by the re-creative activity of the Holy Spirit, the Spirit of Christ sent by the Father. God Himself *acts* in the sphere of the actively

22. *Ibid.,* p. 176.
23. *Ibid.,* p. 177.

doing and celebrating Church, and the result of this divine activity is sacramentally a "new creation" which perpetuates and deepens our eschatological relationship to the kingdom of God.[24]

It should be observed that some interpreters of the new approach to the Eucharist use not only "transignification" but also "transfinalization." They object, as we have seen, to the term "transubstantiation" because they consider it insufficiently dynamic and inadequately human to represent the personal encounter of Christ with humanity in the Eucharist. They insist that "bread" and "wine" do more than denote certain physical objects, for these objects are important as nutriments for humanity and they serve humanity's natural and supernatural needs and purposes. Therefore, their meaning *(significatio)* and their purpose *(finis)* have been changed; thus the appropriate terms for these changes are respectively "transignification" and "transfinalization."

It is also worth noting that both Schillebeeckx and Schoonenberg emphasize that God's presence in Christ and through the Holy Spirit is found in the preaching and hearing of the Word of the sermon as well as in the Eucharist. The advantage of the term "presence" is twofold: it is personal, and as personal it may be intense or relatively remote, as are the interrelations of human persons. Perhaps, however, the supreme benefit of the new approach is the recognition that it is God's gift of himself that is the final category for interpretation, the final and perfect gift of divine love for the undeserving.

Dr. John Huxtable has said that no denomination celebrating the Eucharist has a doctrine of the real absence, so it is absolutely right to affirm that the reality of Christ's presence is a great mystery, which is what the Eastern Orthodox churches have always termed it.[25] At the same time, it is laudable to try

---

24. *The Eucharist* (New York: Sheed and Ward, 1968), pp. 150-51.
25. This was reported by the English Jesuit, Fr. Thomas Corbishley,

to find intelligible indications of what happens in this mystery, as we saw in our sixth chapter.

We may find further illumination of the multiple facets of the Eucharist if we consider the significance of its symbolism.

Signs and Symbols

Both philosophers and social anthropologists have in our day given much attention to the importance of signs and symbols. At the outset, it would be wise to distinguish signs from symbols. It is clearly one of the basic factors accounting for the interest in transignification and transfinalization. In attempting to communicate about God's actions in our midst, it is necessary to use both signs and symbols, but at the deepest level it is symbols that we use.

According to Susanne Langer, signs indicate the meanings we wish to convey — for example, a red light is a warning for motorists to stop — or indicate an obstacle that should be avoided. This is an artificial sign, such as the waving of a flag or the blowing of a whistle as a train is ready to leave the railway station. The sacraments have been defined as "outward and visible signs of an inward and spiritual grace." But, in fact, they can be conceived more helpfully in symbolic terms.

In the important clarification offered by Susanne Langer, symbols "are not proxy for their objects, but are vehicles for the conceptions of objects. To conceive a situation is not the same thing as to 'react toward it' overtly, or to be aware of its presence. In talking about things we have conceptions of them, not the things themselves, and it is the conceptions not the things that symbols directly 'mean.' "[26] Langer believed that there was no

---

in his *One Body, One Spirit* (Leighton Buzzard: Faith Press, 1973), p. 60. Dr. Huxtable has headed the United Reformed Church of the United Kingdom for many years and is a man of wit as well as wisdom.

26. Susanne K. Langer, *Philosophy in a New Key* (Cambridge, MA: Harvard University Press, 1942), p. 25.

one-to-one correspondence between the symbol and the conception, but patterns of correspondence prevent the conception from being entirely arbitrary.

Paul Tillich insisted that it is essential for a religious symbol to participate in the power it symbolizes. According to his view: "The symbol is not a mere convention as is a sign. It grows organically. . . . The symbol opens up a stratum of reality, of meaning and being, which otherwise we could not reach; and in doing so it participates in that which it opens. . . . Symbols open us, so to speak, in two directions — in the direction of reality and in the direction of the mind."[27]

A recent Roman Catholic author affirms that what has been happening in the newer developments after Vatican II is the forgetting of secondary symbolism in order to concentrate on primary symbolism. Thus, Tad Guzie claims that most of the old Roman Rite "was calculated to draw attention to the *objects* of bread and wine; the new rite stresses the *action* of a faith community which is celebrating its redemption."[28] The mystery in the Eucharist will never be totally plumbed, but both primary and supposedly secondary symbols need to be analyzed for the light they throw on this multifaceted diamond — the Eucharist.

The Role of Symbols

Before we discuss the meaning of the symbols used in the Eucharist, it is essential to consider the use of symbols by contemporary thinkers, whether they be historians of religion, sociologists, anthropologists, or philosophers. As an indication of

27. Tillich's "Theology and Symbolism," in F. Ernest Johnson, ed., *Religious Symbolism* (Port Washington, NY: Kennikat Press, 1955), pp. 109-10. I owe these citations, as well as those from Susanne Langer, to Robert L. Browning and Roy A. Reed, *The Sacraments in Religious Education and Liturgy: An Ecumenical Model* (Birmingham, AL: Religious Education Press, 1985), p. 75.

28. *Jesus and the Eucharist* (New York: Paulist Press, 1974), p. 110.

the importance of the modern hermeneutics based upon the recognition of the importance of symbols, it is necessary only to mention the following names: Mircea Eliade, Michael Polanyi, Victor Turner, Mary Douglas, Clifford Geertz, Paul Ricoeur, and Robert Bellah. Despite the variety of their disciplines, they are united in opposing every form of reductionism in their interpretation of symbols, and thus refusing to accept the rationalistic distortions of the Enlightenment that reduced symbols to abstract concepts. They affirm that symbolic consciousness is the distinctively human mode of consciousness.

It is generally acknowledged that Freud and Marx had a profound impact on the modern world and in shaping the modern consciousness. Each had a profound sense of the importance of symbols. Freud rediscovered the symbolic in his interpretation of dreams, which plumbed the unconscious to discover the hidden wishes and inclinations as well as the contradictions of human beings. His interpretation, however, saw humanity only as individuals, not as social beings.

Marx, on the other hand, recognized the power that the social matrix has on individuals through the impact of the social structures of society. These are institutions and spiritual products such as art, religion, ethics, politics, and philosophy, all of which are the material foundation of society. The social function of these institutions and products Marx termed ideology, and this legitimized the existing socio-political order. Marx was unable to see religion as divine revelation or transcendent idea — only as moral sanction and legitimation of the capitalist society of his day with yawning gaps between the haves and have-nots; thus for him religion was an anesthetic, an opiate to make the conditions of slavery bearable for the deprived. His conclusion was: "The abolition of religion as the *illusory* happiness of the people is the demand for their *real* happiness. The demand to abandon the illusions about their condition is the *demand to give up a condition that requires illusions.* Hence criticism of religion is in embryo a *criticism of this vale of tears* whose halo is religion."[29] Yet, according to the insight of William R. Crockett in his *Eucharist: Symbol of Transformation* (1987) there was a double edge to Marx's critique of religion, as expressed in Marx's statement: "Religious misery is in one way the expression of real misery and in another a protest against real misery." Crockett adds: "But Marx never developed the second half of this statement."[30]

Other thinkers, whether anthropologists or sociologists, and including Durkheim, Weber, Mannheim, and Bloch, have acknowledged a positive role for religion in the improvement of society. This could be viewed as the cultivation of an utopian future, or positively employing the charismatic role of religious prophets.

The theological appreciation of symbols is the recognition of their transcendent source or sacred character. And this is not an otherworldly affirmation, but an insistence that the divine is revealed in the finite. Furthermore, it is contended that religious symbols lead to a transformation of individuals and of society through a commitment to a new way of life. In the specific case of the Eucharist, it requires sincere believers to live in conformity with the gospel in the obedience of faith. The Eucharist, as a central symbol of the Christian religion, is an acted parable with an almost inexhaustible set of meanings. The modern world is beginning to realize in a very realistic way the implications of the Eucharist for human justice in a world that flaunts it.

William Crockett writes movingly of what the Eucharist can mean for the transformation of society:

> The community that gathers for a common meal cannot hear the Word of God and share the bread and the cup without

29. Karl Marx, *On Religion,* ed. Saul K. Padover (New York: McGraw-Hill, 1974), pp. 35-36.

30. *Eucharist: Symbol of Transformation* (New York: Pueblo Publishing Company, 1989), p. 254.

reflecting upon what that means for Christian obedience in a
world without sufficient bread, and a world in which injustice,
poverty, and oppression are ever present realities. When we
reflect on the relationship between this meal that we celebrate
and Jesus' meals with outcasts and sinners, we cannot fail to
hear the call to extend our care and love to the outcast and the
marginalized in our own society. To celebrate the Lord's death
until he comes means to accept living under the sign of the
cross in the present. To celebrate this meal as the anticipation
of the meal in the kingdom is to acquire a new social and
political vision. To observe our Lord taking the role of a servant
and serving us at table shakes us out of our usual identities and
roles and shows us a different way of relating to one another
in humble service. To receive Christ's own life poured out for
us is to learn what it means to give of ourselves. The eucharist
as a symbolic action, therefore, provides a model not only for
our meaning, but also for our doing. It is a vehicle both of
disclosure and commitment.[31]

Clearly the primary focus in traditional Roman Catholicism
was the altar of sacrifice, holding the central position in the
sanctuary. Nearly all Roman Catholic churches have brought it
from the back of the edifice to the front, so that it is possible
for the faithful to stand around this table-altar in smaller congregations. In this case, the symbolism expressed is less a
sacrifice than a meal at an open table for Christians. Furthermore, as we have seen earlier, important as Calvary was and is
for our redemption, we also share proleptically in Christ's
victory over the powers of evil in the Resurrection and Ascension to the Father, and in the anticipation of sharing the eschatological banquet, with Christ as host both now and
hereafter. Thus, while the concept and reality of the costliness
of Christ's sacrifice cannot be forgotten, we now emphasize
increasingly the meal, which reflects the frequency with which
Jesus in his earthly life shared bread with the despised and

31. *Ibid.,* p. 251.

marginalized and welcomed those whom the socialites of this world rejected.

Thus the first current symbol is the welcome offered by an open table, encouraging all pilgrims and strangers to feel at home. This is diametrically opposed to any "fencing" of the table to keep out moral lepers, though its meaning will be clear only after some instruction has been given to lead to faith. Moreover, it will give precedence to Christ's high-priestly prayer that *all* his disciples may be one.

But the meal is no ordinary meal. It is the meal of the Messiah, of God incarnate, whose love is unlimited. It is, therefore, a meal of abounding joy and festive hilarity. Browning and Reed have stressed the implications of the meal admirably. They affirm:

> When we push back to the core meaning of communion we find the natural sacrament of the meal and all of the everyday communication which takes place, the sharing of our common lives with one another. It is at the meal that we realize our dependence upon persons and forces other and greater than ourselves from whom the bread and wine have come. Families in every culture have sensed the eternal in the midst of this basic experience of preparing and sharing a meal. Jesus did not "institute" a new ritual or call us to a new sacrament. Rather, he recognized the sacramental nature of the meal which his Jewish friends knew so well that they could never forget it . . . the Jewish meal was always a ritual meal with blessings of bread and wine and thanksgiving prayers at various times during the meal.[32]

Furthermore, we cannot allow ourselves to forget the eschatological dimensions of this messianic meal, which anticipates the banquet of Christ with his own in eternity. Proleptically, we taste — no more — the meal that is to be, the meal that is the pledge of the resurrection of the friends of the risen Lord.

32. Browning and Reed, *The Sacraments in Religious Education and Liturgy*, p. 79.

A useful summary interpretation provided by Browning and Reed is "God's presence in our lives through creation (bread and wine) and through redemption (Christ's giving of his life — body and blood — for all of God's family)."[33]

We must also recall that the Christ who is the genuinely welcoming host is also, very significantly, the servant. While the writer of the fourth gospel omits any reference to the institution of the Lord's Supper, he yet provides eucharistic discourses and shows the extreme humility of the Lord who washed the feet of his disciples. If the host at a meal to which all are welcome is a primary symbol of the Eucharist, we cannot forget that the cross is another, for that marks the deep descent in love made by the co-eternal Son of God (as well as showing the treachery of Judas and all sinners through their disloyalty), and the basin and towel are a third symbol.

But what are we to make of the bread and the cup of wine? The simplest interpretation of these symbols is to take them as representing the body and blood of Christ, the bread broken as the body of Christ on the cross and the wine as the blood outpoured unto death. This is probably what most Protestants would think of these symbols. But, was our Lord's body broken on the cross? Professor J. Gordon Davies finds great difficulties in regarding bread and wine primarily as symbols of Christ's death. He says, "The plain fact of the matter is that death by crucifixion involves of necessity neither the literal 'breaking' of the body nor the shedding of blood."[34] Further, he also argues that John's gospel insists that not a bone of Christ's body was broken, and his elaborate eucharistic theology is associated with the feeding of the multitude. The key word is "life," for the bread is "the living bread" and the new manna that feeds the newly redeemed, just as manna fed the Israelites who had been redeemed from Egyptian slavery. What is celebrated is the estab-

33. *Ibid.*, p. 80.
34. See G. Cope, J. G. Davies, and D. A. Tytler, eds., *An Experimental Liturgy* (London: The Lutterworth Press, 1958), p. 58. But Christ could not be transfixed to the cross without wounds and the shedding of blood.

lishment of the New Covenant (in contrast to the Old Covenant with its blood shedding of sacrificial animals), with its "spiritual blood" symbolized by the wine of celebration and betokening a spiritual sacrifice. Bread is the staff of life, and it symbolizes Christ as the nourishment of the soul. But bread in the form of a loaf or a few loaves symbolizes the union in the Communion of Christians. St. Paul inaugurated the eucharistic unity seen in the one loaf that is fragmented in small pieces, each of which represents a member of the body of Christ, and this idea was fruitfully pursued in the *Didache* in the words: "As this bread that is broken was scattered upon the mountain and gathered together and became one, so let The Church be gathered from the ends of the earth into Thy kingdom."[35] Despite what J. Gordon Davies calls the "crumbly inconvenience" of having real loaves, they, far more than wafers, symbolize Christ, who communicates his life to the faithful as his body.

Bread also has a significant meaning for twentieth-century Christians, who must be appalled by the deaths of so many thousands of human beings through starvation and the lack of any bread, giving evidence of a striking lack of love of the neighbor. There is also a significant contemporary ecological sign in the bread for Christians — it is a reminder that we should be the last persons to spoil God's creation by waste.

The bread also stands for the remarkable cooperation between God and humanity that makes the production of bread possible: it depends on God's gifts of earth, sun, rain, and the seed of the wheat, but it also requires the life and labor of humankind. This is vividly expressed by members of the Joint Liturgical Group in Britain:

> The bread is not simply a loaf; it represents the labour of the farmer who ploughed the field and sowed the seed; it represents the work of harvesting the corn and, in the case of wheat from overseas, its shipment to ports in our own land. Behind the

35. *Didache* 9.4.

loaf stand all the stages from the original planting of the seed to the docking of the ship, the purchase of the flour by the baker, the actual baking of the bread, and its sale in the shop. . . . Likewise the wine . . . and in offering these to God the congregation is offering the whole life and work of its members to Him.[36]

The meanings of wine as a symbol are similar to those attached to bread: it is drink as nourishment for the body, and a sign of divine-human cooperation. But it also carries an additional meaning, as indicated by Edward Schillebeeckx: "Bread and wine, already useful to man as nourishing physical life, have a further function in human intercourse. They have a symbolic meaning — bread is the symbol of life and wine is the symbol of the joy of life."[37] Markus Barth also reminds us that the function of the cup that Christ's guests drink complements the use made of the bread, the drinking of wine "demonstrates the need or the permission to be glad, to relax and to forget the misery in which one is caught (see Psalm 116:13)," and, he adds, "A cup of salvation is mentioned in Psalm 116:13: the people of God need not always eat and drink with tears in their eyes."[38]

But wine is also the color of blood and thus symbolizes pain and agony — the very life-blood of Christ. In the words of Bishop Hugh Montefiore: "Blood, however, symbolizes not only life but death; for blood outpoured, unless staunched, leads to death. And so to drink the consecrated wine is not merely to share in the life-blood of Christ, but also to assert his sacrificial

---

36. Ronald C. D. Jasper, ed., *The Renewal of Worship: Essays by Members of the Joint Liturgical Group* (London: Oxford University Press, 1965), pp. 93-94. In the same volume (p. 54) Stephen Winward writes: "Every eucharist is a Harvest Thanksgiving at which the gifts of God upon which man has laboured are offered to Him to become the means of grace."

37. *The Catholic Tradition: Mass and the Sacraments,* II (A Consortium Book, 1979), p. 305.

38. *Rediscovering the Lord's Supper* (Atlanta: The John Knox Press, 1988), pp. 56-57.

death. Since the blood-shedding of Jesus is sacrificial, it cleanses (like a lustration); it reconciles (like a piaculum); it makes holy (like a sacrificium)."[39]

The very actions of breaking the bread and passing the cup from hand to hand, as ritual gestures, are also profoundly meaningful. Jean-Marie Roger Tillard argues that these are signs of community, of sharing the same destiny and the same act of reconciliation through Christ.[40]

It is in the sharing community of Christ manifested in the Eucharist that we find, or should rightly expect to find, the very deepest solidarity. Here all the members ought to have a profound sense of their individual and communal sins that have been forgiven by Christ, through the reconciliation effected by the sacrifice of the cross that Christ offers up again in the Holy Communion. Here every believer should sense a marvelous union with every other Christian, past, present, and future. Here each member of the body of Christ should find a common sense of exhilaration and joy in contemplating the future privilege of feasting with all the saints at the eschatological banquet of Christ. Here all Christians should rejoice in the inspiration, the sanctification, and the inner power of the gift of the Holy Spirit promised at Pentecost and renewed at every gathering of the church. And here, finally, all Christians should be united in their determination that the equality before God in the Eucharist will be increasingly expressed in a social egalitarianism and social justice as a presage of the culmination of the Kingdom at Christ's *parousia*. The profound sense of solidarity and its social implications were excellently expressed in the Encyclical of Pope John Paul II, *Sollicitudo Rei Socialis:* "Solidarity helps us to see the 'other' — whether a *person, people, or nation* — not just as some kind of instrument, with a work capacity and physical strength to be exploited at low cost and then discarded when no longer useful, but . . . on a

39. *Thinking about the Eucharist: Essays by Members of the Archbishop's Commission on Christian Doctrine* (London: SCM Press, 1972), pp. 77-78.
40. *The Catholic Tradition*, II, pp. 338ff.

par with ourselves in the banquet of life to which all are equally invited by God."[41]

One of the newest concerns emphasized in the reflection on the Eucharist is ecological, as part of the appreciation of the divine creation. The damage to the ozone layer and the excessive warming of the earth's atmosphere threaten to disrupt food production, and, as sea levels rise, thrust millions of people in coastal areas out of their homes and their livelihoods. At the same time, species of animals may become extinct, and many kinds of plants as well. If we add to this the toxic wastes from industrial and military use that are poisoning our waters, it may seem no exaggeration to affirm with the Dominican father Matthew Fox, "Mother Earth is dying."[42]

It is essential to remember the responsibility that God laid on Adam in Eden to care for all living things, for we, too, are stewards under God for all creation. One lively example of what we may expect to see in the near future in our liturgies is the imaginative ecological liturgy produced by a California priest, Scott McCarthy, in his book *Celebrating the Earth*. The Preface of the Prayer of Thanksgiving includes the following section:

> It is good for us at all times and in all places to give thanks to You, O Lord, holy Father, almighty Creator and loving Savior. But especially this Spring when You renew the earth with Your loving care and You renew our hearts as we call to mind all that You do for us. Blessed are You, O God; how great You are! Clothed in majesty and splendor, wearing the light as a robe! Therefore we praise You with angels and all of your Creation.

The Christological section follows:

> When the time was ripe you sent us Jesus, your own Son. He loved your world and delighted to wander in the desert, to

41. Section 39, cited in John J. Walsh, *Integral Justice: Changing People, Changing Structures* (Maryknoll, NY: Orbis Books, 1990), p. 91.

42. *The Coming of the Cosmic Christ* (San Francisco: Harper & Row, 1988), cf. pp. 13-17.

climb the mountains, to bathe in the cool water of the rivers. He taught us to love and to share his love. With a love born of heaven and earth, Jesus gathered his friends together the night before he died. He shared with them a meal of bread and wine, fruits of your earth. . . .

The prayer continues, after the words of Institution:

O Giver of life, present in all your creation, transform this bread and wine into the living presence of Jesus. Transform us into his holy people. Give us wisdom to create a new world where all may share the fruits of the land. Give us knowledge to develop what is lying fallow, to bring forth what is as yet only a seed in our minds. Fill up what is lacking in our lives. May we learn to respect life wherever we find it.[43]

If we are looking for a short expression of the sense of humanity cooperating with God in an important liturgy we shall find it in the Offertory Prayer of the most recent Roman Rite:

Blessed are you, Lord, God of all creation.
Through your goodness we have this bread to offer,
which the earth has given and human hands have made.
It will become for us the bread of life.
Blessed be God forever.
Blessed are you, Lord, God of all creation.
Through your goodness we have this wine to offer,
fruit of the vine and work of human hands.
It will become our spiritual drink.
Blessed be God forever.[44]

Feminism has also left its impact on newer experimental orders of worship, and, as we shall see, the role of women in the Bible is beginning to leave its mark on the most recent

43. Scott McCarthy, *Celebrating the Earth* (San Jose: Resource Publications, 1991), pp. 1109-21.
44. *The Sunday Missal* (London: Collins Liturgical Publications), p. 35.

denominational order for the Eucharist. For a thorough consideration of feminist liturgy and the Woman-Church movement, Marjorie Procter-Smith's *In Her Own Rite: Constructing Feminist Liturgical Tradition* (Nashville: Abingdon Press, 1990) should be consulted. This emphasis will also be reflected in other liturgical developments in coming years.

Finally, it is no exaggeration to claim that the Eucharist has *cosmic* implications. Joseph Ernst urges that the central thought of bringing together into unity in the body of Christ is extended to all domains of the universe and to God. For this, in the perspective of Ephesians, is the last great goal: to "unite all things" in Christ (1:10). The world that has disintegrated in sin is to be led back to the center from which its order flows. In Christ's ascension all things are to be filled up (4:10).[45] The universalism of Christ's salvific love destroys all elitism, snobbery, and self-righteousness in a grand parity of humanity in extensive egalitarianism, which should be reflected in the earthly Eucharist.

Symbolic Expression in Recent Eucharistic Rites

The concepts of sacrifice and the almost exclusive commemoration of the death of Christ fill the Tridentine Rite and the rites emerging from the Reformation, so there is no point in drawing attention to them again. Thus our concentration will be on the new emphases expressed in the post–Vatican II Roman rites and in the Episcopalian and Protestant rites.

The newer prayers highlight the social and ecological impli-

45. P. Bénoît, R. E. Murphy, and B. van Tersel, eds., *The Breaking of Bread,* in *Concilium,* vol. 40 (New York, NY, Glen Ridge, NJ: The Paulist Press, 1969), p. 113. In the same volume, Victor Warnach, O.S.B., claims that the bread and wine are raised up to be Christ himself, to become "his ambassadors," and ultimately "they anticipate something that one day will be shared by the whole cosmos" (p. 101). The technical term for this Pauline conception is *pleroma,* a term found in both Ephesians and Colossians.

cations of the gospel. For example, in Roman Eucharistic Prayer IV, we read:

> To the poor he proclaimed the good news of salvation,
> to prisoners, freedom,
> and to those in sorrow, joy.[46]

It is, however, in the Roman Catholic liturgies for India and for Zaire that the greatest stress is laid on the great variety of creation as the work of God. *The New Order of the Mass for India* combines references to the Bible and to the Vedas to make creation relevant for Indian Christians:

> O Supreme Lord of the Universe, You fill and sustain everything around us; You turned, with the touch of Your hand, chaos into order, darkness into light. Unknown energies You hid in the heart of matter. From You bursts forth the splendour of the sun and the mild radiance of the moon. Stars and planets without number You set in ordered movement. You are the source of the fire's heat and the wind's might, of the water's coolness and the earth's stability. Deep and wonderful, the mysteries of Your creation.[47]

The Zaire Rite for the Mass refers to creation through Christ in strongly visual terms capturing images of the region:

> Holy Father, we praise you through your Son Jesus, our mediator. He is your Word, the Word that gives life. Through him, you created heaven and earth; through him you created our river, the Zaïre. Through him, you created our forests, our rivers, our lakes. Through him you created the animals who live in our forests, and the fish who live in our rivers. Through him you created the things we see, and also the things we do not see. THROUGH HIM YOU HAVE CREATED ALL THINGS![48]

---

46. *The Sunday Missal* (London: Collins, 1984, reprinted 1989), p. 53.
47. Thurian and Wainwright, eds., *Baptism and Eucharist,* p. 189.
48. *Ibid.,* p. 208.

The newer prayers highlight the social rather than the ecological implications of Christian faith, as can be seen in the
second eucharistic prayer in *The American Lutheran Book of Worship,* which recalls Christ's comprehensive compassion:

> . . . the sacrifice of his life;
> his eating with outcasts and sinners
> and his acceptance of death.[49]

Eucharistic Prayer C of the *Book of Common Prayer of the
U.S.A.* expands our awareness of the universe as an astronomer
might do:

> At your command all things came to be: the vast expanse of
> interstellar space, galaxies, suns, the planets in their courses, and
> this fragile earth our home.

> *By your will they were created and have their being.*

> From the primal elements you brought forth the human race,
> and blessed us with memory, reason, and skill. You made us
> rulers of creation. But we turned against you, and betrayed your
> trust; and we turned against one another.

> *Have mercy, Lord, for we are sinners in your sight.*[50]

The Roman Reconciliation Liturgies show how the Holy
Spirit, in a world of desperate divisions, transforms human re-
lations:

> enemies . . . speak to one another, those . . . estranged join
> hands in friendship, and nations seek the way of peace together.

The Holy Spirit effects reconciliation when

---

49. See Frank C. Senn, ed., *New Eucharistic Prayers* (New York and
Mahwah, NJ: Paulist Press, 1987), p. 6.
50. *The Book of Common Prayer . . . According to the Use of the Episcopal
Church* (New York: The Church Hymnal Corporation, 1979), p. 370.

understanding puts an end to strife,
. . . hatred is quenched by mercy,
and vengeance gives way to forgiveness.[51]

Eschatology, which Frank C. Senn states has been a weakness of the traditional Roman liturgy, is now reintroduced, as, for example, in the Intercessions, where the prayer goes:

In that new world where the fullness of your peace will be
    revealed,
gather people of every race, language, and way of life
to share in the one eternal banquet
with Jesus Christ the Lord.[52]

American Presbyterian eucharistic prayers also emphasize the relevance of eternal life to our present life. This can be seen in Prayer A in a sentence leading to the closing doxology:

Fill us with eternal life,
That with joy we may be his faithful people
Until we feast with him in glory.

Prayer B affirms:

We praise you that Christ our life now reigns with you in
    glory,
Praying for us until all things are made perfect in Christ.
In union with your church in heaven and on earth,
We pray that you will fulfill your eternal purpose
In us and in all the world.[53]

The Presbyterians, like the United Church of Christ in the United States, begin on a festive note:

51. Senn, *New Eucharistic Prayers,* p. 46.
52. *Ibid.,* p. 47.
53. *Ibid.,* citing pp. 99, 100, and 101 of the *United Presbyterian Worshipbook* of 1972.

Friends, this is the joyful feast of the people of God!
They will come from east and west
and from north and south,
and sit at the table in the kingdom of God.[54]

All the new liturgies express the union implicit in the communion of saints and the Eucharist as the link between the church in heaven and the church on earth — some briefly, others in expanded form. *The Lutheran Book of Worship* exhibits a commendable brevity in its expression of the concept:

Join our prayers
with those of your servants
of every time and place,
and unite them
with the ceaseless petitions
of our great high priest
until he comes
as victorious Lord of all.[55]

The United Methodist *At the Lord's Table* in Prayer No. 17 for Pentecost has an intercession for the church based on the *Didache* 10. It goes as follows:

Remember, Lord, your Church.
Guard it from all evil,
and preserve it by your love.
Gather it from the four winds
into your kingdom.
By the baptism of water
and your Holy Spirit
send us as your witnesses
unto all the world,

54. Senn, *op. cit.,* p. 110.
55. *Ibid.,* p. 202, from Great Thanksgivings I and II of *The Lutheran Book of Worship.*

in the name of Jesus Christ our Lord,
until he comes in final victory.[56]

The American Episcopal Church has a fine prayer for the faithful departed as part of Eucharistic Prayer D in Holy Eucharist II:

In the fullness of time, put all things in subjection under
your Christ, and bring us to that heavenly country where, with
[_____] and all your saints, we may enter the
everlasting heritage of your sons and daughters. . . .[57]

It is, however, in the new Roman Liturgy that the symbolism
of the bread and wine is most fully and vividly expressed. In the
beginning of the Offertory section of the Mass, the prayer goes
thus:

C. Blessed are you, Lord, God of all creation.
Through your goodness we have this bread to offer,
which earth has given and human hands have made.
It will become for us the bread of life.

P. *Blessed be God forever.*

C. (quietly) By the mystery of this water and wine
may we come to share in the divinity of Christ,
who humbled himself to share in our humanity.
Blessed are you, Lord, God of all creation.
Through your goodness we have this wine to offer,
fruit of the vine and work of human hands.
It will become our spiritual drink.

P. *Blessed be God for ever.*[58]

56. Senn, *op. cit.,* p. 204.
57. Eucharistic Rite II, Alternative Prayer B, p. 369.
58. *The Sunday Missal,* Eucharistic Prayer I, p. 35.

Eucharistic Prayer II of the modern Roman Rite has an *epiclesis* that reads:

> And so, Father, we bring you these gifts.
> We ask you to make them holy by the power of your Spirit,
> that they may become the body and blood
> of your Son, our Lord Jesus Christ,
> at whose command we celebrate this eucharist.

Later, after communion, the petitions and intercessions follow:

> Grant that we, who are nourished by his body and blood,
> may be filled with his Holy Spirit,
> and become one body, one spirit in Christ.
>
> May he make us an everlasting gift to you
> and enable us to share in the inheritance of your saints. . . .
>
> Lord, may this sacrifice,
> which has made our peace with you,
> advance the peace and salvation of all the world.
> Strengthen in faith and love your pilgrim Church on
>   earth. . . .
> Father, hear the prayers of the family you have gathered here
>   before you,
> In mercy and love unite all your children wherever they may
>   be.
> Welcome into your kingdom our departed brothers and
>   sisters,
> and all who have left this world in your friendship.
> We hope to enjoy for ever the vision of your glory,
> through Christ our Lord, from whom all good things
>   come.[59]

The comprehensiveness, concision, clarity, dignity, and charity in these prayers are outstanding. And they make the symbolism of the Eucharist clear as noonday light.

---

59. *The Sunday Missal,* Eucharistic Prayer III, pp. 48 and 49-50.

Apart from the international Roman Catholic rites, we have hitherto concentrated on the American side of the Atlantic. Now we cross the Atlantic to view the new Eucharistic Prayers produced in Britain. The Anglican *Alternative Service Book of 1980* stresses unity effectively, for as the priest breaks the consecrated bread, he says:

> We break this bread
> to share in the body of Christ,

to which the faithful respond:

> Though we are many, we are one body,
> Because we all share in one bread.[60]

Also in Holy Communion B, immediately before the Peace, the priest says:

> We are the body of Christ.
> By one Spirit we are all baptized into one body.
> Endeavour to keep the unity of the Spirit
> in the bond of peace.[61]

Equally impressive is the updating of the Prayer of Humble Access with its metaphor of a meal:

> Most merciful Lord,
> your love compels us to come in.
> Our hands were unclean,
> our hearts were unprepared;
> we were not fit
> even to eat the crumbs from under your table.
> But you, Lord, are the God of our salvation,
> and share your bread with sinners.
> So cleanse and feed us
> with the precious body and blood of your Son,

60. Holy Communion, Rite A, p. 142.
61. Holy Communion, Rite A, p. 189.

that he may live in us and we in him,
and that we, with the whole company of Christ,
may sit and eat in your kingdom.[62]

This prayer indicates the major symbols in the context of a meal, stressing unity with Christ and the whole "company," and even including the eschatological meal.

The United Reformed Church in the United Kingdom (which united the Congregational Churches and the Presbyterian Church of England) has produced an admirable manual or directory for ministers that provides the structure of the service of the Word and of the Eucharist, but permits variations, including four forms of "The Thanksgiving/Eucharistic Prayer." It also recognizes how important gestures are symbolically in the direction it gives for the transmission of the consecrated bread and wine, thus: ". . . as far as possible, the bread and wine should be passed through the congregation, so that each person serves his neighbor and the corporate character of the communion is thus expressed. The sharing is done most simply and meaningfully when a single piece of bread and a common cup are passed."[63]

In the intercessions, prayers are offered on behalf of "those in trade and industry, members of the professions, all who serve the community," with an ecological emphasis included:

and may the resources of the earth be wisely used,
truth honoured and preserved,
and the quality of our life enriched.[64]

There is great warmth in their invocation of the Holy Spirit:

Father, accept through Christ
our sacrifice of thanks and praise:

62. Holy Communion, Rite A, p. 170.
63. *A Book of Services: The United Reformed Church of the United Kingdom* (Edinburgh: The Saint Andrew Press, 1980), p. 15.
64. *Ibid.,* p. 24.

and as we eat and drink these holy gifts,
kindle in us the fire of your Spirit
that with the whole church on earth and in heaven
we may be made one in him.[65]

Thanksgiving III is outstanding for its emphasis on creation and on the ministry of Christ. The first proceeds as follows:

You have created us
and called us in this life
that we should be made one with you
to be your people here on earth.
Blessed are you,
creator of all that is,
Blessed are you
for giving us space and time for living.
Blessed are you
for the light of our eyes
and for the air we breathe.
We thank you for the whole of creation,
for all the works of your hands.

The second emphasis goes as follows:

We thank you, holy Father,
Lord our God,
for Jesus Christ,
your beloved son,
whom you called and sent
to serve us and give us light,
to bring your kingdom to the poor,
to bring redemption to captives

65. *Ibid.*, p. 33. The same expression is found in Eucharistic Prayer II of the French Reformed Church (1982), but its ultimate origin is, of course, the New Testament account of Pentecost with the "tongues of fire."

and to be for ever
and for us all
the likeness and embodiment
of your constant love and goodness.[66]

The English Methodists in their Communion order of worship combine much symbolism in a concentrated expression, as
seen in the ending of their eucharistic prayer:

Grant that by the power of the Holy Spirit
we who receive your gifts of bread and wine
may share in the body and blood of Christ.

Make us one body with him.

Accept us as we offer ourselves to be a living sacrifice,
and bring us with the whole creation to your
heavenly kingdom.[67]

The brief prayer of thanksgiving says all that is necessary:

We thank you, Lord,
that you have fed us in this sacrament,
united us with Christ,
and given us a foretaste of the heavenly banquet
prepared for all mankind.[68]

The 1982 Liturgy of the Reformed Church of France has a
strong ecological implication in its anamnetic prayer:

your universe you put in our care;
your creation you entrust to our hands
with all its wonders and its travail.

66. *Ibid.,* p. 35 for both citations.
67. *The Methodist Service Book* (London: Methodist Publishing House,
1975, with additions 1984), p. 58.
68. *Ibid.,* p. 61.

In addition to its emphasis on unity and strong sense of the communion of saints, and the demand for transformation as a consequence of the Eucharist, it also indicates the importance of Christ's continuing intercession as found in the Epistle to the Hebrews:

> Therefore, Lord, we make before you the memorial
> of the incarnation and passion of your Son,
> of his resurrection from the dead,
> of his ascension in glory,
> of his perpetual intercession.[69]

The Lutheran Church of Sweden's Eucharistic Rite of 1975 stresses the importance of the cooperation of God and human beings in the *epiclesis:*

> Send your Spirit in our hearts that he might work in us a living faith. Sanctify also through your Spirit this bread and wine, fruits of the earth and the toil of people which we bear unto you, so that we, through them, partake of the true body and blood of our Lord Jesus Christ.[70]

As indicated earlier, our modern liturgies show little impact as yet of the feminist movement, but a rectification is manifested in the most recent worship book of the American United Church of Christ. This is titled *Book of Worship: United Church of Christ* and was issued in 1986. It predictably uses inclusive language, but it does more. Its introduction affirms: "The rediscovery of complementarity of female and male metaphors in the Bible and the literature of the early church forbids Christians to settle for literary poverty in the midst of literary riches." It also insists that "The witness of women of faith in the biblical story is treated

---

69. Thurian and Wainwright, eds., *Baptism and Eucharist: Ecumenical Convergence in Celebration* (Geneva: World Council of Churches; Grand Rapids: Wm. B. Eerdmans, 1983), pp. 152 and 154.

70. *Ibid.,* p. 141.

with the same dignity accorded the witness of men of faith."[71]
In the Service of Word and Sacrament I the leader invites the
congregation thus:

> Beloved in Christ,
> the Gospel tells us that on the first day of the week
> Jesus Christ was raised from death,
> appeared to Mary Magdalene,
> on that same day sat at the table with disciples
> and was made known in the breaking of the bread.

To this the response is made:

> This is the joyful feast
> of the people of God.
> Men and women,
> youth and children,
> come from the east and the west,
> from the north and the south,
> and gather about Christ's table.[72]

The same worship book contains some admirable prayers thanking God for creation:

> We give you thanks,
> God of majesty and mercy,
> for calling forth the creation
> and raising us from the dust
> by the breath of your being.
> We bless you for the beauty
> and bounty of the earth
> and for the vision
> of the day

71. Issued by the United Church of Christ Office for Church Life and
Leadership, New York, 1986. The reference is to p. 8.
72. *Ibid.*, p. 44.

> when sharing by all will
> mean scarcity for none.[73]

Even the Blessing is thoroughly inclusive:

> The blessing of the God
> of Sarah and Abraham;
> the blessing of Jesus Christ,
> born of Mary;
> the blessing of the Holy Spirit,
> who broods over us
> as a mother over her children;
> be with you all.[74]

Thus the various eucharists are richly symbolical.[75]

As we reflect on the various liturgical texts for the celebration of the Eucharist — Roman Catholic, Orthodox, Anglican, Lutheran, Reformed, and Methodist — we find a remarkable theological unity in almost every one of them. Without exception, the eucharistic prayer begins with the traditional dialogue, usually emphasizing joy, continuing with gratitude to God for his creation of the world and of humankind, sometimes recalling our misuse of his gifts, commemorating the life, passion, resurrection, ascension, and glorification of Jesus Christ who was the Eternal Son incarnate, recognizing the future coming and reign of Christ, and the promised privilege that all the faithful may join him in the celestial banquet, making the memorial of his institution of the Lord's Supper symbolizing and communicating through his gifts of bread and wine Christ's very body and blood, creating unity in the church that is his body, uniting the church in heaven with the church on earth, and recalling that our Great High Priest ever makes intercession for his own company. The

73. *Ibid.*, p. 45.
74. *Ibid.*, p. 108.
75. The fullest interpretation of its theme known to me is F. W. Dillistone, *Christianity and Symbolism* (London: Collins, 1955).

stress that these are his gifts to us, meant to be shared by the entire world, and through us and others like us to be transformed into the saving community that will help to establish the Kingdom of God, is almost unanimously expressed in all eucharists.

The only cause for sadness in the unanimity of gladness and gratitude is that the churches on earth are not yet united and do not all unrestrictedly open their eucharists to members of every other branch of Christ's universal church.

76. Two excellent books interpreting the Eucharist as Christ's gift to his own are James F. White, *Sacraments as God's Self-Giving* (Nashville: Abingdon Press, 1983), and William R. Crockett, *The Eucharist: Symbol of Transformation* (New York: Pueblo Publishing Company, 1989).

NINE   Conclusion: Agreements and Disagreements

SOME CONCLUSIONS to books are merely concise summa-
tions of the previous chapters, which may please the all too
rapid reviewer but disappoint the thoughtful reader. In this
conclusion we will attempt to show the widespread agreement
that has been reached on the meanings of the Eucharist in the
latter part of the twentieth century, and point out a single, but
serious, disagreement that remains.

First, we must consider the evidence for agreement. The
present relationship between the Roman Catholic Church and the
Anglican and Lutheran and Reformed churches is so changed, at
least among the liturgical leaders of the churches, that it seems as
if the sixteenth-century battle between the proponents of the
Reformation and the Counter-Reformation has been not only
forgotten but also buried, and buried deep. It is very significant
that the book of texts we have consulted most is a product of the
World Council of Churches and bears the significant title *Baptism
and Eucharist: Ecumenical Covergence in Celebration*.[1] One of its
editors was Max Thurian, the liturgist of the French Reformed
Church, who is also a monk and who works as a partner daily with
Catholic priests and nuns at Taizé, the religious community of the
future. The other editor was Geoffrey Wainwright, a Methodist
and an ecumenist who has taught in England, West Africa, Union

1. This work appeared in 1983; it was published by the World Council
of Churches of Geneva and the Wm. B. Eerdmans Publishing Company of
Grand Rapids, MI.

Seminary in New York City, and Duke University in North Carolina. He has also written a book that indicates what has been for too long the missing dimension in both Protestant and Roman Catholic eucharists, *The Eucharist and Eschatology. Baptism and Eucharist* appeared in 1983 and was reissued in 1987. As a commentary on it Thurian edited a series of responses entitled *Ecumenical Perspectives on Baptism, Eucharist and Ministry* (Geneva: World Council of Churches, 1983), in which the expert Catholic liturgist and Dominican J.-M. R. Tillard finds himself in full agreement with the doctrinal teaching on the Eucharist expressed in the Lima Eucharist sponsored by the Faith and Order Commission of the World Council of Churches.

There are, however, other testimonies to the growing ecumenical consensus on the Eucharist. As early as 1973 the Anglican publishing house S.P.C.K. published *Modern Eucharistic Agreement.* This book contains document A, *The Eucharist: A Lutheran-Roman Catholic Statement,* which deals with the hitherto controversial issue in Part I, namely, "The Eucharist as Sacrifice," and Part II, "The Presence of Christ in the Lord's Supper." The second document in this collection, B, is "The Dombes Agreement," the product of French Reformed and Roman Catholic ecumenists. It is entitled *Towards a Common Eucharistic Faith?*, and it contains two unofficial but highly important parts. One is a *Doctrinal Agreement,* and the other is a *Pastoral Agreement.* Document C is titled *An Agreed Statement on Eucharistic Doctrine* and is the product of the Anglican–Roman Catholic International Commission. The last document, D, is that of the World Council of Churches and is entitled *The Eucharist in Ecumenical Thought.* As an indication of the substantial unity of these statements one may note in a comparative table the title headings of the Dombes and the World Council of Churches agreements:

Dombes	**World Council of Churches**
1. The Eucharist: the Lord's Supper	1. The Eucharist: the Lord's Supper
2. The Eucharist: act of thanksgiving to the Father	2. The Eucharist: thanksgiving to the Father

3. The Eucharist: memorial *(anamnesis)* of Christ

4. The Eucharist: a gift of the Spirit

5. The sacramental presence of Christ

6. The Eucharist: communion in the body of Christ

7. The Eucharist: a mission in the world

8. The Eucharist: banquet of the Kingdom

9. The presidency of the Eucharist

3. The Eucharist: memorial *(anamnesis)* of Christ

4. The Eucharist: gift of the Spirit

5. The Eucharist: communion in the body of Christ

6. The Eucharist: mission to the world

7. The Eucharist: end of divisions

While the World Council of Churches Statement lacks nos. 5, 8, and 9 of the Dombes Agreement, each of the other statements in the Dombes Agreement has a parallel in the World Council of Churches Statement. The two approaches display an amazing basic unity. The past twenty-five years have been a period of astonishing liturgical efflorescence. Indeed, in 1976 Leonel Mitchell observed that more eucharistic anaphoras had been composed in the previous ten years than in the preceding millennium.[2] Their convergence — the result of many collections of many eucharistic prayers — is all the more remarkable.

A third testimony to the agreement and convergence is provided by other liturgies. In 1967 the Jesuit, Fr. Michael Taylor, foresaw the remarkable growing together of Christians and edited a volume demonstrating it entitled *Liturgical Renewal in the Christian Churches*.[3] The importance of prior ecumenical forms of church union and their agreement on the Eucharist was empha-

2. L. L. Mitchell, "The Alexandrine Anaphora of St. Basil of Caesarea: Ancient Source of 'A Common Eucharistic Prayer,'" *Anglican Theological Review,* vol. LVIII, no. 2 (April 1976), p. 195.

3. Published by Helicon Press, Baltimore and Dublin. See also Romey F. Marshall and Michael J. Taylor, *Liturgy and Christian Unity* (Englewood Cliffs, NJ: Prentice-Hall, 1965). The writers were respectively a Methodist minister and a Jesuit priest.

sized by a Protestant pastor who converted to Roman Catholicism, Louis Bouyer, in a statement about the Eucharist of the Church of South India that united Anglicans, Congregationalists, Methodists, and Presbyterians. He made this observation: "While it skillfully incorporates quite unexceptional Protestant customs, still, from the point of view of even a conservative Catholic (or Orthodox) liturgist, this eucharistic liturgy seems much more satisfactory than those which emanated from the Reformation. Unquestionably it is much superior to the Prayer Book of the Church of England both on account of its traditional character and its theological soundness."[4] Then in 1984 John Reumann's *The Supper of the Lord: The New Testament, Ecumenical Dialogues, and Faith and Order on the Eucharist* appeared. It stressed that there were five agreed ecumenical emphases in the interpretation of the Eucharist: as Thanksgiving to the Father, as Memorial and Anticipation of Christ, as Invocation of the Holy Spirit, as Communion (*koinonia*) of the Faithful, and as Meal of the Kingdom.[5] In his concluding chapter he claims that both biblical studies and the liturgical movement have led to the convergence. What is important concerning the growing interconfessional agreement about eucharistic prayers is that they stress Christ's presence and the notion of sacrifice, as well as the action of the Trinity in the structure of the eucharistic prayer, and use the term "Eucharist" as the preferred ecumenical term.[6] Most important is the fact that the Christological aspect is dominant in the stress on the *anamnesis* or recalling of the life, ministry, passion, sacrificial death, resurrection, and second coming of Christ, and this is seen as the work of the Holy Spirit — the latter being the contribution of the Eastern Orthodox churches to eucharistic understanding. In addition, they view the communion of the faithful as having two aspects — communion with Christ and with each other — and the

---

4. "A Roman Catholic View of the C.S.I.," in *Theology*, January 1956, p. 4. Cited in The Church of Scotland's Church Service Society's *Annual*, May 1962, p. 47.

5. Published by Fortress Press, Philadelphia.

6. Cf. Thurian and Wainwright, eds., *Baptism and Eucharist*, pp. 182-83.

very concept of the Eucharist as the meal of the Kingdom inevitably suggests its future, eschatological implications. This unity of understanding is all the more impressive in that the author does not hide the burning issues that remain in reference to the age of admission to the chief sacrament, and the threefold ministry in some churches and a single ministry in others.

It remains for us only to show in greater detail what has been exemplified in the citations in each earlier chapter of the recent and contemporary liturgies of the Eucharist, and to consider its overall structure.

As long ago as 1936, the Canadian liturgiologist William D. Maxwell, in his influential *An Outline of Christian Worship,*[7] divided each historic liturgy he analyzed into two sections that he called The Liturgy of the Word (containing lections from the Bible, prayers of adoration, confession, pardon, and intercession, and the climactic preaching or proclamation of the Word of God, with interspersed acts of praise) and the Liturgy of the Upper Room. From the days of the Reformation onward Protestants have exalted the Liturgy of the Word to the disadvantage of the Liturgy of the Upper Room, while Catholics have done the opposite. At the present time the balance of appreciation of both sections of the Liturgy has been very largely restored for both Protestants and Catholics. That in itself is a remarkable rectification.

Two interdenominational English-speaking associations are further pointers to the desire for greater unification in the interpretation of the Eucharist, one British and the other American. There are also several European developments of the same kind, notably the Dombes Group in France and the triennial Kirchentag gatherings in which the laity predominate in West Germany. The British Association knows as "The Joint Liturgical Group" published an "eucharistic canon"[8] in 1978 that represents the work of liturgists of the following eight churches: the Church of England,

---

7. Issued by Forward Movement Publications, Cincinnati.
8. *A Book of Services* (Edinburgh: The Saint Andrew Press, 1980, second impression 1984), p. 14.

the Church of Scotland, the Baptist Union, the Episcopal Church
in Scotland, the Methodist Church, the Churches of Christ, the
Roman Catholic Church, and the United Reformed Church. The
Consultation on Church Union in the U.S.A. is devoted to ecumenical concerns, including among them the production of a
unitive liturgy. This was published in 1978 as *Word, Bread, Cup,*[9]
includes two eucharistic thanksgivings, and is sponsored by ten
churches, including the African Methodist Episcopal Church, the
African Methodist Episcopal Zion Church, the Christian Church
(Disciples of Christ), the Christian Methodist Episcopal Church,
the Presbyterian Church in the United States, the United Church
of Christ, the United Methodist Church, and the United Presbyterian Church in the U.S.A.

As an indication of what might be considered minimally
essential in a contemporary eucharistic prayer, it might be interesting to reflect on the instructions given in the service book of
the United Reformed Church of the United Kingdom, since
both denominations that united to form this church in recent
history were Puritan and therefore, on principle, were suspicious
of liturgies as repressing the gifts of ministers to compose their
own extemporary prayers. The two denominations that were
now united were the Congregationalists and the Presbyterians
of England. For this reason, while they provide liturgies and
several alternative prayers, they also add a list of themes they
consider appropriate for the celebration of the Eucharist. Their
A Book of Services includes the following themes:

> the recital of the mighty acts of God in creation and redemption,
> often with special thanksgivings according to the season of the
> year
>
> the commemoration, with bread and wine, of the sacrificial
> death and the resurrection of Christ 'until he come':

9. Richard Buxton, "The Shape of the Eucharist: A Survey and Ap-
praisal," in Kenneth Stevenson, ed., *Liturgy Reshaped* (London: S.P.C.K.,
1982), p. 87.

invocation of the holy spirit, praying that what we do in obedience to Christ may be united with His perfect sacrifice and that we may be made one in Him, and receive the benefits of His passion and victory.

If we take this synopsis as a series of suggestions, it is interesting to observe what the implications of these statements are because they will give us a summary of the general acceptance of the emphases given in a contemporary eucharistic prayer that attempts to be both ecumenical and reasonably complete. First, we understand that among the thanksgivings there will be a trinitarian structure, acknowledging our gratitude to God the Father as creator, God the Son as redeemer, and God the Holy Spirit as sanctifier.

Next, the mighty acts of God in creation (as well as providence) require an acknowledgment of the creation of the universe and of humanity in it, demanding a concern for ecology and a concern for reconciliation and peace as well as justice and thus reflecting the righteousness of God that guarantees stability for all society.

Then the mighty acts of God in redemption demand the recital of the major events in the life of God the Son, incarnate as a human being, recalling his teaching, his extraordinary love and humility displayed in emptying himself as a servant, ministering specially to the poor, the prisoners, as well as to the sick and the outcasts of society, his miracles, his climactic sufferings both mental and physical culminating in the cross, and the divine vindication of his life in the glorious Resurrection and Ascension, his intercession for the faithful, his coming again to establish his Kingdom on earth, his role as future Judge, and the banquet that he prepares for his own in heaven.

It is also necessary to give special emphasis to Christ's sacrificial death by recalling his gift of himself on the cross and in the bread and wine that become the body and blood of Christ and the nourishment of the church that is his body, and the joyful bond of unity of the church in heaven with the church on earth.

Finally, this Eucharist is, by the invocation of the Holy Spirit, asked to make acceptable to God this our sacrifice of praise, and all that in his institution of it Christ intended it to be, with all his benefits for the faithful, including the forgiveness of our sins, the assurance of everlasting life, and the transformation that may make our lives a way of winning others into this union with Christ and helping to establish the Kingdom of God.

Certain elements of a complete eucharistic prayer, such as the recognition that bread and wine symbolize the cooperation of God the creator and humankind, have been forgotten, and the demand for social justice might have been more forcefully expressed. But basically such a prayer recalls the memorial, the thanksgiving, the sacrifice, the celestial banquet, the communion of saints in joy, the mystery, and social justice. The prayer recognizes the essential symbols and the transignification of bread and wine in this meal, which undergo the wonderful transition whereby they are changed by Christ's will to convey the real presence of Christ in body and blood by the power of the Holy Spirit and still remain a transcendent and glorious mystery.

The gains in the appreciation of the greatest sacrament have been remarkable in our time, and most of them are appreciated across many ecclesiastical boundaries. But it is only right to insist, as we can learn from the history of the understanding of the Eucharist, that there is still much to be learned, which the future will provide under divine guidance. To expect such we have only to consider how differently the Eucharist has been observed throughout the ages and will be in the ages to come.

The early Christians celebrated the Eucharist as a meal at home with joy, enthusiasm, and the belief in the immediacy of their transport with Christ to the heavens.

Then, in the early fourth century, under Emperor Constantine, it became Christianity on parade, with vast congregations meeting in large churches not only recognized but approved by the society surrounding it. Now it was hierarchically celebrated, with the leaders entering in solemn processions in distinctive garb. But they still used the vernacular tongue, and all shared in the rite itself.

The late medieval liturgy, however, caused the Eucharist to lose the shape of a meal, and the vernacular to be exchanged for a learned and remote language familiar only to the priests. The meal symbolism was lost as well, for it was as spectators, not as participants, that the faithful gathered. On rare occasions they took a wafer, but no consecrated wine, and their mediations were private and hardly ever corporate. Sermons were relatively few, but the sense of reverence for the mystery was profound. "Most crucial of all perhaps was the change from the early domestic 'gathered round the table' style to one involving the whole body of worshippers, clergy and laity, being in serried ranks facing the same direction . . . [like] an army on Parade with its officers and its head." And, of course, there was the addition of the musical elements such as chants.

The revolution of the Reformation days made the vernacular available to Anglicans and Protestants, but at the cost of excessive didacticism and frequent verbosity. At the same time hymns gave the people a response of gratitude that the complexities of Gregorian chanting made impossible for the laity in Catholicism and the Counter-Reformation, while it provided many significant religious devotions. Yet the absence of the vernacular meant that the devotions of the common people had no relation to the Eucharist, and there was an excessive concentration on certain supposedly more sacred moments than others in the Mass. It is only with the present century that the scientific study of liturgies has come of age, and that our understanding of the history of worship has become profound. Only now has the combination of the ecumenical and liturgical movements made the production of transdenominational eucharistic canons or anaphoras possible and desirable.

Even so there remains one disastrous source of disagreement — the continuing scandal of the disunity of the churches and the fact that many churches refuse admission to the Eucharist to Christians of other denominations. Perhaps the author may be allowed to cite two liturgiologists, one a Catholic and the other a Protestant. The Catholic is the Jesuit G. D. Yarnold, who wrote over thirty years ago: "Are we content to meet our Risen Lord as we do today around separate tables? is the Church of God a restaurant, or a Father's home?"[10] To that piercing example of wit, we add the plea of the Methodist theologian Geoffrey Wainwright: "From the beginning the modern ecumenical movement has seen Christian unity to be part and parcel of the church's witness to the world: 'that the world may believe' (John 17:20-23). Disunity among Christians is active countertestimony to the gospel of reconciliation."[11] That is the stumbling block of disagreement, ultimately to be attributed to Christian *disobedience*.

10. *The Bread which we Break* (London: Oxford University Press, 1960), p. 110.
11. From Kenneth Stevenson, ed., *Liturgy Reshaped*, p. 98.

INDEX OF TOPICS

INDEX OF PERSONS

271